PENGUIN BOOKS

THE RISE AND FALL OF ALEXANDRIA

Justin Pollard has worked extensively in both British and American television and has worked closely in developing feature films for directors including Shekhar Kapur (*Elizabeth*), Gillies MacKinnon, Sam Mendes, Neil Jordan, and Joe Wright (*Pride and Prejudice*).

Howard Reid worked for the BBC from 1979 to 1991 on many major documentary series, including the Emmy-winning *Story of English*, and has since worked widely in both British and American television. He has written five previous books, including *The Way of the Warrior*, coauthored with Michael Croucher.

THE RISE AND FALL OF
ALEXANDRIA

Birthplace of the Modern World

JUSTIN POLLARD

AND

HOWARD REID

PENGUIN BOOKS

PENGUIN BOOKS

Published by the Penguin Group

Penguin Group (USA) Inc., 375 Hudson Street, New York, New York 10014, U.S.A.

Penguin Group (Canada), 90 Eglinton Avenue East, Suite 700, Toronto,
Ontario, Canada M4P 2Y3 (a division of Pearson Penguin Canada Inc.)

Penguin Books Ltd, 80 Strand, London WC2R 0RL, England

Penguin Ireland, 25 St Stephen's Green, Dublin 2, Ireland (a division of Penguin Books Ltd)

Penguin Group (Australia), 250 Camberwell Road, Camberwell,
Victoria 3124, Australia (a division of Pearson Australia Group Pty Ltd)

Penguin Books India Pvt Ltd, 11 Community Centre,
Panchsheel Park, New Delhi–110 017, India

Penguin Group (NZ), 67 Apollo Drive, Rosedale, North Shore 0632,
New Zealand (a division of Pearson New Zealand Ltd)

Penguin Books (South Africa) (Pty) Ltd, 24 Sturdee Avenue,
Rosebank, Johannesburg 2196, South Africa

Penguin Books Ltd, Registered Offices:
80 Strand, London WC2R 0RL, England

First published in the United States of America by Viking Penguin,
a member of Penguin Group (USA) Inc. 2006
Published in Penguin Books 2007

1 3 5 7 9 10 8 6 4 2

Title page image: SPL/Photo Researchers, Inc.
Map by Jeffrey L. Ward

THE LIBRARY OF CONGRESS HAS CATALOGED THE HARDCOVER EDITION AS FOLLOWS:
Pollard, Justin, 1968–
The rise and fall of Alexandria : birthplace of the modern mind / Justin Pollard and Howard Reid.
p. cm.
Includes bibliographical references.
ISBN 0-670-03797-4 (hc.)
ISBN 978-0-14-311251-8 (pbk.)
1. Alexandria (Egypt)—History. 2. Alexandria (Egypt)—Intellectual life.
I. Reid, Howard. II. Title.
DT154.A4P65 2006
932—dc22 2006044737

Printed in the United States of America
Designed by Nancy Resnick

For Liz, Wilson, Dudley, and Teän

"Ipsa scientia potestas est"

PREFACE

Flotsam . . .

Antiquities are history defaced, or some remnants of history which have casually escaped the shipwreck of time.

Francis Bacon, *The Advancement of Learning*

On most days in the summer of AD 1295 an Eastern Orthodox monk called Maximos Planudes could have been found in the great market of Constantinople, making his way past the spice sellers and the silk traders to the dusty undercrofts where the book merchants piled their own wares in tottering stacks of parchment. Here were codices and manuscripts in Arabic, Syriac, Greek, and Latin, some newly completed, some old. Holy books for all religions, practical treatises, histories, and chronologies. Here too were books still waiting to be written, fresh blank sheets and old volumes that had been scrubbed clean of whatever they once held, ready for a new text.

Walking along the waterfront to the great market, Maximos Planudes might have been reminded of the description in Strabo of Alexandria in the first century AD, which he excitedly called "the greatest emporium in the whole world" (Strabo, *Geography*, book 17, chapter 13). Constantinople, despite the sack of 1204, had since taken on that mantle, which was why this diminutive monk was spending each day of a hot summer there searching through piles of books and manuscripts.

The book dealers must have taken careful note of this unusual creature in their midst. Monks swarmed through the city, but their interest in books was invariably limited to medieval Greek religious works—the biblical glosses and commentaries, the credulous hagiographies, the missals, Psalters, and breviaries whose attraction was as much in the artistic illumination of their pages as in the illuminating quality of their text. But Planudes was after something different. He spent his hours poring over the dreariest-looking texts, from faded Latin fragments to terse Arabic treatises.

Then one day, sometime that summer, he found it. It certainly wasn't much to look at, but there in his hands was a fragment from the wreckage. A rare treasure, finally washed up on a distant shore. He had found Claudius Ptolemy's great lost work on geography—*Geographia*—written in ancient Alexandria, stored for centuries in her library, and believed (at least in the West) to have perished there.

Rumors had been circulating in Europe that a copy had been seen in Arabic translation, just as Ptolemy's other great work was already known to Arabic scholars as *The Greatest,* or, in their language, *Almagest.* Now, here was its companion. The rumors were true.

The survival of this masterful text was a small miracle in itself. The original copies of the *Geographia* had been deposited in the library of Alexandria by Claudius Ptolemy himself, and there they had remained in constant use for centuries. It appears that sometime in the fourth century, however, a copy was made to take to the new Roman capital, Constantinople. When the library at Alexandria was destroyed, this copy thus survived. Now, ironically, the very zealotry that had condemned so many of Alexandria's books would save it. When the patriarch of Alexandria had the patriarch of Constantinople declared a heretic, his followers had taken this copy of the *Geographia* with them into their desert exile. There it had been translated into Syriac and then later into Arabic. The original copy had of course long since perished, but a few of those Arabic translations survived. The last of those had then, somehow, found its way into a bookseller's stock and was now in Maximos Planudes' hands.

The copy of the *Geographia* the monk now so fiercely bartered for was not complete, at least not in the way that he wished it to be, for there was a text, but no maps. We cannot be sure now that Ptolemy's original version even had maps, but that was what Maximos Planudes wanted, and having secured his prize he returned to the monastery at Chora, where he began the painstaking task of noting all the details in the text and turning them back into the thing he craved—a series of maps.

Soon a new rumor was flying around the Mediterranean: Planudes had a map of the world—Ptolemy's map of the world. The story came to the ears of the Byzantine emperor Andronicus II Palaeologus, who ordered a copy made for himself. Soon others were reconstructing, dividing, and improving the maps. By the fourteenth century, the twenty-six maps of the original version had been divided into sixty-four, and one of these copies was obtained in 1400 by the Florentine patron Palla Strozzi, who persuaded a Byzantine scholar to translate the work from Planudes' Greek into Latin.

Now the *Geographia* could at last be read by the academics of Europe, who, thanks to Christianity, retained their knowledge of Latin but had become largely ignorant of Greek. This version, finally finished around 1410, came into the royal courts of Europe at a time when interest in the exploration of the world, an interest that had slept for so long, was finally being rekindled. But none of the Renaissance princes who collected these wonders was more passionate than the pope. If there were new lands to discover, then the papacy wanted to ensure that Catholicism traveled there with the explorers. So the little book that Planudes had discovered years before made its way to the Apostolic Library at the Vatican, along with many of its lavishly illustrated descendants. From the Vatican, copies would then be sent out across Europe.

One of those would change the world.

CONTENTS

xii

CONTENTS

INTRODUCTION

For Alexandria lies, as it were, at the conjunction of the whole world.

Dio Chrysostom, *Orations*, 32

Most of us take it for granted that two cities, Athens and Rome, completely dominated the classical world. We are well aware that their achievements had a profound effect on Western civilization. Their legacy is still apparent, from the architecture of our public buildings to the phrasing of our laws. Even democracy itself was, we are told, their gift. But this is, in fact, a distorted view of history, fueled by generations awed by the might of Rome and the ingenuity of Athens, and perhaps a little too keen to take native historians of both cities at their word.

In fact there was a third city that, at its height, dwarfed both of these in wealth and population as well as in scientific and artistic achievement. Largely overlooked by history, this city had a unique soul. While Greece and Rome spread their influence through trade and war, this city set out on another adventure, not at the point of a sword but on the tip of a pen. Its triumph was to be a conquest of the mind—led not by legions of soldiers but by dynasties of scholars navigating on a sea of books.

This city was Alexandria. Within a few generations of its foundation the city was the marvel of its age, but not just for its size and beauty, its vast palaces, safe harbors, and fabled lighthouse, or even for being the world's greatest emporium, its central market. Alexandria was built on knowledge, and at its heart was not a treasury but the greatest library and museum of antiquity. Encouraged by the ruling Ptolemaic dynasty, this institution became the meeting place and crucible of all the great cultures and minds of the ancient world. It proved an intellectual magnet attracting generation upon generation of the finest scholars, philosophers, poets, and inventors. Egyptians, Greeks, Jews, Babylonians, Persians, Gauls, Phoenicians, and Romans flocked here, stimulating huge advances in mathematics, astronomy and astrology, alchemy, optics, medicine and anatomy, grammar, geography, philosophy, and theology—in short, the sum total of the wisdom of the ancient world. In these halls the true foundations of the modern world were laid—not in stone but in ideas.

There was never anything like the great library and museum before, nor has there been since: the single place on earth where all the knowledge in the entire world was gathered together—every great play and poem, every book of physics and philosophy, the key to understanding . . . simply everything. That institution aimed to accumulate every book written, even from as far afield as India, and at its zenith it was said to contain three-quarters of a million scrolls. Here were not only the works of the brilliant scholars of their own time but also those of their illustrious predecessors—of Homer, Pythagoras, and Herodotus, of Socrates, Plato, and Aristotle—names that might otherwise be unknown to us. Other libraries since have held more books; indeed, today the Library of Congress in Washington and the British Library in London hold between them nearly every book printed in the last two hundred years and many more besides. But they are not complete, not least because most of the knowledge of the first thousand years of Western civilization is missing. These were the books that formed the library of Alexandria, and only a handful have been seen since that library's tragic destruction. All that remains is perhaps 1 percent of the works that were once lodged there, the chance survivors of that shipwreck of human achievement.

The romance of Athens and the might of Rome have overshadowed the Hellenistic civilization spawned by the vast conquests of Alexander. Somehow the people of this place and their extraordinarily modern ideas have fallen down the gap between where classical Greece ended and imperial Rome began.

So our first aim in this book is to look again at Alexandria, to reconstruct the life of the institutions that made it unique—the library and the museum—and to breathe life back into a city that was once the center of the world. Physically there is almost nothing left of ancient Alexandria, but among the drowned ruins in her harbor, in the fragments of the books that survive from her great library, and hidden among the works of later authors lie the keys to this city of wonders.

It was a city of mechanical marvels, of an anatomy school where the circulation of the blood was understood two thousand years before it was previously thought possible, of geographers who knew the earth was spherical and traveled around the sun, of philosophers who even conjectured that everything was made of microscopically small particles called "atoms" (from the Greek *atomos*—"indivisible"). This was the home of Euclid, the father of geometry, whose books are still in print two thousand years after his death, and of Archimedes, of "Eureka" fame. Here too was the young Galen, the greatest doctor and physiologist of the age; and Claudius Ptolemy, the father of both astronomy and geography; and Apollonius, the author of *Jason and the Argonauts*. Stranger names, but no less influential, include Eratosthenes, the first man to measure the circumference of the earth; Aristarchus, the first to envisage a heliocentric solar system; Plotinus, a founder of Neoplatonism; Clement of Alexandria, a father of Christian theology; Arius, perhaps the first great Christian heretic; and Philo, the radical Jewish theologian. These are just a few of the host of geniuses who walked and talked, debated and denounced, read copiously, and finally set pen to paper in the great library and museum attached to the royal palaces of Alexandria. And while some of these legions of scholars are still household names, remembered for their mastery of one or two fields of study, it was the declared aim of all to achieve mastery in all fields of study, all branches of knowledge. And some actually achieved this, turning themselves truly into philosophers—"lovers of wisdom"—and reaching intellectual heights never achieved before or since.

The story of each of these characters tells a part of the history of Alexandria, a history peopled by the political giants of the ancient world: Alexander the Great, Julius Caesar, Mark Antony, and Cleopatra. Our aim in this book is to explore, within the framework of this turbulent political history, the ways in which human knowledge and understanding developed and evolved in this extraordinary city, to trace the evolution of the "Alexandrian Way," which stimulated a dramatic acceleration in our appreciation, not just of science and the material world, but also of literature, metaphysics, philosophy, and religion.

To do this we have had to follow the Alexandrian Way ourselves to some extent, by first reading everything we could find on all the people, subjects, and events in Alexandria's long history—the flotsam and jetsam from the shipwreck of time. We have then laid out those pieces and tried to discover the patterns lying behind them, to fill in the lacunae, the gaps, so that we might explore both the physical and mental worlds of the city and its people.

Wherever possible we have returned to firsthand testimonies and let the people of Alexandria speak for themselves, not merely to restore voices so often drowned out by Rome and Athens, but to try to convey a sense of what it must have been like to actually be there and experience the journey of discovery that was life "at the conjunction of the whole world." In their words we can walk again in the corridors of the world's first and only true "university" and reach out for the long-lost scrolls of the library itself. We can gaze upon the golden mausoleum of Alexander, and discover the cold body of Cleopatra in her quayside palace. We can see the world they knew around them and explore the yet stranger worlds of their minds, in a story that begins with the rise of the Ptolemies—the heirs of Alexander and the last, tragic dynasty in three millennia of pharaohs. We will then pass through the conquest by Octavian into the shadow of the Roman Empire, and end with the triumph of Christianity, the death of the last librarian, and the destruction of the library and the city itself.

In this book we will not only return to the lost wonders of Alexandria, we will also try to enter the "mind" of the city, to discover why it produced such an extraordinary flowering of creativity, knowledge, and understanding. And we will discover that at the core of this dazzling whirlpool of ideas lies the thing you are reading now: the written word. Words encoded in grammars, bound as books, and held in libraries allow the transmission of ideas from one mind to the next over the generations, and the transformation of those ideas into new, fresh thoughts as they travel. While the early Greek scholars and philosophers mostly preferred to establish private schools where their thoughts would be transmitted face-to-face, master to pupil, it was in the great libraries of Alexandria that the real power of the written word burst forth upon generation after generation of scholars who could read—and so hold in their own minds—

the voices of the world's great thinkers, speaking to them across the distant expanses of space and time.

Alexandria was the greatest mental crucible the world has ever known, the place where ideas originating in obscure antiquity were forged into intellectual constructs that far outlasted the city itself. If the Renaissance was the "rebirth" of learning that led to our modern world, then Alexandria was its original birthplace. Our politics may be modeled on Greek prototypes, our public architecture on Roman antecedents, but in our minds we are all the children of Alexandria.

THE RISE AND FALL OF
ALEXANDRIA

CHAPTER ONE

FLOUR AND SAND

History is a child building a sand-castle by the sea, and that child is the whole majesty of man's power in the world.

Heraclitus, *Herakleitos and Diogenes*

From atop the walls of the castle of Qaitbey in Egypt you can look across the rocky coast on which the castle stands to where fishing boats still ride at anchor in the bay and local children fling themselves from the rocks into the warm, clear sea that laps the shore. It is a sight familiar to perhaps thousands of shorelines around the Mediterranean, a timeless scene that, with only a few modifications, could come from just about any century. But few shores have seen as much history wash across them as this one has. The very stones of the castle you look out from once belonged to one of the seven wonders of the ancient world, and the shoreline beyond, boats, children, and all, was a scene that once reached the ears of the Greek poet Homer.

According to Plutarch of Chaeronea, it was through Homer that this place came to the attention of perhaps the greatest general in all history, who, over 2,300 years before you, stood on this same shore, his precious copy of Homer locked in a golden casket in his hands. But when he turned from the sea and looked south he saw only a narrow strip of water separating this island from the mainland, and beyond that an empty coast to which only the smallest of villages clung. When you turn, you will no longer find that scene, for in its place has risen the city founded there by that man, that dreamer—the huge, heaving metropolis of Alexandria.

At the time Homer wrote, there had been some sort of Bronze Age trading post here, almost certainly more impressive than the settlement

Alexander found; but Homer's words echoed through the centuries to Alexander, and the mention of this place changed his mind about a great project he was planning. Plutarch tells us that he had it in mind to build a great Greek city on this Egyptian coast, one which would receive the ultimate honor of bearing his name. His architects and surveyors had thus been dispatched and had selected a suitable site where work was just about to begin. Then, he had a dream:

> . . . as he was sleeping, he saw a remarkable vision. He thought he could see a man with very white hair and of venerable appearance standing beside him and speaking these lines:
>
> "Then there is an island in the stormy sea,
> In front of Egypt; they call it Pharos."
>
> He rose at once and went to Pharos. . . .
>
> Plutarch, Life of Alexander, in Parallel Lives, 26, 3–10

What he found here was a strip of land running east–west, with a large lake to the south and the Mediterranean Sea to the north. Just off that coast stood the island Homer had mentioned—Pharos—and it soon became clear to Alexander, or his architects at least, that by joining this island to the mainland with a causeway, two great harbors would be created, making the safest and largest anchorage on the whole of the north coast of Egypt. Alexander was delighted and "exclaimed that Homer was admirable in other respects and was also an excellent architect, and ordered the plan of the city to be drawn in conformity with the terrain" (Plutarch, Life of Alexander, in Parallel Lives, 26, 3–10).

And so, on this coast in early 331 BC, a strange sight could be seen. On what had once been the quietest of shores the cries of thousands of birds could now be heard. Anyone sailing down this coast might have seen the great flock wheeling in the blinding Egyptian sun and beneath them, on the beach, a small encampment. But these were not desperate, lost desert travelers, patiently circled by the ever watchful vultures; they were Alexander's men, and the birds that dived again and again on them were not harbingers of a death, but of a birth.

Closer inspection might have shown the reason for the birds' interest.

Crisscrossing the sandy shore were lines of barley flour, carefully poured out by workmen walking behind teams of surveyors who calculated angles and distances using tools unchanged since the days of the pyramid builders. The entire area now lay under a net of these white lines, attended to by countless small birds that did their best to eat them as fast as they were laid. Had we been able to see this work from on high, as the birds did when they flew up, we might have seen their purpose—to lay out a new harbor. And around this harbor they were to describe an entire city. It seemed like madness—but an inspired, perhaps even divine lunacy.

The idea to use flour had come from one who now stood among them. It was a practical solution to the lack of chalk in Egypt but, typically, an impulsive and perhaps not wholly thought-out one. As fast as the lines were laid, the birds descended and ate them. Some of the workmen muttered that it was an omen, and a bad one at that. What good could come from a city that the gods tried to eradicate the very moment it was first laid out? However, Alexander's personal soothsayer, Aristander, countered that it simply showed that Alexandria would one day feed the whole world, and according to an ancient source known today as "the pseudo-Callisthenes" in the *Alexander Romance*, when the great man consulted the Egyptian gods himself on the matter, he was told: "The city you are building will be the food-giver and nurse of the whole world" (Arrian, *Anabasis*, book 3a, chapter 2).

So the work on the shore opposite the little island of Pharos progressed, painfully slowly. Alexander, however, could not wait. Within a few days he had gone, perhaps a little bored by the daily drudgery of deciding where palaces and temples should go, but also tempted away by a new idea that had seized him while designing his city. It had been suggested to him by some Egyptians that he might not be a man at all, but a god, for surely only a god could achieve what he had done. It was flattery of course, but in a heroic age and on the lips of an ancient people perhaps it was more. Either way he set off with all speed to the desert shrine of Ammon to discover if it was indeed true.

Thus Plutarch describes the foundation of the city of Alexandria by its first and greatest son, Alexander the Great. As with so much about Alexander's life, it can be difficult to separate fact from myth in a story filled with omens and peopled by gods. The ancient sources do not even agree on whether Alexander founded his city before or after he spoke to the oracle at the shrine of Ammon in Siwa, but what all do agree on is that he alone chose the place, and the choice was a spectacularly good one.

Lying on the Mediterranean coast west of the Nile, this was an area that had not been well integrated into the ancient Egyptian states of the Old, Middle, and New Kingdoms. This is not to suggest that the area was completely empty, however. Excavations have shown that a small fishing village called Rhakotis had existed here since the thirteenth century BC, and the value of the anchorage was indeed known to Homer, whether or not he appeared to Alexander in a dream to remind him, as he wrote in the *Odyssey:*

> *Now off Egypt,*
> *About as far as a ship can sail in a day*
> *With a good stiff breeze behind her*
> *There is an island called Pharos*
> *It has a good harbour*
> *From which vessels can get out into open sea*
> *When they have taken in water*

Homer, *Odyssey,* book 4

Some evidence of the prehistoric harbor that Homer knew of has even been found off the shores of the island of Pharos. In the early years of the twentieth century Gaston Jondet, the chief engineer of ports and lights in Egypt, noted an extensive series of breakwaters beneath the present sea level which were unmentioned in classical texts. These had formed a Bronze Age harbor at a time when the Egypt of Rameses the Great and Tutankhamen traded extensively with the Minoan world, providing a port free from the choking silt of the delta. But they had already fallen into disuse and disappeared beneath the waves by the time Alexander arrived here. It is apposite, perhaps, that it should be Homer, a Greek source, who first makes mention of this place, for it was a Greek who was about to transform it.

Alexander was born in late July of 356 BC into the royal family of an ascendant Macedonian state. Under his father, King Philip II, the nation of Macedon, to the north of classical Greece, had extended its influence south and east across the Mediterranean, becoming a key player in Greek international politics. Greek culture mattered to Philip, and he ensured that his son received the very best Greek education available; indeed, Alexander's personal tutor was Aristotle, one of the most influential philosophers in all of Western thought. The tales of Alexander's promising childhood are legion, from his taming of the supposedly uncontrollable horse Bucephalus to his father's exhortation that he should conquer a land suitable for his ambition, as Macedon was too small for him. Most of these legends grew up after the events, of course, to help explain the extraordinary rise of the young Macedonian. After the assassination of Philip by his bodyguard Pausanias at a wedding banquet (possibly at the instigation of the new king of Persia, Darius III), Alexander was quickly proclaimed king by the Macedonian army. He was clearly already held in high regard. And so, at just twenty years of age, began the most remarkable military career in history.

If Alexander's father had been assassinated on Persian orders, Darius III would come to regret the decision. With an army of over forty thousand men Alexander first marched south to consolidate his hold over the city-states of mainland Greece and then crossed over the Hellespont into Asia to confront Darius in person. After defeating a Persian force at the battle of Granicus he stormed down the Ionian seaboard like an avenging angel, "liberating" the wealthy Greek trading ports that lined the coast on the way. He besieged Halicarnassus, then turned inland to the ancient Phrygian capital of Gordium, where, so legend has it, he chose to tackle the problem of "the Gordian Knot."

The legend goes that at a time when Phrygia found itself without a king, an ancient oracle prophesied that the first man to enter the capital in an oxcart should be their next king. That man was the peasant Gordias, who, in return for his sudden change in fortune, dedicated his cart to the gods, tying its shafts to a post in an elaborate knot. The oracle then further prophesied that whoever could undo the knot would be king of all Asia. It had been a problem that had bothered would-be rulers of the world from that moment on. The knot was allegedly fiendishly complicated, without protruding ends and hence impossible to unpick. But

Alexander found a simple solution. He drew his sword and sliced the knot in half, and as the oracle predicted, he did indeed go on to become master of all Asia. That at least is how Alexander's friends and propagandists told it.

From Gordium he then passed through the Cilician gates—the high pass in the Tarsus Mountains of modern-day Turkey—and into central Anatolia to face the Persian Empire head on. At the battle of Issus in 333 BC, Darius III was defeated and fled the field, leaving his mother, wife, and children to be captured by Alexander. Also among the spoils was the golden casket, belonging to the Persian king, in which he placed his beloved copy of Homer.

Alexander chose not to pursue the fleeing Persian across the Euphrates, but instead continued south, besieging coastal cities as he went. Where he was heading became clear in 332 BC, when he was welcomed into Egypt as the nation's liberator. Possibly with the connivance of the Persian governor of Egypt and certainly with the active support of the native Egyptian bureaucracy, the country was ceded to him without so much as a skirmish, and Alexander was king of Egypt at the age of twenty-three.

By the time Alexander first set foot on Egyptian soil, that civilization was already some three thousand years old. But this was not the Egypt of Khufu and Rameses. The pyramids of the Old Kingdom were already over two thousand years old, while the magnificence of the New Kingdom courts of Amenhotep III and Tutankhamen had faded and passed a millennium before.

Egypt's recent history had been crueler. Since 525 BC it had been a subject nation of the Persian Empire and its nominal pharaoh (the Twenty-seventh Dynasty) was in fact the Achaemenid shah, currently Darius III. The proud and ancient nation of Egypt had not taken kindly to Persian rule, and throughout the period links between native Egyptians and Greek merchants had been growing, fostered by their mutual antipathy toward the occupying superpower. Some Egyptian cults had even taken root back in Greece. In 333 BC the Athenians had allowed Egyptian merchants to buy land for a temple to their goddess Isis, wife of the god of the underworld, Osiris. There were also Greek merchants living in Egypt and adopting elements of its religion, particularly the worship of Isis, which in the following centuries would spread across the Mediterranean and, under Roman rule, reach as far as Britain. There were even Greeks in the civil administration, and so, though Alexander was a foreigner, the Egyptians welcomed him with open arms, as a Greek and their nation's liberator.

That Alexander wanted Egypt as part of his expanding empire was obvious. Despite the fact that so many of her glories were centuries if not millennia in the past, Egypt still retained a highly complex, literate culture with a wealth of esoteric knowledge, especially in astronomy, mathematics, and alchemy—knowledge which Greeks such as Pythagoras and Herodotus had sought out in the recent past. But more important for Alexander, Egypt was still a very wealthy nation with access to gold, slaves and exotic African imports from the south, and rich in grain. The irrigated fields around the Nile were a huge source of food that not only kept Egypt itself fed but also provided a surplus that could be exported for profit or used in military adventures. Then there was Egypt's position, directly across the Mediterranean from Greece, with a major river navigable far into the south. A pharaonic canal cut between that river and the Red Sea would provide access to the Indian Ocean for a ruler with the ambition to attempt a conquest of India—a ruler with the ambition of an Alexander.

And so it was with these thoughts in mind that Alexander first came to the tiny village of Rhakotis. In the heyday of the Egyptian pharaohs, life had been concentrated on the Nile Valley, and while some New Kingdom rulers had ventured beyond her borders to carve out empires, Egypt was traditionally insular and inward looking. It focused on the Nile Valley, not the Mediterranean, and thus little effort had been spent on developing the northern coast outside the delta. But for Alexander things were different. The Mediterranean, not the Nile, bound his world together, and a port on this coast would provide the quickest way of supplying his army and controlling his empire.

Here then he found a unique location on a dangerous coast. To the south of the site lay Mareotis, a 100-square-mile lake; to the east was the mouth of the Canopic branch of the Nile and the rest of the delta, offering access to Egypt's wealth and connections on to the Red Sea. To the north, just offshore, stood the island known as Pharos. Aside from the two harbors created by a causeway from Pharos to the mainland, canals could connect the Canopic Nile to the lake and the lake to the sea. In terms of trade it was simply a perfect location. The geographer Strabo, who visited the city some three hundred years after its foundation, also noted another great benefit:

> . . . and in addition to the great value of the things brought down from both directions, both into the harbour on the sea and into that on the lake, the salubrity of the air is also worthy of remark. And this likewise results from the fact that the land is washed by water on both sides and because of the timeliness of the Nile's risings; for the other cities that are situated on lakes have heavy and stifling air in the heats of summer, because the lakes then become marshy along their edges because of the evaporation caused by the sun's rays, and, accordingly, when so much filth-laden moisture rises, the air inhaled is noisome and starts pestilential diseases, whereas at Alexandria, at the beginning of summer, the Nile, being full, fills the lake also, and leaves no marshy matter to corrupt the rising vapours. At that time, also, the Etesian winds blow from the north and from a vast sea, Alexandrians pass their time most pleasantly in summer.

> Strabo, Geography, book 17, chapter 1

This might seem like little more than a pleasant conceit, but finding a healthy location away from the slow-moving and polluted waters of the delta, where disease was rife in the summer, was a masterstroke. The site was cool, clean, and accessible from abroad, and that in Egypt was rare. It must have seemed to be the perfect location for a provincial capital, and so, with the decision made, Alexander moved off again.

There was one further place the Macedonian king had to visit while in Egypt, and this visit would have profound implications both for Alexander and for the dynasty of Greek pharaohs that would soon be established in his city of Alexandria. As he rode through the Western desert toward the shrine of Ammon at Siwa, he could hardly have imagined that he would never return alive to the city he had just founded. He had left behind a capital of sand and flour—just a preliminary sketch—before dashing off once more in his endless, restless pursuit of yet greater achievements.

But what he did next would help secure the future of that sketch and ensure that this city would be his home in death if not in life.

Even today the oasis of Siwa is an extraordinary site. Standing lost between the Qattara Depression and the Great Sand Sea, it lies in one of the most remote and inhospitable parts of the country. Legend has it that when King Cambyses II of Persia first conquered Egypt his entire army of fifty thousand men vanished somewhere in the emptiness of the surrounding desert as they marched in search of the oasis. Under Roman rule its very remoteness made it famous as a place of banishment.

It is only after mile upon mile of dunes and dry rock that the oasis suddenly appears, a great swath of green, filled with a forest of palm trees, over which towers the old fortress of Shali. Here also, in the now nearly abandoned village of Aghurmi, stand the remains of what brought Alexander and perhaps Cambyses to this place—the temple of Ammon.

In the temple was an oracle popular among the Egyptians (although no pharaoh had ever visited the site) and widely respected in the Greek world. The deity worshipped here was clearly Egyptian, as Diodorus Siculus's description makes clear:

> The image of the god is encrusted with emeralds and other precious stones, and answers those who consult the oracle in a quite peculiar fashion. It is carried about upon a golden boat by eighty priests, and these, with the god on their shoulders, go without their own volition wherever the god directs their path. A multitude of girls and women follows them singing paeans as they go and praising the god in a traditional hymn.
>
> Diodorus Siculus, *Library of History*, book 17, chapter 50

But if the god was worshipped here in a particularly Egyptian form, the spread of the cult across the Mediterranean to Greece, where it was known as the cult of the Libyan Ammon, made this a perfect bridge between Alexander's Greek roots and an Egypt he needed to rule in a manner Egyptians would accept.

The oracle, we are told, had news for Alexander about his lineage—news that not only would cause ructions in the Greek world but would begin the process of turning Greek conquerors into Egyptian pharaohs. We are told that as Alexander approached the temple the priest welcomed him, calling him "Child of the God." He then invited him into the adytum—the interior of the temple usually reserved exclusively for the priests. The rest of the king's entourage had to wait in the courtyard. Just what Alexander asked the oracle in the darkened silence of the temple of Ammon is disputed. According to Plutarch, citing an anonymous source, the king asked two questions:

> He inquired whether any one of his father's murderers had escaped, to which the priest answered that he must not ask such questions, for his father was more than man. Alexander now altered the form of his inquiry and asked whether he had punished all the murderers of Philip: and then he asked another question, about his empire, whether he was fated to conquer all mankind. On receiving as an answer that this would be granted to him and that Philip had been amply avenged, he made splendid presents to the god, and amply rewarded the priests.

> Plutarch, *Life of Alexander,* in *Parallel Lives,* 27

But even Plutarch is suspicious of this story, though he is happy to repeat it. He and many other ancient authors felt that what passed between Alexander and the oracle was almost certainly kept secret. But what mattered to the Greeks in the king's party and what would matter to later generations of Egyptians is that from this meeting grew the idea that Alexander was not the son of Philip of Macedon but the son of the god Ammon himself.

The idea that Alexander was a living god was treated with great skepticism by the ancient Greeks, who generally thought only the dead were worthy of deification. Indeed, by the time of Plutarch there was even a story current that the whole idea of Alexander's immortal ancestry came about through a misunderstanding at Siwa. Plutarch tells us that some believed that the priest who emerged from the temple to greet Alexander mispronounced the Greek *"O paidion"* (Oh, my child!), and instead called out *"O paidios,"* which could to a Greek ear sound like *"O pai Dios"* (Oh, child of the god!).

By the second century AD the author Lucian found the idea of the divine Alexander humorous enough to make fun of him in one of his *Dialogues of the Dead* (13), in which Alexander discovers in the underworld, somewhat to his surprise, that he is not a god:

DIOGENES: *Dear me, Alexander, you dead like the rest of us?*

ALEXANDER: *As you see, sir; is there anything extraordinary in a mortal's dying?*

DIOGENES: *So Ammon lied when he said you were his son; you were Philip's after all.*

ALEXANDER: *Apparently; if I had been Ammon's, I should not have died.*

DIOGENES: *Strange! There were tales of the same order about Olympias too. A serpent visited her, and was seen in her bed; we were given to understand that that was how you came into the world, and Philip made a mistake when he took you for his.*

ALEXANDER: *Yes, I was told all that myself; however, I know now that my mother's and the Ammon stories were all moonshine.*

DIOGENES: *Their lies were of some practical value to you, though; your Divinity brought a good many people to their knees.*

Lucian, *Dialogues of the Dead*, 13

And in that last line from Diogenes lay Alexander's genius. While the Greeks could not easily accept that they were ruled by a living god, the Egyptians had kept this central to their beliefs for three thousand years. Herodotus said that the Egyptians were the most religious of all peoples, and their beliefs imbued every element of their society. Egypt was a theocracy where the majority of the large agricultural estates were owned by temples and managed by an elite caste of priests whose positions were often hereditary. The power built up by these institutions had grown century by century as the god-kings of the three ancient Egyptian kingdoms had granted them more and more land and rights. Between the pharaoh and the temples not only was the economy organized, but, in Egyptian eyes, the relationship between humans and gods was also managed. The ruler of Egypt was seen as Horus, the son of the god Osiris and the mediator between the worlds of the everyday and the divine. Through his interaction with the temples and his performance of the kingly rites in those temples, a state of harmony (*maat*) was maintained in the world—the stars would continue to circle in the heavens, the Nile would flood once a year, and so life in Egypt would go on as it had for thousands of years.

While the Greeks sneered at men who called themselves gods, the Egyptians actively required it of their rulers, so it served Alexander well to be considered divine in their eyes. Whether he believed it to be true himself is another and perhaps unknowable matter.

God or not, the oracle of Ammon inspired Alexander to keep up his relentless pace of conquest. Leaving Egypt, he finally and comprehensively defeated the Persians at the battle of Gaugamela before striking out east, through Medea, Parthia, and Scythia, on through Afghanistan and into India. His fleet crossed the Indian Ocean, from west to east and then back again—restless, relentless, and as unstoppable as the ever-shifting mind that drove it onward.

But he was chasing a desert mirage. By the time he was thirty-two years old his vast empire was already tottering, weighed down by self-interest and riven with factional infighting. As he returned to Babylon, omens of his impending death began to appear. Just outside the city a Chaldean astronomer appeared before him and warned him that entering the city (or in some versions of the story, entering the city from the east) would bring about his death. Alexander lived in a world of omens and oracles, and the prophecies of the celestial seers of Babylon, the "writers of the Book of Heaven," were not lightly cast aside. Their *Astronomical Diaries* had proved so accurate that Alexander had ordered them translated into Greek and sent to his old tutor Aristotle for inspection. This led within a year to the complete reform of the Greek calendar. So powerful, so widely believed, were the prophecies of these men that they could easily become self-fulfilling. Their predictions of Darius's doom may have helped to unsettle his army and hence put Alexander on the Persian throne in the first place. Now those prophecies were aimed against Alexander himself.

Alexander did, however, finally enter the city and in doing so embarked on the last days of his life, just as the astronomers had predicted. In these final moments legends begin to crowd in even more thickly around the man. The ancient sources now tell a strange tale. According to Arrian, Alexander went to inspect his soldiers, and while he was away from the throne room an escaped convict broke in, put on the insignia of the king, and sat on his throne. When discovered and asked why he was doing this he made no reply (or according to Plutarch he claimed he had been released by the supreme god). Alexander was troubled and consulted the wise men in Babylon, who advised that the man should be put to death so that the bad luck this foretold might fall on his shoulders and not the king's. Recent research suggests, however, that this peculiar legend may be the surviving echo of an eyewitness account of an ancient Babylonian ritual which neither Alexander nor later classical writers understood. When Babylonian astronomers predicted inauspicious times it was the custom for the priests to release a convict and place him on the throne as a "substitute king" in place of the real ruler. Then, any bad luck that befell the kingdom during this ominous time would fall on the shoulders of the criminal, not the king and hence the state. When the danger passed, the criminal would be executed, taking his ill fortune to the grave with him.

This was then perhaps the scene that Alexander stumbled upon, but its resolution did not ease his foreboding. He now fell into a dark mood, mistrustful of his friends and fearful for his future. Plutarch says that the Babylonian palace soon filled with soothsayers and sacrifices and that the slightest strange thing would be taken by Alexander as an omen, and a bad omen at that. And he had every right to worry.

Alexander's final illness came on during a drinking party, and his decline was then rapid. Diodorus Siculus takes up the story:

> *There he drank much unmixed wine in commemoration of the death of Heracles, and finally, filling a huge beaker, downed it at a gulp. Instantly he shrieked aloud as if smitten by a violent blow and was conducted by his friends, who led him by the hand back to his apartments. His chamberlains put him to bed and attended him closely, but the pain increased and the physicians were summoned. No one was*

able to do anything helpful and Alexander continued in great discomfort and acute suffering.

Diodorus Siculus, *Library of History,* book 17, chapter 117

He died in the palace of Nebuchadnezzar II on the afternoon of June 10, 323 BC. He was thirty-two years old. The cause of Alexander's death has been disputed since the moment he breathed his last, and a full investigation is outside the scope of this book. Some ancient authors maintain he died of an illness, perhaps malaria or typhoid; others report that he was poisoned, perhaps with belladonna, since Plutarch states that he was unable to speak shortly before the end, and paralysis of the vocal cords is a symptom of poisoning with deadly nightshade. He further suggests, as does Arrian, that some thought the poisoning to have been carried out at the instigation of Aristotle, who feared that the king's imprisonment of the chronicler Callisthenes for complaining about the king's growing arrogance signaled that Alexander's success had made him uncontrollable. In this version of events Aristotle procured a poison which was conveyed to Alexander's court in the hoof of a mule. These possibilities have since been elaborately embroidered by centuries of storytellers until the astonishing tale of Alexander's death has become filled with weeping horses, total eclipses, and speaking birds.

What did matter, regardless of the cause of his death, was that the largest empire on earth was now effectively leaderless, and there was a limited amount of time in which the king's surviving family and generals could make their pitch for part or all of his inheritance. Exactly who should now rule in his place was not clear. Alexander had a half brother, Philip III Arrhidaeus, who was the son of Philip II and Philinna of Larissa, but he seems to have been simpleminded and incapable of taking on sole rule of so great an empire in anything more than name. Despite this he was the choice of the army in Babylon and hence nominally became Alexander's heir. A few months after Alexander's death his Bactrian wife, Roxana, gave birth to his son, who was immediately declared king and joined his uncle on the throne as Alexander IV of Macedon. So it came to pass that the heirs of the greatest ruler of the ancient world were a fool and a baby.

The vast empire he had held together with little more than the power of his own will almost immediately began to disintegrate. Infighting erupted among Alexander's once loyal generals as each grasped feverishly for a piece of his crumbling inheritance. But there was little concrete to grab. For all his military brilliance, Alexander's attempts at governing his empire had bred hostility and dissent. In Persia his willingness to take on Persian customs, both in government and in dress, might have helped him to hold on to those lands, as his adoption of a pharaonic style of government in Egypt ensured his popularity there, but both practices were highly distasteful to other Macedonians. They were the conquerors, and few saw why they shouldn't rule the empire they had won in a Macedonian way. Their arrogance would ensure the fragmentation of Alexander's world.

Only one man had realized the true nature of Alexander's legacy—his childhood friend, confidant, and senior general, Ptolemy. He had been with Alexander from the start, and even accompanied him to the oracle of Ammon at Siwa. He was also present in Babylon when Alexander died, and a few days after the death called together the two other generals closest to Alexander. His view was that there was little hope in trying to maintain a leaderless single empire spanning Asia, North Africa, the Middle East, and the eastern Mediterranean. Better to divide it up into its three principal constituent parts, which each one of them could rule. He suggested they form a ruling council which would meet regularly to keep affairs on an even keel.

This extraordinarily farsighted proposal anticipated the inevitable frictions between what were at that moment the three most powerful people in the world, and offered a solution to the problem. But both the other generals dreamed of succeeding Alexander as sole supreme emperor. They rejected Ptolemy's proposal outright, thereby setting the stage for the centuries of interfactional warfare which would follow. Ptolemy, realizing full well that it was now each man for himself, left immediately for Egypt, the richest and most self-contained part of Alexander's empire.

Meanwhile, Alexander's body, already taking on the attributes of divinity, was prepared for travel, as Curtius Rufus recounts (although he claims that he for one does not believe the story):

> *Although the king's body had lain in the coffin for 6 days in scorching heat, there was no sign of decay when the Egyptians and Chaldeans came to embalm it. A golden sarcophagus was filled with perfumes, and on Alexander's head was placed the insignia of his rank.*

Quintus Curtius Rufus, Alexander the Great, book 10, chapter 10

Diodorus adds that after the embalmers had made the body sweet-smelling and incorruptible with the embalming materials of the region—frankincense, myrrh, beeswax, and honey—the whole body was wrapped in linen and sealed in exquisitely beaten gold sheets, so finely figured to his form that his features were still recognizable through them.

It was widely assumed that his corpse would be returned home to his birthplace—Macedon, in northern Greece. But Ptolemy realized that this was no ordinary body. Alexander, if not a god himself, had certainly seemed to have been touched by the gods, and the magical aura that surrounded him in life might also remain in death, in much the way that the bones of saints held a remarkable power over living minds in the Middle Ages. Other than an empire which was already tottering on the brink of civil war, the most valuable thing of Alexander's, for any successor, was not his lands or money or fame, but his body—the ultimate icon of the ultimate ruler. Here was an object whose value would only grow as the years passed and the myths evolved. This realization had not been lost on Alexander's friends even during his lifetime, when, according to a legend retold by Aelian, Alexander's favorite soothsayer, Aristander, had predicted "that the country in which his body was buried would be the most prosperous in the world" (Aelian, *Varia Historia,* 12.64).

Ptolemy knew what he had to do. He had to take for himself a part of Alexander's empire he could rule and defend alone. And the jewel he would set in that new nation's crown was the gold-clad body of Alexander himself.

CHAPTER TWO

STEALING A GOD

Fear no more the heat o' the sun
Nor the furious winter's rages;
Thou thy worldly task hast done,
Home art gone, and ta'en thy wages;
Golden lads and girls all must,
As chimney-sweepers, come to dust.

William Shakespeare, *Cymbeline*

While the fighting between the heirs of Alexander intensified, Ptolemy quietly secured his position as ruler of Egypt, as he was uniquely well equipped to do so, having been with Alexander from childhood. He had watched the man at work, learned from his successes, and learned still more from his failures.

Ptolemy was the son of a nobleman called Lagus, a member of a relatively obscure Macedonian family. Indeed, so obscure was it that when Ptolemy eventually achieved greatness himself, wild stories quickly became embroidered around the prosaic facts of his ancestry. The pro-Ptolemaic faction even claimed that he was the illegitimate son of Philip II. For their part, those ranged against Ptolemy told the story of how he had once asked a grammarian the famously difficult question "Who was the father of Pelops?" only to receive the reply "I will tell you as soon as you tell me who was the father of Lagus."

But for all the obscurity of his ancestry, Lagus did ensure that his son received an education at Philip II's court. Here he was appointed a page, during which time he became a close friend of the young Alexander and one of the group of five youths charged with mentoring the king's son.

In this situation he was able to watch the impressive Philip at work, carving out a Macedonian empire and building the army that his son would one day unleash on the world. He must also have enjoyed the culture of the court and perhaps shared the privilege of being taught by the tutor Philip had appointed for his son Alexander—the great Aristotle.

But he had shared in Alexander's tribulations as well as in his good fortunes. In the Pixodarus affair, Alexander had nearly been gulled into marrying the daughter of one of the heirs of King Mausolus, whose capital at Halicarnassus Alexander would later besiege. It was a match Philip knew to be inappropriate, and he managed to forbid it despite Alexander's having apparently already agreed. For this the prince and his mentors, including Ptolemy, were exiled, only to return upon the old king's death.

This turbulent childhood and youth molded Ptolemy into an extraordinarily shrewd young man, and his prince's ablest companion, as they set out to conquer the world together. He had been appointed one of Alexander's seven personal bodyguards and had played key roles in the campaigns in Afghanistan and India, although Arrian's descriptions of his heroics (drawn from Ptolemy's own account of Alexander's life) betray a tendency to exaggerate his importance. But most important of all, Ptolemy had learned to watch and wait, to see but remain silent. That was the great advantage he had over his old friend Alexander. Ptolemy was not in a hurry.

After Alexander's death the situation became delicate, and, having been with Alexander at Siwa and in Memphis, Ptolemy knew the Egyptian people had to be treated carefully if he was to retain their loyalty in the dangerous years ahead. As such he made no pretense of kingship, made no bid for the pharaonic throne so recently vacated by his friend and master. Instead he contented himself with the old Persian title "satrap"—effectively making himself governor of Egypt.

Even this careful move did not leave him without enemies. Alexander had appointed a man called Cleomenes to administer the delta area and raise the funds for the building of Alexandria. Cleomenes was a businessman, an extortionist, and a crook. Of those who wrote about him none had a good word to say for him. Demosthenes called him a "dishonest manipulator," while Arrian pulled even fewer punches and just branded him "an evil man." The cause of such hatred was, at least in part, his sheer success. He had been so successful indeed, and felt so confident, that he had declared himself satrap while Alexander was still in India. On returning, the king had admonished him for his presumption but, extraordinarily, hadn't dismissed him for it—he'd generated far too much money for that.

As part of the initial settlement among Alexander's generals upon his death, Ptolemy had now taken the title of satrap of Egypt for himself, but in doing so he was taking a risk. Alexander's empire was crumbling and Cleomenes had already shown that he had the nerve to take on the Macedonian state. How long would this hugely wealthy individual put up with Ptolemy as his master? For now this powerful but increasingly unpopular man could not be unseated, so in taking the title satrap for himself, Ptolemy appointed Cleomenes as his assistant (*hyparchos*). Most likely neither felt content with this, but the final resolution would have to wait.

And waiting is what Ptolemy was becoming good at. The end of Alexander's reign had been marked by confusion, and time seems to have done little to clarify the situation. As such the preparations for Alexander's body's final journey home were anything but quick. Indeed it was two years before news came from Babylon that the sarcophagus of Alexander was finally on the move.

The procession must have made quite an impression. The king's body had been placed inside two golden caskets, the outer one draped with a purple robe on which lay Alexander's armor. This coffin was then mounted on a specially constructed golden carriage with a vaulted roof supported by slender Ionic columns. Diodorus describes the scene:

> *At the top of the carriage was built a vault of gold, eight cubits wide and twelve long, covered with overlapping scales set with precious stones. Beneath the roof, all along the work was a rectangular cornice of gold from which projected heads of goat-stags in high relief. Gold rings two palms broad were suspended from these, and through the rings there ran a festive garland beautifully decorated in bright colours*

of all kinds. At the ends there were tassels of network suspending large
bells, so that any who were approaching heard the sound from a great
distance. On each corner of the vault on each side was a golden figure
of Victory holding a trophy.

Diodorus Siculus, *Library of History*, book 18, chapter 26

But that was only the beginning. Diodorus goes on to explain how
the carriage lavishly advertised the already partly mythical achievements
of Alexander: On the vault over Alexander's body was strung a golden
net on which were suspended long painted tablets, one on each side. On
the first of these was a chariot carved in relief, on which sat Alexander,
scepter in hand, surrounded by Macedonian and Persian attendants. On
the second tablet were carved war elephants complete with mahouts and
regular Macedonian troops. The third tablet portrayed Alexander's impressive cavalry in battle formation, while the fourth showed his navy,
ready for combat. At the entrance to the chamber itself there were golden
lions whose eyes, so Diodorus tells us, turned to watch those who would
enter this holy of holies. Above the chamber, he adds,

there was a purple banner blazoned with a golden olive wreath of great
size and when the sun cast upon it its rays, it sent forth such a bright
and vibrant gleam that from a great distance it appeared like a flash of
lightning.

Diodorus Siculus, *Library of History*, book 18, chapter 26

Here then, condensed into one fabulous vehicle, was the achievement
of Alexander—a glittering advertisement for all that he had been and all
that he could have been. Its single remaining task was to bear away the
body of the man whose life it portrayed. Finally, in 321 BC the carriage,
drawn by sixty-four mules and accompanied by a great procession, wound
its way through the streets of Babylon and out into the countryside beyond. The question now was, where was it going?

Ancient historians cannot agree on where Alexander himself wanted
to be buried, but that is perhaps hardly surprising when his heirs couldn't
agree either, though each would claim he was doing Alexander's will.
The traditional burial place for a king of Macedon was the ancient capital

of Lower Macedonia, Aigai on the slopes of the Pierian Mountains in what is now northern Greece. Here, by the modern village of Vergina, lie the remains of a great Macedonian palace whose veranda once commanded a majestic view over the plains of the Haliakmon River, and where, among the ruins of the temple of Eukleia, can still be found the bases of two votive statues dedicated by Alexander's grandmother Queen Eurydice. All around among the elm trees can be seen the memorials of ancient Macedonians of all classes and levels of fame, right up to the magnificent royal tombs of the Great Tumulus, whose contents are now impressively housed in their own subterranean museum. Here lie the finds from the "tomb of Philip II," discovered in 1977, perhaps the last resting place of Alexander's father, although more recent archaeological work suggests that perhaps it is the tomb of his simple half brother Philip III Arrhidaeus. But whoever the occupant actually was, this was clearly the last resting place of Alexander's ancestors and hence perhaps as close as this restless soul might have come to a final home.

But other thoughts had crowded into Alexander's mind in his last years. The trip to Siwa had given him alternative and far more illustrious ancestors—the gods of Egypt. While we do not know to what degree Alexander actually believed that he was a god, Diodorus says his last wish was to be buried not with his earthly ancestors in Aigai, but at Siwa, where he could be with his divine father, Ammon.

But with Alexander dead there were considerations far greater than his dying wishes—indeed all his last wishes were soon forgotten. Whatever he believed or wanted his people to believe, the mummified contents of his golden coffin were worth as much as the coffin itself—literally its weight in gold—wherever it finally ended up.

When the procession left Babylon, that body was nominally under the control of Philip III Arrhidaeus, but as such it must, in truth, have been under the control of Perdiccas. Perdiccas, one of Alexander's faithful bodyguards, had, according to some ancient sources, been given Alexander's ring on his deathbed—as close as the great man came to nominating an heir. Since then he had done his best to try to hold the whole of his old master's dream together—to keep the empire as one entity. Of course he was not ruling in his own right, merely as regent for the dead king's simple half brother and infant son, but he was certainly in control. So we must imagine that the procession struck out for Aigai, in the lands directly ruled by the people over whom Perdiccas had control. But they would not stay that way for long.

Ptolemy was clearly tipped off about the removal of Alexander's body, and he acted quickly. As the funerary cortege wound its way across Asia Minor back toward Macedon, Ptolemy struck, possibly in or near Damascus. Seizing control of the somber procession, he ordered it to turn south down the Mediterranean coast and across Sinai into Egypt. Alexander wasn't going home to Macedon, he was going back to the city he'd founded by the island of Pharos, and there, though dead, he was going to found a new empire—not a crude military conquest but an empire of the mind.

The kidnapping of the body of Alexander was Ptolemy's masterstroke. While the other generals still jostled for wealth and position in the Near East and Persia, he had realized that the one treasure still worth having was the body of the king himself. Ptolemy had decided that Alexander would quite literally be the centerpiece of the new Egyptian empire he planned to rule, and where better to rule from than the city his old master and friend had founded?

But again patience was necessary. Alexandria was not yet a thriving city and Egypt was not yet so pliable that its people would accept anything their satrap ordered. Ptolemy needed the Egyptians to believe in him and what he stood for. He knew dangerous times were coming. Having stolen the body of Alexander he had finally severed his links with Perdiccas, showing clearly that he had no belief in the maintenance of Alexander's empire as one coherent entity. He had effectively shouted "Every man for himself" and must have known that Perdiccas would now come after him and the treasure he had taken for his own.

Egyptian protocols now had to be carefully followed. After a sweltering journey across Sinai, Ptolemy ordered that the body first be taken to the old pharaonic capital of Memphis, twelve miles south of the modern Egyptian capital of Cairo, and interred in an Egyptian-style tomb near his divine "father," Ammon, while work on both his Alexandrian tomb and his city progressed.

Memphis was a city of pharaohs, an ancient center of Egyptian religion and regal power, and the place where Alexander had been crowned king. This had been Egypt's first great city in what, even then, was the distant past. Legend had it that it had been created by the founder of the Old Kingdom, Menes, close to the necropolis at Saqqara, where the first pyramids had been built. Since then its fortunes had waxed and waned, having lost its role as capital in 1300 BC and having only recently returned to prominence under the Persian satraps. But for Ptolemy's purpose what Memphis had in its favor was history. When the funeral procession of Alexander wound through the gates, it was entering a city that was already 2,750 years old.

The presence of his body here announced that he had been a legitimate heir to the pharaohs who had built this place; that he had supported the priests of Ptah here; that he had honored the Apis bull, Egypt's most sacred animal, who lived here; and that he had respected the ancient temple system that ran the country. His burial in an Egyptian-style tomb was also of the greatest importance. This spoke to Egyptians, telling them that Egypt—long-suffering, invaded, and despoiled Egypt—was what had mattered most to Alexander and that the greatest general for centuries, perhaps of all time, had known that his spiritual home was here in the greatest of ancient civilizations. That alone proved to them that he must have been born of the Egyptian gods, and reminded them that they were once, and would be again, a great nation.

But Ptolemy did not intend to leave Alexander in Memphis. This ancient city in the delta was not ideally suited as the capital of the type of modern state he had in mind, and the monolithic religious presence there might prove stifling to his plans. Though he wanted to rule Egypt in a way Egyptians understood, this did not extend to being a puppet of Egyptian officials and priests in Memphis. No, the site for his new capital had to be Alexandria. Not only had this place been selected by the divine Alexander himself but it also fulfilled Ptolemy's strategic and cultural requirements. Ptolemy needed a capital that had access to the Mediterranean world, the Greek world, which could dominate trade and diplomacy as well as grant a military advantage against enemies. He needed a port which had access to Egyptian wealth *and* that of the world beyond. Ancient Egypt had often been an inward-looking culture, suspicious of foreign contact. Ptolemy intended to plug it into the Greek world and in the process reinvent it.

There were also purely military considerations. This Egypt was not going to be part of a greater empire. Ptolemy had seen firsthand how difficult it was to rule vast territories with their huge cultural differences. He instead chose a place with one cultural identity, but he would have to defend it from the other heirs of Alexander who still believed in Alexander's dream and would, no doubt, attempt to bring Egypt back into the fold. As Egypt's wealth was the Nile Valley, this meant protecting the country's flanks, setting up buffer zones in the east and west to prevent attacks across Sinai or from the other city-states along the Libyan coast. For this Alexandria was ideally situated, so he urged its builders on.

The man charged with laying out Alexander's city was Dinocrates of Rhodes, who hence takes his place as the first in that long line of Alexandrian scholars. He had the task of following with surveyors where Alexander had once strode with barley flour, placing temples here and palaces there with the sweep of his hand and turning that vague idea into functioning reality. As the city's planner he devised a design based on the principles of the great Greek architect Hippodamus of Miletus, the man who had been employed by the Athenians to build their harbor at Piraeus. Hippodamus had been a flamboyant character, if the none-too-flattering sketch furnished by Aristotle can be relied upon:

> Hippodamus, the son of Euruphon a Milesian, contrived the art of laying out towns. . . . This man was in other respects too eager after notice, and seemed to many to live in a very affected manner, with his flowing locks and his expensive ornaments, and a coarse warm vest which he wore, not only in the winter, but also in the hot weather.

> Aristotle, *Politics*, part 8

Despite these affectations Hippodamus and his school were held in high regard when it came to planning towns. For them town planning was about much more than just laying out public squares and markets. For them the job of an architect also included suggesting how a town should function, what the structure of its government should be, and how its citizens should work together for the common good. Aristotle, in a more generous mood, tells us that Hippodamus was

> *the first who, not being actually engaged in the management of public affairs, set himself to inquire what sort of government was best; and he planned a state, consisting of ten thousand persons, divided into three parts, one consisting of artisans, another of husbandmen, and the third of soldiers; he also divided the lands into three parts, and allotted one to sacred purposes, another to the public, and the third to individuals.*
>
> Aristotle, *Politics*, part 8

He even seems to have gone as far as suggesting the rudiments of a welfare state, when he

> *made a law, that those should be rewarded who found out anything for the good of the city, and that the children of those who fell in battle should be educated at the public expense; which law had never been proposed by any other legislator, though it is at present in use at Athens as well as in other cities.*
>
> Aristotle, *Politics*, part 8

Of course Hippodamus had rarely had the opportunity to build a city from scratch, having instead to change towns piecemeal and persuade their inhabitants of the merits of his ideas. At Alexandria, however, Dinocrates had a clean slate, and as he paced the burning sand he must have thought of not just how to build a city but how to make it work as well.

The physical system Dinocrates built was based around a grid of roads, each cell of which was then to be filled in with housing, public buildings, and royal palaces. This gridiron provided the maximum road access and commercial frontage while also allowing for privacy within each cell. It was a simple but hugely innovative design, forgotten in the modern world until recent centuries. Today, of course, it is a plan that forms the backbone of some of the greatest cities on earth, from Tokyo to New York.

The most important work, however, was to create the two sea harbors and for this major engineering work was necessary. This took the form of a 600-foot-wide mole, or causeway, stretching between the mainland and the island of Pharos, which divided the bay in half. As this land bridge was seven times the length of a Greek stadium (around 4,200 feet) it was known as the *heptastadion*. The heptastadion was cut and bridged at its top and bottom to allow shipping to pass from one harbor to the other. To the east was the Great Harbor, running from the isle of Pharos over the heptastadion, along the coast, and out via another promontory, the Lochias. Across its narrow neck lay dangerous reefs, making the approach extremely difficult; but inside the harbor, shipping was almost entirely protected from the elements. For a ship finding passage into this haven, an extraordinary new vista now opened up. Ahead lay the tiny island of Antirrhodos, with its own miniature royal harbor, and embracing this, the walls of the harbor proper, where the palaces, apartments, and gardens of the royal quarter spilled down to the edge of the sea. Here the still blue waters ran so deep that even the largest ships could tie up at the walls without fear of grounding.

To the west lay the port of Eunostos in the curve from the other end of the Pharos across the heptastadion and on to the mainland coast. With its wide mouth it made for an apparently much easier approach from the sea, but again the harbor opening was littered with reefs and shoals, making sense for any sailor of the port's name, Eunostos—the "Port of Good Return." From here there was also a canal cut across to Lake Mareotis. Finally, there was a third, very small sea harbor, on the far side of the island of Pharos itself, known as the Port of Pirates, suitable for small fishing boats perhaps but, thanks to a string of rocks across its entrance, of no use in Dinocrates' magnificent plan. Nor was the name purely fanciful. The inhabitants of Pharos and the users of her harbor retained something of a reputation for piracy even as the city began to thrive, and ships approaching and leaving port were warned to give the island a wide berth.

To provide water for the city, another canal stretched from the Nile near the town of Canopus to great underground communal cisterns in the city. For those fortunate to be living in the wealthier sections of the city, the larger private houses were fitted with their own cisterns giving their owners the unique advantage in a desert land of having fresh water "on tap." Nor were the inhabitants of Pharos forgotten, and an aqueduct carried water for the island from the Nile canal, through the city, and across the heptastadion.

Within these boundaries it was Dinocrates' task to fit this perfect city, and the results were spectacular. Imagine the traveler whose ship puts in at Alexandria's Great Harbor in these early days. He would walk along the new wharves and pass south through the Gate of the Moon into the city itself. Ahead lies a 101-foot-wide boulevard known later as the Street of the Soma, or "body," after the mausoleum of Alexander and the Ptolemaic kings that stood on its flank. Down each side the dazzling white of marble colonnades leads the eye to the southern gate of the city—the Gate of the Sun—and, glittering beyond it, the waters of Lake Mareotis. Here Nile transports laden with Egyptian grain might be seen tying up alongside the marsh harbor, while distant sails carry Greek treasures away to the Nile Valley. Walking down the granite-paved street, our visitor eventually comes to the major crossroads where the great east–west Canopic Way intersects the Street of the Soma. In years to come this will be the chaotic, noisy heart of the city, filled with street philosophers, tradesmen, and hawkers, but for now it is still quiet. To the left along the way, in the far distance, stands the Canopic Gate, beyond which a dusty road leads east toward the Nile and "old" Egypt. To the right the colonnades stretch out to the Necropic Gate at the threshold of the City of the Dead. Beyond lie the gardens and embalming houses in which the inhabitants of this city will be buried in centuries to come, a silent otherworld of incense-laden air and voiceless mausolea. Along both these streets and the grid of smaller roads that spread out from them, plots are already being divided up. There will be a theater and a stadium, a riding track, a gymnasium, and a host of temples and shrines. The large space needed for the hippodrome will have to be found outside the city limits, beyond the Canopic Gate, while the royal quarter will quickly fill with ever more lavish palaces and lodges.

Other wonders too would soon come to Alexandria, but with the building of the heptastadion and the laying out of the main roads, the fundamental plan of the greatest city in the ancient world was complete. Plutarch in his *Life of Alexander* commented that the overall shape was, appropriately enough, like that of a military Macedonian chlamys, the Macedonian short cloak—gathered in the middle between the

Mediterranean and Mareotis and splaying out to east and west. Long before the lighthouse shone out from Pharos, before the foundation of the
library or museum, before even Alexander's body was entombed in its
marble-and-rock-crystal vault, his city was already a miracle. The flour
and sand had become marble and granite.

The people who gazed out from their new marble porticoes in the
nascent city were as varied in origin and wealth as the peoples Alexander
had conquered. The city had been laid out not in three "classes," as Hippodamus had suggested, but in three main ethnic districts: the original
village site of Rhakotis became the native Egyptian quarter, the Brucheum
was home to both Greek immigrants and the Greek rulers of the city, and
a Jewish quarter was populated with both local Jewish residents and traders and a large population (some report it as one hundred thousand people) of captives, brought here by Ptolemy after he had conquered
Jerusalem. Later other districts would follow, but already this blend of
European, African, and Near Eastern peoples was unique.

We have no contemporary description of the early city, but later travelers visited and described what this seed would become. Strabo, a Greek
geographer, whose name is actually an insulting Roman term meaning
"squinty," visited the city during Julius Caesar's lifetime and recorded
how by his time, every space within the plan laid out by Dinocrates had
been filled with buildings:

> The city contains most beautiful public precincts and also the royal
> palaces, which constitute one-fourth or even one-third of the whole
> circuit of the city; for just as each of the kings, from love of splendour,
> was wont to add some adornment to the public monuments, so also he
> would invest himself at his own expense with a residence, in addition
> to those already built, so that now, to quote the words of the poet,
> "there is building upon building." All, however, are connected with
> one another and the harbour, even those that lie outside the harbour.

> Strabo, *Geography*, book 17, chapter 8

But if it was the whim of Alexander that had founded the city and the
will of Ptolemy that made it his capital, it was something more powerful
than both of them that made it a success from the start. The reason people

from across the ancient world were settling here was trade. Alexandria was rapidly becoming the entrepôt of the world. Sited between two harbors, the city stood at the crossroads of the ancient world, where the fine art and technology of the Greek city-states could be traded for the vast food resources of the Nile Valley, the treasures of Africa, and the luxuries of Asia. By the time Diodorus visited sometime around the middle of the first century BC it was unsurpassed:

> *The city in general has grown so much in later times that many reckon it to be the first city of the civilized world, and it is certainly far ahead of all the rest in elegance and extent and riches and luxury. The number of its inhabitants surpasses that of those in other cities. At the time when we were in Egypt, those who kept the census returns of the population said that its free residents were more than three hundred thousand, and that the king received from the revenues of the country more than six thousand talents.*

> Diodorus Siculus, *Library of History*, book 17, chapter 52

Alexandria was a commercial success, and once the body of the hero himself was installed as its centerpiece it would gain an electrifying additional significance. It would become a city of God.

While Alexander's great plan seemed to be coming together, Ptolemy's place in succeeding to this patrimony was by no means yet certain. Ptolemy's retiring to Egypt with the body of Alexander sent out a clear message to any Macedonian generals who might dispute the succession. If Perdiccas or anyone else wanted to reintegrate Egypt into that empire, he would now have to fight Ptolemy for it. Egypt was hence the first fragment to fall away from the Macedonian Empire, beginning a sequence of collapse that would lead to years of internecine warfare.

But in the last remaining days of peace there was one other problem in Egypt to clear up. It was time for Ptolemy to turn to that other festering sore, that other dangerous reminder of the old times. Cleomenes of Naucratis was still a powerful official in Egypt, and still the man in charge of funding the building of Ptolemy's new city. But as that dream came to fruition, so the potentially dangerous Cleomenes' usefulness was coming to an end.

It was perhaps an old face from Ptolemy's childhood, Aristotle, who suggested the solution. Cleomenes had somehow come to Aristotle's attention, and in the great man's economic treatise *Oeconomica* he describes at length some of the hyparchos's more "unusual" methods of raising funds. In one instance he threatened to attack the sacred crocodiles who ate one of his servants, forcing their priests to produce a large quantity of gold in order to buy off his wrath and so protect the sanctity of the reptiles.

In particular Aristotle reports the unique approach he took to funding and filling the new city of Alexandria by persuading the inhabitants of the nearby market town of Canopus to move to the city: "Sailing therefore to Canopus he informed the priests and the men of property there that he was come to remove them. The priests and residents thereupon contributed money to induce him to leave their market where it was" (Aristotle, *Oeconomica*, book 2, 1352a).

Cleomenes was not about to forgo a substantial bribe, so he took the money and left the inhabitants of Canopus in peace, at least for a little while. But in fact the residents of the city had just bought some time while the finishing touches were put to Alexandria. Then Cleomenes returned "and proceeded to demand an excessive sum; which represented, he said, the difference the change of site would make to him. They however declared themselves unable to pay it, and were accordingly removed" (Aristotle, *Oeconomica*, book 2, 1352a).

Aristotle went on to list numerous other cons, tricks, and elaborate extortions by which this rather faithless financial adviser lined the imperial pocket and his own. Whether this information had come to Aristotle from Ptolemy, or whether it was common knowledge, is unknown. Perhaps Cleomenes felt invulnerable enough even to boast of his financial "achievements." If he did so, however, he was a fool, for Aristotle was writing his death warrant.

Perhaps, standing in front of the beautiful city now growing up around him, Cleomenes thought his work, his reputation, or even his money could protect him. He was quite mistaken. In fact, making money—his great talent—would be his undoing. His sharp financial practices had been overlooked for years by rulers eager to line their own coffers, but Ptolemy now turned with righteous indignation on the man who had built Alexandria for him. The financial wizard who, more than any other person, had actually turned Alexander's orders into architectural reality was charged with embezzling the staggering sum of eight thousand Egyptian talents. To put that into the context of the day, it was enough money to have paid one of the laborers building the city for over sixty-six thousand years. It was also of course a charge which undoubtedly had a certain ring of truth to it, even if Ptolemy had massaged the exact figures. As a result Cleomenes was tried, found guilty, and promptly executed.

It was another astute move on Ptolemy's part. He had removed a dangerous and wealthy rival and at the same time made himself hugely popular in Egypt for bringing "justice" to bear on a man who had bled the country dry. But Ptolemy had no intention of returning the money. Alexandria was built, the population was moved, and the money in the state (and Cleomenes') coffers would now be at his command. It was a most fortunate situation for Ptolemy, and he needed good fortune, for war was coming.

Alexander would have wept to see what followed his death. Perdiccas, his old friend, could not stand by quietly while provoked by Ptolemy. Ptolemy had Alexander's body and was clearly carving out a piece of his empire for his sole use. And so, in a vain attempt to hold together the whole idea of a unified empire, the regent attacked Egypt with the full might of the Macedonian army—Indian elephants, mahouts, and all. But his high-handed arrogance and his failure to appreciate the impossibility of ruling this vast, messy collection of conquests alone would prove his downfall. Although others of the friends and companions of Alexander marched through Sinai into Egypt with Perdiccas, not all of them still believed that the empire could be maintained. Fewer still believed, or wanted to believe, that it should be maintained by Perdiccas. Thus, the army that burst into the eastern delta was not the happy, all-conquering band of brothers that had only recently fought its way across Asia to India.

On reaching the Nile, Perdiccas ordered his army across, the elephants in the front, then the shield bearers and ladder carriers who were to be the vanguard of his attack on a fort known as the Fort of Camels. However, Ptolemy was not far away, and he and his army dashed to the fort and quickly took up positions, prepared to repel the assault: "At once the shield bearers set up the scaling ladders and began to mount them while the elephant borne troops were tearing the palisades to pieces and throwing down the parapets" (Diodorus Siculus, *Library of History*, book 18, chapter 34).

According to Diodorus, who describes the scene, Perdiccas did not use his war elephants with the tactical brilliance of his old master, and seeing a weakness, Ptolemy personally seized the initiative:

> *Ptolemy, however, who had the best soldiers near himself and wished to encourage the other commanders and friends to face the dangers, taking his long spear and posting himself on the top of the outwork, put out the eyes of the leading elephant, since he occupied a higher position, and wounded its Indian mahout. Then with utter contempt of the danger, striking and disabling those who were coming up the ladders, he sent them rolling down, in their armour into the river.*

Diodorus Siculus, *Library of History*, book 18, chapter 34

His men followed suit and began targeting the Indian mahouts, leaving the elephants out of control and useless, although Perdiccas sent wave after wave of attackers, having the advantage of numbers. The battle (and Ptolemy's personal heroics) lasted all day, but in the end Perdiccas was forced to call off the assault and retreat to his former camp. Ptolemy was victorious.

We don't know Diodorus's source for this episode, but the wild heroics of Ptolemy himself suggest it was somewhat biased. In fact Ptolemy had delayed Perdiccas long enough for something far more powerful to come to the rescue—doubt.

Perdiccas had failed to cross the Nile, and now the whispering campaign began. Ptolemy had secured a jewel for himself—something manageable, defendable. Why shouldn't Alexander's other old friends do the same for themselves? Forget the greater empire, forget Perdiccas, and seize something tangible for their own. And so they did. In the late spring of 321 BC a mutiny broke out among those same Macedonian troops who had once conquered the world, and Perdiccas's own officers assassinated him.

This would not bring an end to the wars among Alexander's heirs, but it did mark the end of the idea that any of them could rule everything their old master had. By the end of the fighting, which lasted until nearly the end of the century, Alexander's dreams lay in ruins—his mother, wife, half brother, and infant son all murdered. In their place stood three families. In Greece and Macedon, the Antigonids would rule the old homeland; in the Asian satrapies, the descendants of Seleucus (who had been one of the assassins of Perdiccas) would govern this part of the former Persian Empire; while in Egypt, Ptolemy intended to found his own dynasty.

Ptolemy had set the tone for the new order in Egypt and, fired by the same drive that had taken him and his master to the Indian subcontinent, set about subduing the city-states of North Africa.

By 321 BC the wealthy but isolated city of Cyrene, lying between Egypt and Tunisia, had fallen to him. As one of Alexander's conquests it was a state Ptolemy rightfully felt was his for the taking, having only recently come under the rule of a Spartan adventurer in the chaos following Alexander's death. But in retaking the city he showed himself to have learned from his master's diplomatic mistakes. He did not replace tyrant Spartan rule with a dictatorship of his own but with a liberal constitution. Under the "Ptolemaic constitution" the state was to be ruled by ten thousand privileged citizens arranged into two councils and a popular court, in a plan not dissimilar to that proposed by Hippodamus. He did not go so far as to let the Cyrenians think they could rule themselves alone, of course, appointing himself as their guardian in perpetuity.

In an age which celebrated outright conquest, this defensive imperialism was not only novel, it was successful and sustainable. Ptolemy pushed on farther west beyond Cyrene to take control of the profitable trans-Saharan trade routes bringing gold, ivory, and slaves from Central and West Africa. To the east and north he seized Palestine and parts of Syria, as well as Cyprus and the Aegean islands of the Cyclades. This gave him control of lucrative trade routes but, more important, created a buffer zone where he could contest disputes with his Persian and Macedonian rivals, leaving the Egyptian heartland stable and free from warfare for generations to come. Ptolemy had been the only successor to Alexander not to want to inherit that whole empire. He did not want new territories, just enough friendly or subject states around him to protect the core of his plan—Egypt. He had taken a dependent satrapy and forged it into an independent nation. The physical structure for the Ptolemaic age was now in place; it simply needed to be brought to life.

CHAPTER THREE

EGYPT REBORN

Egypt has more wonders in it than any other country in the world and provides more works that defy description than any other place.

Herodotus, *The Histories*

During Ptolemy's lifetime, the body of Alexander was not the only god resting in Memphis. Apis, the bull god of the city, was, at least to the native Egyptians, easily as important as the mummified remains of the conqueror of the world, and the representation of this deity was a living bull kept in its own temple and treated with the respect due to the earthly manifestation of a god.

It was a peculiarly Egyptian idea. The Apis bull had been a powerful symbol in Egypt since the very first dynasties well over two thousand years earlier. Originally it had represented the power and will of the pharaoh himself, later being thought to represent the god Ptah, whose center of worship was at Memphis. By Ptolemy's day, however, the animal had come to represent the incarnation of Osiris, the lord of the dead, who was usually depicted in human form, wrapped and mummified for burial. According to Plutarch, the bull was then the living aspect of this dead god or, as he put it, "the beautiful image of the soul of Osiris" (Plutarch, *Isis and Osiris,* chapter 20, in *Moralia*).

To Egyptians the presence of this living creature was a manifestation of a god on earth, more holy than the sacred cows that walk unmolested through the streets of Indian cities. When the bull died, the whole of Egypt went into seventy days of mourning and fasting, during which time the carcass of the huge animal was mummified and prepared for a lavish funeral. The body was then carried down the sphinx-lined processional

way from Memphis to the great funerary complex at Saqqara, where some
of the earliest pharaohs had been buried. Here the line of sphinxes directed the mourners to a temple and catacomb where the dead Apis, now
known as the Osiris Apis or Serapis, would be laid to rest—the Serapeum.
Today the majority of the site lies buried deep under the sand, something
that was already a problem in 24 BC, when Strabo paid a visit:

> One finds a temple to Serapis in such a sandy place that the wind
> heaps up the sand dunes beneath which we saw sphinxes, some half
> buried, some buried up to the head, from which one can suppose that
> the way to this temple could not be without danger if one were caught
> in a sudden wind storm.

Strabo, *Geography*, book 17, chapter 1

After Strabo the sands seem to have continued to pile up and the
complex disappeared from historical view for 1,875 years until, in a scene
that could have come from a children's adventure book, the French archaeologist Auguste Mariette stumbled upon those same sphinxes that
Strabo had recorded disappearing beneath the sand:

> Did it not seem that Strabo had written this . . . to help us rediscover,
> after over eighteen centuries, the famous temple dedicated to Serapis?
> It was impossible to doubt it. This buried sphinx, the companion of
> fifteen others I had encountered in Alexandria and Cairo, formed with
> them . . . part of the avenue that led to the Memphis Serapeum.

Auguste Mariette, *La Serapeum de Memphis*, 1856

The tantalizing line of sphinxes led to one of the most important funerary sites in Egypt, into the presence of animals whom the Egyptians, at
least, believed to be gods. Mariette was transfixed by thoughts of what lay
beneath his feet:

> Undoubtedly many precious fragments, many statues, many un-
> known texts were hidden beneath the sand upon which I stood . . . and
> it was thus, on 1 November 1850, during one of the most beautiful
> sunrises I had ever seen in Egypt, that a group of thirty workmen,

working under my orders near that sphinx, were about to cause such
total upheaval in the conditions of my stay in Egypt.

Auguste Mariette, *La Serapeum de Memphis,* 1856

What Mariette found as he dug was that the line of sphinxes led to a sand-filled courtyard in which sat one of the most exquisite Egyptian statues in existence—the Squatting Scribe. Beyond this, behind a rockfall of rubble which he removed with explosives, lay seemingly endless subterranean galleries cut into the living rock beneath Egypt's oldest pyramids, which had once contained the mortal remains of the Apis bulls. Each one had been buried in a giant sarcophagus, cut from a single piece of granite and weighing sixty to eighty tons. Inside had lain the doubtless bejeweled and gilded bodies of the bulls themselves, though Mariette noted that all the coffin lids had been pushed aside and the remains robbed.

Two millennia before, in the time of the Ptolemies, few would have dared enter the catacombs where Mariette now walked, and none would have disturbed the sleep of the recently deceased Apis. After their lavish, almost pharaonic burial, word would have gone out to the priests that a new Apis had to be found, and the Nile Valley would be scoured in the search for a calf born under just the right circumstances. Herodotus says the priests were looking out for the "calf of a cow which is never afterwards able to have another. The Egyptian belief is that a flash of lightning descends upon the cow from heaven, and this causes her to receive Apis" (Herodotus, *The Histories,* book 3 [Thaleia], chapter 27).

In practical terms this meant a black calf with a white diamond on its forehead, an eagle on its back, a scarab mark under its tongue, and double the usual number of tail hairs. When such an animal was found, there was rejoicing through the country because the living god had returned to them. The calf's mother was immediately revered as the Isis Cow, while her calf was transported down the Nile to Memphis, housed in a golden cabin on its own barque.

From now on the bull would live like a king, appearing to an adoring public during the seven days of the annual Apis festival, being led through the crowds by his priests. It was said that a child who smelled the breath of the Apis would be granted the gift of foreseeing the future, as the bull was an oracle. Those without access to such a fortunate child could ask the

bull itself about their future by holding out food for it. If it took the offering, then their future was bright; if it refused, then the omens were bad.

To the Greek Herodotus, this worship of a farmyard animal seemed
strange, to say the least. Although the Greek gods might take on animal
form when it suited them, there were no sacred animals in their pantheon. Most Greeks had enough trouble with the idea of a living human
taking on the characteristics of a god, as we've seen in their response to
Alexander's claim of divinity, so a living animal god was simply ludicrous
to them.

But antagonizing Egyptians' millennia-old beliefs was a foolish undertaking, as Ptolemy well knew. The Apis rituals were a link with that un-
imaginably long Egyptian history that this country's people held so dear,
and Ptolemy saw that this could make or break his attempt to rule successfully here. Herodotus went on in his description of the Apis cult to
describe how the hated Persian rulers of Egypt had mocked the cult.
Their king Cambyses had heard of the birth of a new Apis and demanded
that this living god be brought before him. The priests of Apis had duly
done this, but

> when the priests returned bringing Apis with them, Cambyses, like
> the harebrained person that he was, drew his dagger, and aimed at the
> belly of the animal, but missed his mark, and stabbed him in the
> thigh. Then he laughed, and said thus to the priests: "Oh! blockheads,
> and think ye that gods become like this, of flesh and blood, and sen-
> sible to steel? A fit god indeed for Egyptians, such a one! But it shall
> cost you dear that you have made me your laughing-stock."
>
> Herodotus, The Histories, book 3 (Thaleia), chapter 27

The humiliated king was true to his word and ordered the priests of
Apis whipped. Then, according to Herodotus, he went about dismantling
the whole cult, instituting the death penalty for any Egyptian found cel-
ebrating the Apis festival. But the real damage had been done to the sacred bull itself: "Apis, wounded in the thigh, lay some time pining in the
temple; at last he died of his wound, and the priests buried him secretly
without the knowledge of Cambyses" (Herodotus, The Histories, book 3
[Thaleia], chapter 27).

The Egyptians were very clear about what happened next. The crime drove Cambyses mad, leading him into a downward spiral of events. He is said to have murdered his own brother and sister (who was also his wife), while his attempt to intimidate the oracle at Siwa led to his losing an entire army in the desert sands. Eventually he received a self-inflicted sword wound in his thigh, in exactly the same location where he had wounded the Apis. It became infected and he died.

But more important than Cambyses' fate was the survival of this story among the Egyptians. The moral of the tale they had recounted to Herodotus was one of a bad foreigner ignoring their ancient rituals and hence, quite rightly, coming to grief. Egyptian records actually show that between 525 and 522 BC Cambyses was involved in the dedication of the sarcophagus of the dead Apis, implying that the story Herodotus was told had been made up by his Egyptian sources. But what mattered was that Persian rule had been a humiliation, and in the Egyptian consciousness, this could easily be equated with the maltreatment of an Apis bull. Alexander had also been a foreigner, but in lifting Persian dominion he had gained favor in Egypt. To keep that favor, however, his successors would have to "walk like Egyptians."

All of this was known to Ptolemy as he prepared the final parts of his plan for a new Egypt. Back in Alexandria, the first phase of Alexander's—and now Ptolemy's—dream was nearing completion. In the Brucheum the great wealth of Egypt had been put to good use building palaces suitable for her new ruler. The mud brick of the early buildings had been encased in polished stone and alabaster. The Ptolemaic household was furnished with chairs and beds in the Egyptian style, carved from cedar of Lebanon and inlaid with ivory from equatorial Africa. Outside, royal parks with their marble fountains and shimmering lakes proclaimed the largesse and power of this "pharaoh in all but name."

But that was just the problem. Alexander had already been a great king when he appeared in Egypt, and the confirmation from the oracle at Siwa that he was a son of Ammon told the Egyptians everything they needed to know to crown him pharaoh. For Ptolemy it was different. He could declare himself a Greek king—a *basileus*—indeed, that was an essential part of making his claim to Egypt as one of the successors of Alexander. But that title meant precious little to the Egyptians he intended to rule, and regardless of what esteem he held those native people in, he knew that they drove the economy that would make or break his dream.

What Ptolemy needed was a means of combining Greek and Egyptian religious traditions in a way that would leave him a king in Greek eyes but a god in Egyptian ones—no mean feat when one considers the trouble Herodotus had coming to terms with the differences between their cultures. But in the Apis bull he saw an opportunity, and he seized it.

His plan was to create a new cult, one that combined elements of Greek and Egyptian practice and symbolism, that would serve to tie together seamlessly the fates of the Greek rulers and their Egyptian subjects. It would clearly be extremely difficult to impose himself upon ancient native beliefs, and equally the Egyptians were unlikely simply to throw away thousands of years of religion to turn to Greek beliefs. But if he could invent a new religion that combined the two, then he could insert his family into the heart of it, granting them the godlike rights due to the heirs of Alexander and the heirs of the pharaohs.

To do this Ptolemy needed the help of local Egyptian priests and Greek thinkers, and he was quick to foster connections between the two. He began by encouraging Greeks to write *Aegyptica*—Egyptian histories which drew on the centuries-old traditions of the priests of Memphis and Thebes. Of course this required the active cooperation of those priests. The historian and Skeptic philosopher Hecataeus of Abdera, who accompanied Ptolemy on a Nile journey as far as Thebes (Diogenes Laertius 9, 61), was one of the first to take up the challenge, and he tells us that Ptolemy ordered the priests to "provide the facts from their sacred records" (reported in Diodorus Siculus, *Library of History*, book 1, chapter 46.8). Another papyrus document from around this date (c. 300–298 BC), known as Hibeh Papyrus 27, records in Greek how the writer spent five years as a disciple of a "wise man," almost certainly an Egyptian astronomer-priest, who taught him how the Egyptians measured time with an instrument called a gnomon—a staff for measuring the length of shadows cast by the sun. Clearly the lesson was well learned, for within a hundred years a Greek scholar at Alexandria would use this simple tool to make a far more spectacular measurement—the circumference of the earth.

This cultural exchange program between Greek and Egyptian scholars had a number of benefits. Not only did it provide Ptolemy with detailed information about how Egypt was run, but it gave his Greek academics access to the centuries of scientific (particularly astronomical) and religious thinking of the Egyptians. It also encouraged exchange the other way, helping to Hellenize the priestly caste in the temples and make them look more favorably on Greek rule. One such Egyptian who would prove vital in Ptolemy's religious plans was Manetho.

Manetho was an Egyptian high priest in Heliopolis, one of the ancient cult capitals of the country since the days of the pyramid builders, which lies today engulfed in the urban sprawl of Cairo. He was also a historian, which gave him added benefits when it came to legitimizing Ptolemy's rule. Indeed the chronological lists of pharaohs used by Egyptologists today is still based on one drawn up by Manetho, one which seamlessly integrates the Ptolemies, of course. The plan the two devised was to create a new cult based in the temple that stood over the tombs of the Apis bulls in which a personification of those dead animals could be worshipped as Osorapis—a fusion of the god of the dead, Osiris, and the living bull, Apis.

The results must have sounded thoroughly Egyptian; but it was in their interpretation by Ptolemy and his Greek-influenced helpers that we begin to see how the fusion was enacted. The great cult statue of Serapis was commissioned by Ptolemy from the Greek master sculptor Bryaxis, who, with three others, had been responsible for a side each of the mausoleum at Halicarnassus. His Serapis was represented not in Egyptian form with combined human and animal elements, but as a benign, bearded man, seated on a throne and wearing the crown of fertility (the *modius*). To represent his power over the dead, the power of Osiris, the three-headed dog of the Greek underworld, Cerberus, crouched at his right knee. In his left hand he held aloft a wand similar to the staff of the Greek god of healing, Asclepius. In fact his image must have looked remarkably similar to Zeus, but this was Zeus imbued with thousands of years of Egyptian religious power. To the Greeks he could easily be seen as a Greek god ruling an alien land, but to the Egyptians his outward appearance was simply a new manifestation of the age-old truths that Egyptians, and Egyptians alone, had always known.

Ptolemy wanted not only to establish this Greco-Egyptian cult as quickly as possible but also to locate its center in his new capital, Alexandria, away from the powerful influence of the old temple administrations. It must also have seemed appropriate that this new city should have its own, new and unique god protecting it, housed in a temple which bore the same name as the last resting place of the Apis bulls—the Serapeum. But the inhabitants of Alexandria—Greeks, Jews, and Egyptians—would require some convincing. To do this Ptolemy not only had to call on the right people to support his idea but had to frame his new deity in a way that appealed to the eclectic audience of his new city.

As such, the new god Serapis had to combine many of the best features of a number of gods. Importantly, he was cast as a god of healing, a deity who had a practical everyday value that would bring him into the lives of anyone who was (or knew someone who was) sick. This power was indicated by his Asclepius-like staff, which indicated to the Greeks this facet of his being. For the Egyptian audience he was equated in this to Imhotep, the supposed architect of the first pyramid who was later worshipped as a god of healing. He was also given some of the personal appeal of Asclepius in that it was said that he was a god who came privately to people and spoke to them in their dreams. He was thus someone who could be appealed to personally, rather than simply through the offices of a priestly caste cut off from the normal population in the forbidden realm of the adytum, the exclusive priestly inner sanctum.

These healing powers and his association with the dead Apis, and hence Osiris, god of the netherworld, also gave him different powers that would appeal to the Alexandrian audience. He was a god who stood outside the realms of fate, beyond the fickle chances of the everyday world. He was a god who had beaten death, like Osiris. As such he could see into the future and hence could be appealed to as an oracle, a hugely popular idea in both the Greek and Egyptian worlds. Creating another oracular center in Alexandria would be a real coup, bringing wealth and prestige to the city, perhaps making it a place to rival Delphi or Siwa and granting whoever controlled it (namely Ptolemy) enormous power over those who might make important political decisions based on its pronouncements.

But there was a danger that all these powers made the new god seem a somber and frightening character, particularly to the Greeks. The Egyptian and Greek attitudes to death stood at extreme ends of the spectrum, so a unified god of death had to tread carefully. In the Hellenistic world the afterlife was a dull, gray place—a dusty land of regret where the dead looked back in sorrow at what they had, and hadn't, done in life. For the Egyptians it was quite the opposite. Egyptians looked forward to death as a time and place where the very best in life was made eternal. Planning for death—building tombs and preparing grave goods—was not a solemn undertaking but often a hobby, something to be done in one's spare time and enjoyable. They did not wish for death but knew that after death, when they had, in the idiom of the day, "gone to the west," all that was good in life could await them there (provided they had prepared carefully beforehand).

To compensate for the negative image that Serapis's associations with death created in Greek minds, he was also cast for them as a Dionysian character. He was an ebullient, festive god, filled with life and the love of life, who indulged in banquets and festivals: a Bacchic figure who, in the knowledge that a Greek afterlife was much less fun than an Egyptian one, encouraged his followers to seize the day and enjoy this life to the full. In short, he was all things to all men and women.

If the Alexandrians still needed persuading, Ptolemy had another weapon in his armory—philosophers. Demetrius of Phalerum had been a philosopher of the Peripatetic school, a pupil of Aristotle, and an Athenian statesman. His ten-year rule in Athens had brought peace to the city until its invasion by one of the heirs of Alexander forced him from power and overseas to Alexandria. He arrived here with an extraordinary reputation as a thinker and a politician, the protector of Athenian liberty, the regulator of her laws, and a fine orator and writer. As such he was later to play a key role in turning Alexandria into the center of the ancient world; but before any of the real work began, Ptolemy wanted him to support the new cult of Serapis. And Demetrius seems to have been glad to help.

The story that went around the city shortly after his arrival was that he had been struck blind. This of course was a disaster for Demetrius, Ptolemy, and Alexandria. But good news followed rapidly on the heels of bad when the announcement was made that through a miracle, his sight had been restored. And how had this miracle come about? He had simply prayed to the new god Serapis, in his role as god of healing, and Serapis had done the rest. To celebrate, Demetrius then put his considerable lyrical skills to use in composing the first of his paeans, in which he demonstrated his gratitude for the god's intervention.

There is, of course, a chance that events happened exactly as the story said, but the arrival of an old friend of Aristotle's at Ptolemy's court at this time, in need of friendship and protection but with an astute and practical knowledge of the politics of the Hellenistic world, was perhaps more likely to have been a public relations opportunity too good to miss.

Nor was Demetrius the only Greek thinker to be held up as an acolyte of Serapis in an attempt to persuade the Alexandrians. One of the most popular Greek cults of the time was the Eleusinian mystery cult of Demeter and Persephone. The annual festival in Eleusis, near Athens, was considered to be one of the most important in the ancient world, and, as with all cults, the secrecy which surrounded it attracted adherents by the thousand. Central to these were the five clans whose families had, so the legend had it, from the first provided the priests who administered these undisclosed rites. Ptolemy managed to persuade one of these clan members, Timotheus from the Eumoplid family, to support his new god Serapis. Backing from such an important official must have influenced Alexandrians and Greeks throughout Egypt, and not only that, but as Timotheus's own cult was a secret, there would never have to be an explanation of how the "truth" of Serapis had been revealed to him.

With Serapis established, Ptolemy could now make his final move, the final political maneuver that would ensure that his Egypt would become the only true legacy of Alexander's dream. His city was nearing completion, his religion was in place (or at least beginning)—it was time to make his last great gamble and bid for the throne.

For some time Ptolemy had been preparing his Egyptian subjects for an announcement. He had been encouraging his family to live in a more overtly Egyptian manner, adopting Egyptian modes of dress, attending traditional rituals, and even going as far as to contemplate the father-daughter and brother-sister marriages which had been common among the great dynasties of the New Kingdom some seven hundred years before.

He didn't want to be seen by his new hosts as a foreign ruler, another Cambyses. He was not, however, simply going native. Egypt offered his family some things money could not buy—history, tradition, and a civilization so old that it made the Hellenistic world look like an afterthought—but he also had something to offer it. He was holding out the prospect of Egypt's becoming the center of the world once again.

Ptolemy had a dream of a new kind of city and country, a place of universal knowledge where the thoughts of the greatest minds could be turned to the creation of the perfect state, under the benevolent eye of a dynasty of rulers who would gain wealth, fame, and immortality from their patronage of this greatest of human projects. If Ptolemy could cherry-pick the highlights of that ancient culture and fuse them with the modern thinking of his Greek world, then he would be more than both. He would look like an Egyptian but speak like a Greek (indeed, he and most of his descendants refused to learn the Egyptian language). He would be something new, the founder of not just a new dynasty but a new kingdom.

And so the final, logical stage in Ptolemy's progress from childhood friend of Alexander to pharaoh was put into motion. As the new cult of Serapis was built up in Alexandria, so the traditional role of Memphis was run down. Along with the decline in religious importance, the main arms of administration were also moved from the old capital to the new city. From here the state was reorganized. Registers of houses, land, slaves, cattle, and taxpayers were ordered to be drawn up in every village, then summarized and returned to what was now officially the new capital—Alexandria.

Then in early 304 BC Ptolemy set the seal on his achievements by sending out another declaration to the people of Egypt. The days of Persian domination—of foreign domination—were in the past. Egypt had awoken, stirred by a new leader. He was to be no longer their satrap, but their savior—Ptolemy Soter—the first in a new dynasty of Greek pharaohs who would oversee the greatest explosion in thought and innovation the world has ever known. And at its heart would be Alexandria.

CHAPTER FOUR

THE LEGACY OF ARISTOTLE

All men by nature desire to know.

Aristotle, *Metaphysics*

I f it was Egyptian religion and Macedonian tactics that placed Ptolemy on the throne of Egypt, it would be Greek thought that kept him there. The state he envisaged ruling was unlike anything else in the ancient world—a country of the mind built in an alien land from the rubble of Alexander's empire.

Ptolemy simply didn't share Alexander's ambition to rule the world, as he had seen how hopeless the idea really was. What he did share with his old friend was glimpses of a way in which at least a single country might be governed. Ptolemy and Alexander had been close as children and young men; indeed, the rumor in the Egyptian court was that the two men were half brothers following a liaison between Ptolemy's mother, Arsinoe, and Philip II (after which she was quickly married off to the minor nobleman Lagus). The story was almost certainly false, but it served the new pharaoh well to be thought of as related to the founder of the new city and as a man in whose veins the blood of the god Alexander flowed. But what Ptolemy had learned of government in the Macedonian court had not come from watching Alexander's father, whose autocratic rule would end with his assassination, or from observing the increasingly tyrannical government of Alexander's final years. Instead, it came from the man whom Philip had employed to educate his son and who had by default educated Ptolemy as well. He was Aristotle, one of the greatest thinkers of the ancient world, and it was to memories of his tutelage that Ptolemy turned when he thought about bringing his new kingdom to life.

Aristotle had always been there in the background, in the calmer, more considered parts of Alexander's and Ptolemy's minds, and through this his influence spread far beyond his own writings and into his pupils' actions. He'd informed Alexander's whole way of thinking, promoting a love of investigation and discovery which not only drove the conqueror across vast physical territories but encouraged his journeys into all areas of knowledge. Alexander was a great devourer of books, often running out of material on campaigns and frantically sending for more. He read histories, scientific treatises, the plays of Euripides, Sophocles, and Aeschylus— everything from his precious "casket copy" of the *Iliad* (as corrected by Aristotle) to the dithyrambic odes of Telestes and Philoxenus. He also liked to put his knowledge to use, as Plutarch describes:

> *Doubtless also it was to Aristotle that he owed the inclination he had, not to the theory only, but likewise to the practice of the art of medicine. For when any of his friends were sick, he would often prescribe them their course of diet, and medicines proper to their disease, as we may find in his epistles.*

> Plutarch, *Life of Alexander,* in *Parallel Lives,* 8

So great was Aristotle's influence on him that, if we are to believe Plutarch, he was often heard to say that he loved and cherished his tutor no less than if he had been his own father, "giving this reason for it, that as he had received life from the one, so the other had taught him to live well" (Plutarch, *Life of Alexander,* in *Parallel Lives,* 8).

It was an interesting distinction—two fathers, one for a physical life and one for the life of the mind—but it was a conception that would finally bear fruit not in Alexander's empire but in Ptolemy's Alexandria. Ptolemy had his physical kingdom, his throne, his army, his defenses, and in those he was the inheritor of at least a part of Alexander's world. Now he would combine that physical inheritance with an intellectual one and create something unique. In this Aristotle might claim to be the true father of Alexandria, closer than the rumored links between Ptolemy and Alexander, and more a father to his pupil's city than to the man himself.

Aristotle, the man on whose thoughts Alexandria's intellectual foundations—and hence the intellectual foundations of the whole Western world—were built, was himself a member of a great dynasty, connected not by blood or marriage but purely by thought and reason. He was the heir to a revolution in philosophy, building on the work of his old master, Plato, who in turn had built his philosophy on the foundations of his tutor—Socrates, whom the eighteenth-century classicist John Lemprière characterized as "the most celebrated philosopher of all antiquity" (Lemprière, *Classical Dictionary Writ Large,* p. 588).

Philosophers, literally "lovers of wisdom," had guided and shaped the Greek intellectual world from at least the time of Pythagoras in the sixth century BC, but with the coming of Socrates (469–399 BC), Plato (429–347 BC), and Aristotle (384–322 BC) came a subtle shift in approach. Whereas many of the early philosophical questions were concerned with the nature of reality, of the world and universe, and the role of the divine in the greater scheme of things, the new notion initiated by Socrates was more concerned with the philosopher's own role in the world, in how to live correctly and set an example for others. Ethics and morality began to extend the fundamental concerns of philosophy, and so philosophy became not simply speculation but a practical tool of government and a cornerstone of civilization.

As a young man Socrates had distinguished himself as a soldier, fighting in three major battles and being decorated for saving the life of a wounded friend. These expeditions with the military were, however, the only occasions on which this unusually sedentary philosopher ever left Athens. After the campaigns he led a highly ascetic life, going barefoot and without a coat in the winter. He had no interest in money or material goods and claimed that he was not paid for his teaching, though as he had no other means of financial support this seems unlikely.

Socrates was a controversial figure with new and sometimes startling things to say, so he made enemies as well as attracted friends and followers. His methodology was to initiate a series of questions to an individual or a group to reveal the extent of their knowledge (or ignorance), seeking to expose contradictions in their beliefs. This was all well and good when addressing pupils or followers, but when this method was applied to people who thought of themselves as important, perhaps even great, Socrates' proven ability to show that they in fact knew nothing easily caused offense. Writing in his *Lives of the Philosophers*, Diogenes Laertius explains:

> *And very often, while arguing and discussing points that arose, he was treated with great violence and beaten, and pulled about, and laughed at and ridiculed by the multitude. But he bore all this with great equanimity. So that once, when he had been kicked and buffeted about, and someone expressed his surprise, he said, "Suppose an ass had kicked me, would you have had me bring an action against him?"*
>
> Diogenes Laertius, *The Lives and Opinions
> of Eminent Philosophers (Socrates)*

Not that Socrates initiated these dialogues out of spite or arrogance. He always maintained that his own philosophical strength was rooted in the fact that he at least knew that he himself knew nothing. He was merely frustrated that others thought they really did know and understand the world and each other.

While his reputation grew—the oracle at Delphi declaring that there was none wiser in the land—so too his concerns with ethics and the right ways to live inevitably drew him and philosophy into the political arena, where, during a period of considerable political instability, he could hardly avoid being seen as taking sides. In the 390s BC his enemies finally brought charges against him, alleging that he had corrupted the Athenian youth, made innovations in the religion of the Greeks, and ridiculed their gods. As was the practice in Athens, where there were no professional judges, Socrates was summoned to answer the charges before a full jury of 501 citizens elected by ballot. The jury expected Socrates to put up an eloquent, self-effacing defense and finally sue for forgiveness, but this went entirely against the grain of his moral philosophy. Instead, he challenged the whole foundation of the trial and the supposed justice upon which it was based. He complained that these were trumped-up charges supported by false witnesses, which was almost certainly true, and his eloquence almost won the jury over. In the end he was found guilty by only three votes.

The next step in this "people's trial" was rather unusual. Instead of handing down a set sentence for the crime, the jury was required to ask Socrates how he himself considered he should be punished. But Socrates was still not prepared to humble himself before his accusers, and, perhaps buoyed by the close vote in the trial itself, he suggested that because he had so helped to develop the intellectual caliber of the people, he should be granted free meals for life and pay a very modest fine. The jurors were not in a joking mood, however, and the mocking of their judicial process turned them savagely against him. The motion to put him to death immediately was passed by 441 to 60.

He was duly sentenced to death by drinking hemlock, though his execution was delayed for thirty days by a local religious festival. Pressed by his followers to change his mind, he is said to have exclaimed, "Would you then have me die guilty?" He died aged seventy in 399 BC.

In holding firm to his beliefs to the point of death, Socrates had a phenomenal impact on the Greek mind and Greek civilization. The philosophy of Pythagoras had not concerned itself with how a society should operate. But after Socrates philosophers would interest themselves in the state and politics. Their subject had taken on a moral dimension and become something worth dying for.

Lemprière summarizes his achievements with admirable clarity:

> *The philosophy of Socrates forms an interesting epoch in the history of the human mind. The son of Sophroniscus derided the more abstruse inquiries and metaphysical researches of his predecessors, and by first introducing moral philosophy, he induced mankind to consider themselves, their passions, their opinions, their duties, actions and faculties. From this it is said that the founder of the Socratic school drew philosophy down from heaven upon the earth.*

Lemprière, *Classical Dictionary Writ Large*, pp. 588–90

There is one other aspect of Socrates' death well worth noting. This is simply that it happened at all. That a philosopher should be put to death for holding views and expressing them orally (he did not set his views down in writing) merely because they were different from currently accepted norms attests to how seriously this new philosophy was being taken. Indeed, the shift in emphasis from metaphysical to moral philosophy which Socrates pioneered had the effect of making philosophy's subject area even more politically loaded than it had been, to the point where Socrates' immediate successors became actively engaged in working out the ideal form that not just individuals but entire societies should take.

Ten years or so before his death, it is said, Socrates had a dream one night. A young bird fell exhausted into his lap, and then in front of him it grew at great speed into a fully fledged swan and flew away. The next day Plato appeared at Socrates' school and asked to enroll as a pupil. He stayed with Socrates right through until his death, though he says he was not present when his master swallowed the poison.

After his master's death Plato decided to travel, visiting Sicily several times and venturing as far as Egypt, in search of the basic tenets of Pythagorean philosophy, which he knew had their origins there. Once he had satisfied himself that he understood their essence, he returned to Athens and went about establishing his own school. The remains of that school can still be found today in what is now a suburb of Athens but was then a sacred grove of olive trees on the outskirts of the city. Here low stone foundations still mark the site of one of the city's gymnasiums, along with a cluster of earlier buildings, one of which is claimed as the original home of the legendary hero who gave his name to this place—Academus. This was where Plato founded the Academy; the word itself has since become synonymous with learning and centers of education around the world. It was here that he undertook to teach young Greek men how to rule. The school attracted pupils from across the Mediterranean world, and its work extended far beyond the confines of politics. From its foundation, perhaps as early as 385 BC, it would last, intermittently, until AD 529, when its final closure by the emperor Justinian is said by many to mark the very end of antiquity.

Unlike Socrates, whose parents were artisans, Plato was from a noble and literate family, and once he had settled in Athens he began to write prodigiously. His philosophy was based on the physics of Heraclitus, who held that everything was in a state of continual flux and that change was the ultimate reality; his metaphysics he took from the Egyptian Pythagorean school, and his ethics and morals from his master, Socrates.

Socrates had not chosen to put any of his philosophy in writing himself, so Plato saw his first task as setting down his master's dialogues. As no comparative records exist, it's impossible to tell whether these early works are straightforward transcriptions of Socrates in action (they are written in that form, with Socrates the inquisitor unraveling the beliefs and knowledge of his subjects), or Plato is already using the Socratic dialogues to put his own thoughts in the mouth of his dead master.

It is clear, however, that as Plato's writings progress, still couched in the form of Socratic dialogues, the voice we are hearing is more and more that of Plato himself. Because these works take the form of questions and answers, it is to some extent left to the reader to determine exactly what his philosophy consists of, but there are some basic notions which underlie his vision, and these would inform the physical and cultural life of Alexandria in years to come.

At the most profound level Plato perceived everything in the universe as having two manifestations. On the one hand there is the physical world which we recognize all around us. This is composed of ordinary matter, which the Greeks believed was made up of the four essential elements—earth, fire, water, air—constantly transforming themselves from one state into the next. This world is unstable and in a constant state of flux, essentially imperfect, giving rise to the endless disorders and deceptions which create the errors and miseries of human life.

But behind this perceived sensory world lies a quite different world of ideal "forms" or "ideas." In the fullest expositions of Plato's theories these forms are perfect, unchangeable, pure, and immortal. The human soul is composed of such divine stuff, though it is surrounded by the unstable elements of the sensuous world. It is the task of the philosopher to recapture his divine origins by moving away from the material world, curbing and governing his physical passions, and embracing the inner world of form and the mind.

For Plato this was much more than a simple philosophical construct; it was a way of life, both for the individual and for the state. The perfect state was one where the rules he was deducing were put into perfect practice, making philosophy not the preserve of ethereal academics, but an essential and practical tool of government. Plato believed he could divide up the types of government just as he could divide earth, fire, water, and air, or the polluted "material" from the pure "form." According to Diogenes Laertius, Plato divided the political world into five species: democracy, aristocracy, oligarchy, monarchy, and tyranny. He goes on to explain:

> *Now, the democratic form of constitution exists in those cities in which the multitude has the chief power, and elects magistrates and passes laws at its own pleasure. But an aristocracy is that form in which neither the rich nor the poor, nor the most illustrious men of the city rule, but the most nobly born have the chief sway. An oligarchy is that constitution in which the magistracies are distributed according to some sort of rating: for the rich are fewer in number than the poor. The monarchical constitution is either dependent on law or on family. . . . But a tyranny is that kind of government in which the people are either cajoled or constrained into being governed by a single individual.*

> Diogenes Laertius, *The Lives and Opinions*
> *of Eminent Philosophers (Plato)*

This was the sort of philosophy that must have been impressed on the young Alexander and Ptolemy at the Macedonian court—practical information for the future rulers of the world. In the monarchical setting of his father's palace, Alexander likely mused on the relative values of democracy and monarchy, aristocracy, oligarchy, and tyranny. Athens had embraced democracy but often had fallen to foreign rulers. Carthage was a land of oligarchs set soon to clash with a Roman republic ruled by an aristocracy. But how would he rule the world? Did he dream of becoming monarch of the world? Would he rule through an aristocracy? Would he allow democracy to thrive in Greece? Whatever his decision, in the end, in trying to hold together one vast empire he chose the last and Plato's least favored route—tyranny.

For Ptolemy, the decision had been different. Born into an aristocracy ruled by a monarchy he could join only through mythmaking, he would choose the route of monarchy, reinventing his family as the legitimate successors to the most ancient court on earth. His empire was to be a family affair, not fought over by his generals, but bound to the age-old traditions of the Egyptian royal house.

But Plato had more to say on government. He went on to describe justice as being of three species—justice toward God, men, and the dead—but it was in one last division that he really struck a chord with Ptolemy, giving him the chance when building his new kingdom to put into practice the philosophical ideas he had learned as a child at the court of Philip. This was in Plato's conception of the three types of knowledge: "In the same way, there are also three species of knowledge. There is one kind which is practical, a second which is productive, a third which is theoretical" (Diogenes Laertius, *The Lives and Opinions of Eminent Philosophers [Plato]*).

It was this thought that electrified Ptolemy—bringing together the productive, the practical, and the theoretical in one state. Plato went on to define his three species. House building and shipbuilding were productive knowledge in that one could see the work produced by them. Playing a flute or harp, by contrast, was practical knowledge, for although there was no visible result produced by playing the instrument, something was clearly being done. The same was true of political science. Geometry and astronomy, by contrast, concerned themselves with abstractions and hence were purely theoretical.

It was by combining the three that Ptolemy hoped to create a new model city in Alexandria and a new country beyond. It would feed and be fed by productive knowledge—the ships in the Great Harbor and the markets beyond. It would be governed by practical knowledge in the application of the very best and most efficient forms of government and administration. And set at its heart would be the world's greatest center for Plato's third species—theoretical knowledge—which seeks out the truths of the universe and reaches out for the perfect forms of God and soul that lie behind the chaos of the everyday world. This would be a community that had mastered its sensual passions and, in knowing the miseries which arise from unjust conduct, could aspire to excellence and perfection through the exercise of rational and morally sound judgment.

In 1929 the British philosopher Alfred North Whitehead, when considering Plato's contribution to Western philosophy, could not avoid the opinion that "the safest general characterisation of the European (modern) philosophical tradition is that it consists of a series of footnotes to Plato" (Alfred North Whitehead, *Process and Reality*).

It happens very rarely in the history of any branch of knowledge that three of the greatest masters of a subject follow each other in direct descent, each one in many ways outshining his master and predecessor. Just as Plato first recorded, formalized, expanded, and developed the Socratic philosophy, so would Aristotle take the ideas of his master, Plato, and forge from them systems of thought which have affected the entire development of Western civilization. It was also through Aristotle that the ideas of the perfect state were brought to the attention of young Ptolemy, and through Aristotle's own unique way of gathering knowledge that Alexandria's preeminent institutions—her museum and library—came into existence.

Aristotle came to Athens to study under Plato when he was about eighteen years old, but he came with certain predispositions. His father had been court physician to King Amyntas II of Macedonia, father of Philip, grandfather of Alexander the Great. Although his father died when Aristotle was only ten, medicine was the traditional occupation of certain families, passed down from father to son. It is therefore very likely that the young Aristotle had already received medical training from his father at home, and that training would have emphasized the importance of investigation and objective observation of the patient and the physical world.

So his family background connected him directly to the Macedonian royal family, trained him as an empirical observer, and also, incidentally, left him with an intense dislike of courts and princes. Unlike Plato, who was an accomplished athlete, the young Aristotle was small in stature, thin-legged, with small eyes and a lisp, which may well have left him prey to the scorn of the noble athletes of the Macedonian court, for whom outward disfigurement was a sign of inner decay.

Aristotle remained at Plato's Academy in Athens until the death of his master, and most people assumed that he would inherit the position as head of the Academy, but the post was eventually given to a nephew of Plato's. However, Aristotle had certainly not been idle during his fifteen years at the Academy. On the contrary, his insatiable appetite for knowledge had led him to study literally every subject that existed at that time.

Plato himself had felt that he needed to restrain the young man rather than encourage him in his researches. But though there was never any serious rift between the two, and Aristotle always remained highly respectful of his master, intellectual differences had begun to emerge. Plato remained convinced that only the refinement of the soul would give access to the underlying, ideal forms of the universe and existence, the world around being merely an imperfect copy of the forms. He was therefore in essence an idealist, a rationalist.

But Aristotle came increasingly to place value on the knowledge he gained through his senses, making him an empiricist, trusting what he could see and test, ignoring or dismissing speculation. Here, then, lay the path which would lead directly to the "scientific" method, though it would not gain that label until nearly two thousand years later.

After Plato's death Aristotle accepted an invitation from a former fellow student at the Academy to travel to Assos near Troy, which his colleague ruled, and he stayed there until his patron was overthrown and killed. He then traveled on to Lesbos, where he carried out biological research of such outstanding quality that it was not superseded until the eighteenth century AD. Even Charles Darwin was an unqualified admirer of Aristotle's biology. Writing up his findings in *On the Generation of Animals,* Aristotle lays bare the fundamentals of all scientific inquiry, stating boldly that facts can be established only by observation and that theories are valid only insofar as they are supported by observed facts.

And this was the approach he applied as he systematically surveyed the whole of human knowledge as it was in the Mediterranean world in his time. Not content with pioneering the observational method in biology and inventing the study of formal logic, Aristotle both studied and wrote definitively about physics, chemistry, zoology, botany, anatomy, embryology, astronomy, geography, geology, and meteorology. He also explored almost every known aspect of psychology, government, politics and political theory, ethics and moral philosophy, economics, aesthetics, metaphysics, history, literary theory, rhetoric, and religion. And in so doing he created a model of the philosopher as a man of knowledge and wisdom in all fields, which acted as a beacon for generations of scholars, researchers, and philosophers who would later throng the halls, lecture theaters, and libraries of the museum in Alexandria.

These then were the three generations of exceptional scholarship, the pedigree of thought that came to bear on the practical rule of the world in 342 BC, when Philip II of Macedon summoned Aristotle to become his fourteen-year-old son Alexander's personal tutor. Aristotle performed this role until Alexander assumed the throne on Philip's death in 336, and remained as personal adviser to the young king until Alexander set off in 333 on his Asian campaigns. During these critical years Aristotle prepared Alexander to be a military leader, using as models great Greek heroes like Ajax and Achilles as they appear in Homer's *Iliad,* paragons of classical valor.

Alexander's subsequent career shows that his old tutor had prepared him well, but in his hurry to dominate the whole world the conqueror and his teacher began to drift apart. Perhaps to the most powerful man on earth, the strict admonitions of this old-school master no longer seemed relevant or dignified. Equally Aristotle can only have felt unease with the stories coming back from Asia of his old pupil's growing autocracy and superstitious paranoia. The imprisonment and subsequent death of Aristotle's nephew Callisthenes at Alexander's order cannot have helped. Callisthenes, sent with Alexander to record the greatest military campaign of all time, had proved to be an outspoken critic of some of Alexander's decisions, particularly his adoption of Persian customs, which alienated his Macedonian troops and commanders. In response Alexander accused him of treachery and threw him into prison, where he died, either from torture or disease. When that news got back to Aristotle it must have given rise to foreboding as well as grief. He had always maintained to his young pupil that a ruler over vast swaths of the earth must be as superior to ordinary men as we humans are superior to beasts. In Alexander he could now see a man who believed every day that he was closer to this godlike state, but whose actions betrayed a cruelty and arrogance that in reality took him further from it. Plutarch notes that Alexander, having in his youth treated Aristotle as a second father, once out on his campaigns "suspected him somewhat, yet he did him no hurt, neither was he so friendly to him as he had been; whereby men perceived that he did not bear him the good will that he was wont to do" (Plutarch, *Life of Alexander,* in *Parallel Lives,* 8).

It is perhaps this that led to the tales that Aristotle determined to put a stop to his protégé's rise, his unseen hand controlling events in Babylon during Alexander's last days, bringing him to his death.

But if Aristotle and Alexander grew apart in later years with regard to their views on kingship and rule, Aristotle's methods were still close to the young king's heart, and Pliny and others suggest that he remained imbued with a love of practical observation, of the finding and collecting of examples of everything. It was something that Aristotle dreamed of and that Alexander, master of the world, could bring to pass, and it would have a vital role in the creation of Alexandria. Pliny tells us that Alexander gave Aristotle control of all the hunters, fishermen, and fowlers in his empire, and made him overseer of all the royal forests, lakes, ponds, and cattle ranges, as recognition of his tutor's masterly knowledge of all things natural. It's also reported that Alexander sent many books and treasures back to Aristotle from the libraries of Babylon, Persia, and India.

Even after Aristotle left the service of the Macedonian state, Alexander continued to feed him with the information and objects that he so desired. Indeed, Alexander had sent out orders to the fishermen, hunters, and farmers of his lands to send all the strange devices they possessed or interesting objects they found to Aristotle for his study and for use in his lectures. At the same time, and for many years previously, Aristotle, who had inherited wealth from his father, had become an avid collector of books. He collected them on any subject and in any language; it didn't matter what they were about, it just mattered that he had a copy—a copy of everything. It was a passion he had held ever since he entered the Academy—Plato's nickname for Aristotle was "the Reader."

These two collections—of objects and books—were, though it seems strange today, something entirely new. Aristotle was the founder of modern empirical science, the first man to attempt to study and systematize the things he observed around him, and the result bore fruit in the philosopher's own school, which he founded in Athens on the banks of the Ilissus River. Here, in the sanctuary to the Lycian Apollo, he established a school and research institute that was to become the prototype of all subsequent educational institutions: the Lyceum. Today there is little left of the Lyceum to see, just an archaeological site between the Museum of Modern Art and the British embassy, but in Aristotle's time the sanctuary was surrounded by covered walkways where he strolled as he taught, giving rise to the name "Peripatetic" for his school of philosophy. Here for twelve years he would lecture his students on metaphysics and logic in the mornings (*esoteria*), while in the afternoons he would present public lectures on ethics, politics, and rhetoric (*exoteria*). Here also resided his great collection of objects, which inspired his thoughts and demonstrated his theories. This was the first museum in Western history, a resource for scholars to study and demonstrate as they walked through the stoas—the great halls where the philosophers taught, hence "Stoics"—and gardens of the Lyceum.

Likewise his collection of books, brought from all over the known world, was the first attempt to gather all written knowledge in one place, the first true, if private, library. These were the seeds of the modern world, first planted in the Lyceum, but which would grow to maturity not long after Aristotle's death, in the soil of Alexandria.

The death of Alexander in Babylon also ushered in the last sad year in Aristotle's life. After Alexander's death a wave of hostility against Macedonians swept through Athens, and he was accused of impiety—the same charge that had been brought against Socrates. Placed in an impossible position, with the stark fate of Socrates before him, Aristotle chose to leave Athens and his beloved Lyceum, saying he would rather abandon the city than give the Athenians another chance to sin against philosophy. Aristotle retired to his house at Chalcis in Euboea, where he died within the year from a stomach complaint.

But if relations between Aristotle and Alexander had been strained and the strange intertwining of their fates had brought an end to both men, both their legacies were being kept alive across the Mediterranean by that other pupil of both—Ptolemy. What level of correspondence existed between Aristotle and Ptolemy is unknown, although Aristotle's writings against Cleomenes perhaps suggest that the old master was still guiding his pupil's hand. But regardless of how actively Aristotle was involved in Ptolemy's plans, it was in Ptolemy's Egypt that the ideas of philosophy's great triumvirate—Socrates, Plato, and Aristotle—would be tested in the real world. If there was ever to be a land of philosopher-kings, it would be here and now.

CHAPTER FIVE

CITY OF THE MIND

The great pagan world of which Egypt and Greece were the last living terms . . . once had a vast and perhaps perfect science of its own, a science in terms of life. In our era this science crumbled into magic and charlatanry. But even wisdom crumbles.

D. H. Lawrence, *Fantasia of the Unconscious*

There had been nothing in the way Ptolemy came to power to suggest that he intended to behave differently from any of the kings of the ancient Mediterranean. He had gained his kingdom through battles, grave robbing, and murder, yet by the time of Aristotle's death on March 7, 322 BC, word was already circulating that the great work starting in Egypt was not, unlike her neighbors', simply directed at building armies and war machines. Instead, the focus was on creating something far more unusual: a vast body of knowledge. In an age when most of the great philosophers and poets frequently moved between cities and countries, looking for new patrons and avoiding the endless wars, here was a place of continuous protection and patronage, a place where the armories were being filled not just with weapons but with the tools of pure reason. And so the greatest minds of the day—indeed some of the greatest minds of all time—began to answer the call.

One of the first to send Ptolemy word of his support for the project was, perhaps not surprisingly, Theophrastus, Aristotle's successor at the Lyceum. Theophrastus had been Aristotle's close friend, both in Macedonia and later in Athens. Indeed, Aristotle had given him that name, meaning "divine speaker," because of his graceful conversation; when he had first come to study philosophy he was simply Tyrtanius from Lesbos.

Theophrastus had also been a close friend of Aristotle's nephew, the historian Callisthenes, and must have shared his master's discomfort at his arbitrary and ultimately fatal treatment at the hands of Alexander. The depth of the friendship between the two scholars of the Lyceum can be seen from Aristotle's will, in which he appointed Theophrastus as guardian to his children as well as confirmed him as his successor. And Theophrastus did not disappoint his old friend. At the Lyceum he became renowned as a brilliant polymath, and in a lifetime of scholarship he surveyed nearly every branch of knowledge, producing works which were still consulted well into the Middle Ages. Hailed as a "Father of Botany," Theophrastus developed Aristotle's empirical approach to the study of nature by means of observation, collection, and classification, making him perhaps history's first true scientific researcher.

An example of his practical approach to problem solving comes in the story that he invented the "message in a bottle." He had been considering the problem of where the water in the Mediterranean Sea came from and believed that it must flow into the basin from the Atlantic Ocean. To test this he sealed a message in a bottle, asking its discoverer to send news of where he or she had found it, and threw it into the sea to see where the currents would take it. We do not know if he ever received a reply, if his bottle was lost, or if it is still lying on some forgotten Mediterranean beach awaiting discovery.

At the Lyceum, Theophrastus had become a star, an international scientific celebrity, attracting students from all over the ancient world. At one time he is said to have had two thousand pupils. During his thirty-five-year tenure there he became so popular with the Athenians that when the old charge of impiety was brought against him he, unlike Socrates and Aristotle before him, simply brushed it off and continued teaching. Besides his great works on botany, Theophrastus also wrote treatises with titles like *On Fire, On Sweat, On Swooning, On the Difference of the Voices of Similar Animals,* and *On Signs of Weather.* His book *On Stones* is the oldest known work on geology. When he died he was granted a public funeral, and Diogenes Laertius tells us that "the whole population of Athens, honouring him greatly, followed him to the grave" (Diogenes Laertius, *Life of Theophrastus,* chapter 11, in *The Lives and Opinions of Eminent Philosophers*).

No doubt remembering the privilege of his own education from Aristotle, Ptolemy was quick to invite Theophrastus to become tutor to his own son (also called Ptolemy)—not that that was the only attraction to having the philosopher in the city. For Theophrastus was not simply the inheritor of Aristotle's philosophical legacy. In his will Aristotle left all his personal library—his collection of books by other authors, his own published works, and, critically, his unpublished lecture notes—to his friend.

But Ptolemy's hopes of securing both Theophrastus and the collections of Aristotle were to be disappointed. Athens was still the home of the Lyceum, still the great hope of Greek philosophy, despite the terrible treatment many of her finest sons had received at the citizens' own hands. So the news came back that the great philosopher and the library of Aristotle would not be moving to Alexandria. In his place Theophrastus sent the seeds of a new academy in the form of his most brilliant pupil, Strato of Lampsacus. If anyone could infuse the future Ptolemy II with a love of learning, it would be Strato. Another polymath whose interests spread to all areas of life, he wrote three books on

> *Kingly Power; three on Justice; three on the Gods; three on Beginnings; and one on each of the subjects of Happiness, Philosophy, Manly Courage, the Vacuum, Heaven, Spirit, Human Nature, the Generation of Animals, Mixtures, Sleep, Dreams, Sight, Perception, Pleasure, Colours, Diseases, Judgements, Powers, Metallic Works, Hunger, and Dimness of Sight, Lightness and Heaviness, Enthusiasm, Pain, Nourishment and Growth, Animals whose Existence is Doubted, Fabulous Animals, Causes, a Solution of Doubts, a preface to Topics; there are, also, treatises on Contingencies, on the Definition, on the More and Less, on Injustice, on Former and Later, on the Prior Genus, on Property, on the Future.*
>
> Diogenes Laertius, *Life of Strato,* chapter 4, in
> *The Lives and Opinions of Eminent Philosophers*

Strato would be to Ptolemy II what Aristotle had been to Alexander, or at least that was his father's hope. But just as Strato was stepping ashore in the Great Harbor to take up his position at court, another Athenian, albeit a refugee, and another friend of Theophrastus was also making his way toward Alexandria, and he would begin to formalize Ptolemy's grand plan to make Alexandria the intellectual center of the world. Demetrius of Phalerum understood philosophy from both sides, having walked with Aristotle through the stoas of the Lyceum but also having ruled Athens and attempted to put those theories into practice. His arrival in Alexandria had been fortuitous for Ptolemy, giving him the opportunity to ally a well-known statesman and philosopher to his new cult of Serapis. We do not know if he came from Athens bearing copies of the books of Aristotle and the Peripatetic school. We do not know if he brought some of the strange objects from the museum that Alexander had ordered sent to his old tutor. But what he certainly brought with him was an idea. Demetrius knew that the fame of Athens was not its democracy, but its philosophers. He knew the center of a city, the center of a state, should be more than a palace, a parliament, or an armory. It should be a museum—literally the "place of the Muses," goddesses of poetry, music, dance, and the liberal arts and sciences, where these subjects should be both taught and extended by observation and experiment, and all manner of knowledge contemplated. Here the greatest minds could come to have their great thoughts, where strange and wonderful things could be studied and considered, and where all the ideas of every thinker who had come before could be consulted in a single collection of books. This was the true key to being master of the world, and if Ptolemy sought greatness then he would have to create the greatest museum.

Ptolemy was inspired. He had probably already been collecting the books he required to write the great history of Alexander he was planning. He still possessed Alexander's own campaign diary as well as the works of his other historians, including the unfortunate Callisthenes. Now Demetrius challenged him to supplement these with other works, any works, for everything might add some detail or throw light into some dark corner of the tale. Demetrius recommended that the king gather about him all the books about kingship he could muster, along with books on the geography of the lands they had crossed, on their ancient and recent history, and on the customs of the various peoples the Macedonians had encountered in their Asian campaigns.

Soon the shelves of the palace were filling with books (the term *bibliotheka* literally means "bookshelf"), and by 300 BC they were overflowing.

So the area around the recently completed royal residence had become a building site again, this time for dormitories and assembly halls, laboratories, observatories, and zoological gardens. The city of the mind, like the dream of Alexander, was being turned from an idea into a physical reality. The huge wealth of Egypt, Ptolemy's wealth, was being focused in a new direction. The museum and library of Alexandria, two of the greatest institutions the world would ever know, were under construction.

It was into this inspired chaos that one of the most famous names from all antiquity was about to step, a man whose personal life is all but lost to us but whose name is still known in just about every school and college across the world. We have little idea when Euclid of Alexandria was born, or when he died (the most educated guesses suggest he was born around 325 BC and died sometime about 265 BC); Alexandria was where he chose to work, and his impact on mathematics catapulted the city into the scientific stratosphere. For at least 750 years after his death, if you wanted to be anything in mathematics, you simply had to study the subject in Alexandria. His book the *Elements* remained a standard text on geometry well into the twentieth century, even providing the basis of some of the calculations that NASA needed to put a man on the moon. Even now the knotty problems Euclid set his Alexandrian students remain the bane of schoolchildren and the delight of mathematicians. It is also now reckoned that his *Elements* is the most translated, most published, and most studied book in existence after the Bible. Since its reintroduction into Europe in AD 1482, having been lost in the West for nearly the whole medieval period, at least a thousand different editions of the work have been published.

Our only glimpse of this extraordinary man comes from the writings of Proclus, a Greek philosopher and head of the Athenian Academy, writing around AD 450, some seven hundred years after his subject's death. Therefore, even this scrap cannot be relied on for its accuracy; but in its recollection of one personal story it may perhaps hold an echo of the man himself. "They say that Ptolemy once asked him if there was a shorter way to study geometry than the Elements, to which he replied that there was no royal road to geometry" (Proclus, *A Commentary on the First Book of Euclid's "Elements"*).

Given the near-complete absence of information on Euclid's life, Proclus had to do some detective work to discover even this. He tells us that parts of the *Elements* are based on the work of his predecessors Eudoxus and Theaetatus and that Euclid was younger than Plato's circle, but older than Eratosthenes, while the mention of Euclid's name by Archimedes, who Proclus knew was writing during the reign of Ptolemy II, helped him to narrow down the date. Even this is debatable, however, as some scholars believe the mention by Archimedes was inserted into his works after his death. Indeed, other scholars have gone on to doubt the very existence of the man at all, arguing that his name was a cover for a team of mathematicians working in Alexandria who took the name from the philosopher Euclid of Megara, who had lived a century earlier.

However, the only evidence for this assertion is that there is some stylistic variation in different sections of his book. Given that correct academic procedure in those days consisted of gathering up your predecessors' findings and working on from there, this provides a perfectly adequate explanation for the stylistic variation in the *Elements*. So, regardless of whether he was one man or many, the simple fact is that from the earliest days of Alexandria there emerged one of the most important books of all time produced by one (or more) of the first great minds of the city and who, under the name "Euclid," would go down in history as perhaps the greatest mathematician of all time.

What, then, was this great work about? The obvious answer to the question is of course geometry, but that is far from a summary. The thirteen books of the *Elements* open with a series of definitions and five propositions. Some seem deceptively simple: The first is merely that it's possible to draw a straight line between any two points. To the points and lines are added circles, and then the existence of other geometrical objects is deduced from these. Proposition 4 states that all right angles are equal. This may seem obvious, but underlying this bland statement is the assumption that space is homogeneous—a figure is independent of its position in space. In short, Euclid was defining space—the whole canvas of the mathematical universe on which geometry could then be inscribed.

The famous fifth proposition is concerned with parallel lines and states that only one line can be drawn through a point parallel to a given line. It was only when this postulate was dropped in the nineteenth century that non-Euclidean geometry could emerge.

Books 1 through 6 of the *Elements* explore planar geometry—triangles, parallels, circles, and the like. Books 7 through 9 deal with number theory; book 10 deals with "irrational numbers"; and finally books 11 through 13 deal with three-dimensional geometry, the last being concerned with the five regular polyhedra (multisided 3-D figures). This book was used extensively by Johannes Kepler as he struggled to unravel the workings of the solar system in the seventeenth century AD.

Like so many of his contemporaries, Euclid didn't stop at mathematics. Other surviving books include the *Elements of Music* and his *Optics*, which is the first extant work on perspective. The intriguing *Book of Fallacies* has sadly not survived, but Proclus describes it:

> *Since many things seem to conform with the truth and to follow from scientific principles, but lead astray from the principles and deceive the more superficial, [Euclid] has handed down methods for the clearsighted understanding of these matters also. . . . The treatise in which he gave this machinery to us is entitled* Fallacies, *enumerating in order the various kinds, exercising our intelligence in each case by theorems of all sorts, setting the true side by side with the false, and combining the refutation of the error with practical illustration.*

> Proclus, *A Commentary on the First Book of Euclid's "Elements"*

Euclid was, according to Proclus, a Platonist, and it was this philosophy, the philosophy that would come most to represent Alexandrian thought, that drove the "Father of Mathematics" to devote his entire life to the exploration of those forms and ideas which Plato saw as underlying the untidy jumble of the observed world. Plato had himself said that "the knowledge of which geometry aims is the knowledge of the eternal" (Plato, *Republic,* book 12, chapter 52).

For Euclid, mathematics was not simply an abstract idea but a method for seeking out the harmonies of shape which revealed the sublime, even divine, forms of creation. In his *Elements* Euclid began to set down a method by which Plato's world could be explored and in doing so set Alexandria on a journey of discovery far beyond anything taken by the ships which came and went each day through the Great Harbor.

Years before, it is said, Plato had a motto written above the door to the Academy: "Let no one ignorant of mathematics enter here." Now Euclid was showing the reason why.

Euclid's work remained pivotal to the development of the European intellectual tradition for at least two thousand years, and one of the reasons for its longevity was that it was coherent and substantially accurate. For the story of Alexandria this is of critical importance. Here, in the reign of the first Ptolemaic pharaoh, his protolibrary and museum were invested with a completely trustworthy compilation of a major science which generations of succeeding scholars could call upon, not just for academic study but as a means of enhancing their own work. Then as now scholars returned again and again to the shelves holding Euclid's works to compute, test, and verify their own research, in fields ranging from physics to geography and astronomy. The *Elements* is, even today, an anchor of mathematics, first dropped over two millennia ago into a sea of ignorance from the ship of Alexandria.

Mathematics was not the only early love of Alexandrians, however. Another great area of exploration in these early days of the museum was medicine.

It was Alexandria's geographical and cultural position that would make it so pivotal in the development of medicine. Here in Egypt, Greek scholars could draw upon a complex body of Egyptian traditions and practices regarding the preservation of the human body after death by mummification. Whereas in the classical world Greece, Rome, and the states of the Near East maintained strong taboos on the study of the dead, for thousands of years the Egyptians had done their best to preserve corpses through mummification, which, of course, required an intimate knowledge of the inner workings of the human body and a high level of skill in dissection.

Mummification entailed the removal of the brain and all the soft organs of the body cavity except the heart (which was considered the center of intelligence and feeling) and was standard practice at the time of the Macedonian conquest. Now in Alexandria two young scientists, Herophilus of Chalcedon and Erasistratus of Ceos, seized upon this breach of normal mortuary taboo and began to explore the human body in minute detail, thus founding the great Alexandrian tradition of anatomy and physiology.

Though human dissection was still anathema to Greeks, here in Alexandria such things were hugely more open. Not only were the two physicians allowed to carry out their work (some say they were master and pupil, others that they headed rival schools), they were actively encouraged and even given live condemned prisoners to vivisect. The scene must have been disturbing and bloody, but it was taking them into another world, one that was secret and unknown. Guided by the mortuary technicians with their centuries of experience in mummifying the dead, these Greeks were now opening up the world of the living body, seeing for the first time into the machine that housed the soul, discovering by experiment its form and function.

Their progress was amazing. Casting aside the magical and mystical beliefs and superstitions of their predecessors, Herophilus first described the linked functions of the brain, spinal cord, and nervous system, rightly relocating the center of thought from the heart to the brain. He went on to distinguish correctly between motor and sensory neurons and to establish the link between the eye and the brain in the optic nerve. As well as making detailed observations of the physiology of the eye, he explored and described all the internal organs—heart, liver, pancreas, intestines, and reproductive organs. He was also the first to distinguish between veins and arteries, to show that blood rather than air flowed through these vessels, and to examine the valves of the heart in detail. This in turn led him to link the heart to the pulse and to use the latter diagnostically. Through his extensive (and public) dissections he established the heart as not the center of feeling but the center of the circulatory system, thereby anticipating William Harvey's "discovery" of the circulation of the blood by nineteen hundred years.

Erasistratus refined Herophilus's work, making minute observations of the bicuspid and tricuspid valves of the heart and establishing their one-way flow system. He then went on to consider the digestive, respira-

tory, and vascular systems and made a bold attempt to show how sub-
stances vital to our functioning were channeled around the body.

Perhaps more basic and important than the specific details of their
work (all of Herophilus's work is lost, but he is quoted at length by followers of his school) was that they were the first to establish a new concept of the causes of disease and illness. At a time when it was commonly
held that sickness and ill fortune descended on mortals from the gods, as
divine punishment, these Alexandrians insisted that illnesses had natural
causes and should therefore be addressed by secular, scientific means. For
them good health was the key to human happiness, and understanding
the operation of the human machine was the key to achieving this.

Their methods are summed up by Celsus, a Roman physician and poet
of the first century AD:

> Moreover, as pains, and also various kinds of diseases, arise in the
> more internal parts, they hold that no one can apply remedies for these
> who is ignorant about the parts themselves; hence it becomes necessary
> to lay open the bodies of the dead and to scrutinize their viscera and
> intestines. They hold that Herophilus did this in the best way by far,
> when they laid open men whilst alive—criminals received out of
> prison from the king—and while these were still breathing, observed
> parts which beforehand nature had concealed, their position, colour,
> shape, size, arrangement, hardness, softness, smoothness, relation, pro-
> cesses and depressions of each, and whether any part is inserted into or
> is received into another.

> A. Cornelius Celsus, *Of Medicine*

Already the scope of the museum and library of Alexandria were extending far beyond Demetrius's exhortation to gather the materials for
Ptolemy's own book, but by now the desire to know more—to try to
know everything—seems to have gripped them both. How these two
men worked together in these early days, and what persuaded Ptolemy to
extend the scope of his project from simply collecting personal research
materials to making his city the center of the academic world, is something of a mystery. But there is one clue.

For once we appear, at least at first glance, to have remarkably detailed information on this dramatic and decisive period in the formation of the city and its schools, though as we shall see, not all is as it seems. To appreciate the context of the work we need to backtrack a little into Jewish history.

Persian rule in Egypt before the arrival of Alexander had been profoundly unpopular, but not every aspect of it had disappeared entirely under the rule of the Ptolemies. The Persians had relied heavily, and successfully, on large numbers of Jewish administrators to run Egypt on their behalf. Ptolemy I had continued this program during his early wars, bringing as many as one hundred thousand Jewish prisoners from Israel to Egypt (and Alexandria in particular). Many of these he treated very well, and they became an important element in his army and in the administration. Living and working in a Greek-speaking world (indeed, many may have come from the Greek-speaking world), some of these Jews had become very Hellenized, although no pressure seems to have been put upon them to change their religious customs and practices. Contact with the Jewish population only increased Ptolemy's interest in further expanding his book collection, as Demetrius was encouraging him to look beyond the confines of Greek literature to the other great books of Egypt and the Near East, and large sums of money had been set aside for their acquisition. The problem of course was that most of these texts were not in Greek, but Syriac, Persian, Egyptian, and Hebrew, and this didn't suit either the Greek masters of Alexandria or the increasingly Hellenized immigrants whose native tongue was slipping away, leaving them unable to read the literature and holy books of their native land. How Ptolemy I, Demetrius, and the immigrant population of Alexandria went about solving this problem survives in a document that claims to be by a Jewish scholar named Aristeas living during the reign of Ptolemy's son. There is no trace of the supposed original of this account, but it is apparently faithfully reproduced in full by the early Greek church historian Eusebius of Caesarea (c. AD 260–339) in his *Praeparatio Evangelica* (Preparation for the Gospel), dating to approximately AD 314–318.

In it he tells the remarkable, indeed largely fabulous story of how one of the most important books in history came to be translated into Greek and from there spread across the world. Aristeas, the author, tells us that

Demetrius was called before Ptolemy to give an account of the progress
with collecting books for the library. Demetrius told the king that twenty
thousand books had been collected so far and that he had set a target of
increasing this to fifty thousand as quickly as possible. He then added,
almost as an aside: "It has also been notified to me that the customs of the
Jews are worthy of transcription and of a place in your library" (Eusebius,
Praeparatio Evangelica, book 8, chapter 2).

The king was intrigued, as Demetrius no doubt knew he would be,
and demanded to know more. Demetrius obliged and told him that the
Hebrew books of law would be a valuable addition to the library, as the
law they contained was divine and hence "very full of wisdom and sin-
cerity." There was, however, a problem, Demetrius told him:

> *An interpretation also is required; for in Judaea they use characters
> peculiar to themselves, just as the Egyptians use their own position of
> the letters, inasmuch as they have also a language of their own. And
> they are supposed to employ Syriac, but this is not so, for it is a dif-
> ferent kind of language.*

> Eusebius, *Praeparatio Evangelica*, book 8, chapter 2

The king was certainly not going let a little problem like translation
get in the way of his obtaining a copy of such a vital text, so Demetrius
was given the job of not just finding but arranging for the translation of
the Jewish holy books. In a memorandum to the king, also recorded by
Aristeas, he then tells us how he intended to go about this:

> ## TO THE GREAT KING FROM DEMETRIUS
> *In accordance with thy command, O king, that the books which were
> wanting to the completion of the library might be collected, and that the
> parts which had been damaged might be properly restored, I have very
> carefully given my attention to these matters and now present my report
> to thee. . . . If therefore it seems good, O king, there shall be a letter
> written to the High Priest in Jerusalem, to send elderly men who have
> lived the most honourable lives, and experienced in matters of their
> own Law, six from each tribe, in order that we may test the agree-*

ment by a large number, and after receiving the exact interpretation,
we may give it a distinguished place, in a manner worthy both of the
circumstances and of thy purpose. Good fortune be ever thine.

Eusebius, *Praeparatio Evangelica,* book 8, chapter 3

In short, Demetrius was suggesting gathering a group of the finest
Hebrew scholars from Jerusalem to come to Alexandria, where each
would produce his own translation, all of which could then be compared
to produce one synthesized and corrected Greek version. Ptolemy duly
wrote the letter to the high priest Eleazar in Jerusalem:

> *I have determined that your law shall be translated from the Hebrew*
> *tongue which is in use amongst you into the Greek language, that*
> *these books may be added to the other royal books in my library. It*
> *will be a kindness on your part and a regard for my zeal if you will*
> *select six elders from each of your tribes, men of noble life and skilled*
> *in your law and able to interpret it, that in questions of dispute we*
> *may be able to discover the verdict in which the majority agree, for the*
> *investigation is of the highest possible importance. I hope to win great*
> *renown by the accomplishment of this work.*

Eusebius, *Praeparatio Evangelica,* book 8, chapter 4

So far this seems like a plausible, if extraordinary, hint at how Ptolemy
and Demetrius worked together, but now the tale begins to take on a
more mythical tone. Aristeas tells us that these seventy-two wise men did
come to the city, and the king wept with joy at their arrival. For a week
he put philosophical questions to them before ordering them taken to the
island of Pharos. Here they were placed in seventy-two separate cells, and
each was told to make his own translation of this great work—the first
five books of the Bible (known as the Pentateuch). Being kept apart
would ensure that no one scholar copied or consulted another, and so the
work each produced would be entirely his own.

After exactly seventy-two days all of these scholars then emerged simultaneously with their Greek translations. Each one was identical. And
so the legend of the creation of the awesomely authentic Septuagint, as it
is still known, was born.

It seems almost incredible that we have the actual correspondence which would lead to translation of the first five books of the Bible into Greek, and alas, it is too good to be true. It is a wonderful story, but in it credibility is stretched to breaking point as we are asked to believe a literary miracle as hard fact. And this is not the only problem with the text—there is a problem with the mention of Demetrius in the first place.

Other reliable sources state clearly that Demetrius had indeed dedicated himself to establishing the library and museum for Ptolemy I, but he also recommended that a different son should succeed his father to the Egyptian throne. When Ptolemy II succeeded, he had Demetrius sent into exile in Upper Egypt—some claim he was even imprisoned there—where he died just a year later, possibly from the bite of an asp. Yet this correspondence purports to be between Demetrius and Ptolemy II. In his letter to the high priest Eleazar of Jerusalem, the king states quite clearly: "Whereas it happens that many Jews who were carried away from Jerusalem by the Persians in the time of their power, have been settled in our country, and many more have come with my father into Egypt as prisoners of war" (Eusebius, *Praeparatio Evangelica,* book 8, chapter 4).

Aristeas claims that Ptolemy I was writing to the high priest, but the letter was clearly from Ptolemy II. The authenticity of this correspondence must hence be seriously challenged by the apparent conflation of two Ptolemies into one. In fact the veracity of the "Letter of Aristeas" was questioned as early as the seventeenth century, where it was pretty conclusively shown to be the work of a much later Hellenistic Jew from Alexandria who wished to stress the authenticity of the Septuagint version of the Old Testament and its miraculous translation as described by Aristeas.

However, it does seem that the letter dates from between 200 and 90 BC and, despite its errors, may contain, at least in its less mythical passages, a memory of the zeal of those early years of collecting books in Alexandria. Certainly the version we have today has been wildly embroidered by later Christian writers such as Saint Augustine, Eusebius, and Irenaeus. But in summing up the putative dialogues of Demetrius and Ptolemy, Aristeas, whoever he was, was making a point that both men would have understood: that the mysteries of the world lie not, as Alexander thought, over the horizon in yet unconquered territories, but in the minds of his own subjects.

Ptolemy II, if not his father, did oversee the first translation of the first sections of the single most important book in the history of the world—the Bible—during the first half of the third century BC in Alexandria. In truth, what is far more extraordinary than Aristeas's miraculous translation story is the fact that the religious books of the Jews were translated in the first place. However inaccurate Aristeas's words are and whatever his real purpose in writing, the sentiment is entirely of the period. The Ptolemies wanted to know everything, not just their own history or their own religious texts, and in wanting to know what lay outside their world they were stepping into the unknown.

So in its first seventy years or so, Alexandria acted as host to the greatest mathematician in the world and published his finest work, a book destined to become the second most successful book of all time. It also saw the establishment of the ancient world's most successful school of anatomy, physiology, and medicine, along with the finest library and museum to be found anywhere in the ancient world. And there its scholars began to undertake the enormous task of copying, editing, translating, and cataloging the entire compendium of written knowledge as it existed at that time, including the first translations of what would become the most published book the world has ever known: the Bible.

With the spirit of scientific inquiry firmly enshrined here, Alexandria's scholars were set to push the boundaries of knowledge way beyond the limits recorded in all those ancient scrolls. And this was barely the beginning.

CHAPTER SIX

GREEK PHARAOHS

For good ye are and bad, and like to coins,
Some true, some light, but every one of you
Stamped with the image of the King.

Alfred Lord Tennyson, "The Holy Grail," *Idylls of the King*

By 285 BC Ptolemy I felt that his work building his kingdom was coming to an end. To ensure a smooth dynastic transition, in that year he appointed his son Ptolemy II as joint ruler, charged with taking over the day-to-day affairs of state. It was time to concentrate on the project that had begun it all, his own firsthand account of the life and campaigns of Alexander the Great.

It's a clear indicator of the intellectual tide of the times that Ptolemy I, one of the most powerful individuals in the world, chose to crown his achievements not by basking in luxury, but by writing a book. Sensing the enormous power which the foundation of the museum and library was engendering, Ptolemy formulated his swan song in writing his own version of the momentous events he had lived through. His book survived for centuries, and its eventual loss is one of the greatest literary tragedies of all time. Yet the very fact that he, a divine king, should dedicate his last years not to statecraft but to literature was a near-perfect sign of the times.

The nation he left in his son's care was the strongest of any of those seized by the successors of Alexander. His attempts to stabilize the regional situation had involved not just fighting but subtle and effective diplomatic campaigns which saw many of his children married to neighboring, often rival heads of state. It was an extraordinary achievement and one which might have received more recognition both in his time and today if it had not been a life lived in the very long shadow of his old master. And yet it was a life that in many ways was far more successful. Alexander had no heirs, his empire was fragmented, his generals were alienated, his family was dead. Ptolemy had created a new state, a new dynasty, a new religion, a new form of government, and a miraculous new city. The terrible irony of his reign is that his own great work, in which he told the story of the conquest of the world through his own eyes, has not survived. In that we might have seen a more personal side to Ptolemy, and hence history might well have weighed the two men's contributions differently.

Three years after appointing his son co-regent Ptolemy I died, aged eighty-four, and the fledgling dynasty faced its first crucial test. Following his father's lead, Ptolemy II acted swiftly and decisively. He was crowned pharaoh of Egypt in the ancient capital of Memphis on January 7, 282 BC, without any real challenge; yet with the cold calculation that his family would become famous for, he promptly had two of his half brothers murdered, probably with the connivance of his sister and future wife, Arsinoe. In this way the prospect of sibling rivalry was nipped in the bud.

But if Ptolemy II was ruthless he was certainly not uncultured. His father had been keen to ensure that his son enjoyed an education as privileged as his own. So, like Alexander, he could claim to have had two fathers, one for his body—Ptolemy I—and one for his mind—Strato of Lampsacus. Just as Ptolemy I had seen the flaws in his old master's reign, so his more educated son began to see the flaws in his father's. Ptolemy I had enjoyed the wealth of Egypt and used it both to shore up his position militarily and to fund a revival in Greek learning, but the actual administration of Egypt had remained largely a mystery to him. The details of how Egypt operated economically were of little interest, provided that it operated smoothly. It had been left to others, mainly the Egyptian temples, actually to administer the collection and sale of the grain upon which his wealth was founded. So it was to the great good fortune of Alexandria and the forthcoming Ptolemaic dynasty that the second Ptolemy would turn out to be one of the greatest and most able administrators in the ancient world.

The young Ptolemy threw himself into the development of the Egyptian economy with gusto and in the process created the most sophisticated planned economy until the formation of the Soviet Union more than two thousand years later. The first step in this process, repeated several times in his reign, was to understand just what it was that he had inherited. To do this he ordered a comprehensive census of all his domains. Typically, a survey would cover all water sources, the position and irrigation potential of all land, the present state of cultivation, crops grown, and the extent of priestly and royal landholdings. Armed with what was, in effect, an ancient Domesday Book, Ptolemy and his ministers set to work.

Their first problem was trade. For centuries in Egypt there had been no true currency with which to buy and sell goods. Most markets operated on a barter-and-exchange system. For very large-scale transactions it was possible to pay in gold or other precious metals, but the idea of coinage was still relatively new. True monetary economies had emerged in the city-states of the Mediterranean beginning around 650 BC, probably first in Lydia, whose later king Croesus had made himself a byword for fabulous wealth. Ptolemy I had made some attempts to follow suit, issuing coins called staters just as Alexander had, but outside Alexandria these were as much demonstrations of royal power as they were useful coins. His son, however, now massively extended this scheme with the creation of a state-run banking system with local branches throughout the towns and villages of the country, all reporting back to the central bank in Alexandria. From these banks a coin-based currency was introduced, backed up by a system of written "bills of exchange"—promissory letters which could be exchanged for real money, or, as we would call them, banknotes. The entire rural economy was to be centered on these local branches, which provided the capital—seed grain and tools—that the farmers needed. They also provided massive state-aided infrastructural schemes such as the creation of a reservoir in the Southern Fayyum oasis which held 360 million cubic yards of water and irrigated 60 square miles of arable land. This was not pure largesse, however. Nearly all the grain produced by farmers was taken into the royal treasury in the form of tax. More land under cultivation meant more grain, and more grain meant more money in the Alexandrian coffers.

The driving force behind this economy was, of course, the immense quantity of grain produced in the Nile Valley. The annual flooding of the Nile, which ran through an almost rainless desert, made this the most productive agricultural land in the known world, where the sun always shone on the crops, but never dried their roots. Such valuable land was largely owned by the crown or the temples and leased to farmers, who were free men and women who often used slave labor to maintain their estates. Such estates produced a vast surplus, much of which the state took. Yet Ptolemy's system also allowed for a degree of individual enterprise, as banks could handle private financial transactions, provide loans, and broker deals.

Whatever capital was left could be spent in the thriving open markets. Traditionally Egyptians had acquired the necessities of life they couldn't produce for themselves by direct barter—effectively swapping a loaf for a pint of milk. The Greek immigrants, however, greatly encouraged the development of markets throughout the whole country. These were often held in the precincts of temples, and records exist of the temple taxes levied on the traders. In the town of Oxyrhynchus, for example, had you taken a stroll into the courtyard of the temple of Serapis on market day, a chaotic vista would have opened up as you passed through the first pylon. That day the peace of the temple would have been shattered by the cries of stallholders, all hoping to relieve you of some of the coins in your pocket. Here the local farmers and traders sold local vegetables, wood, olives, rushes, bread, fruit, wool yarn, and plaited garlands from wooden stands, each of which had been licensed (for a fee) by the temple. Among the crowd you might pick out the priests of Serapis, moving between the stalls, checking their goods and imposing the appropriate import duty on everything from olives, dates, cucumbers, squashes, beans, spices, and rock salt to pottery, green fodder, wood, and dung. The throng would also have attracted other traders offering more sophisticated wares, from the bulk grain dealers looking to turn a profit back in Alexandria, to the tailors, leather embroiderers, tinsmiths, butchers, and brothel keepers who always gravitated toward a crowd.

Even in this controlled economy there would be signs of real wealth. Though all land was nominally owned by either the state or the temples, Ptolemy reserved the right to present land to individuals, from which they could collect substantial revenues. These favors were usually accorded to courtiers like Apollonius, Ptolemy II's finance minister, who was granted 10,000 arourae (about 6,800 acres) of highly productive land in the Fayyum, giving him a huge income. Here then, dressed in his finery, was a man who could never walk through a market without attracting the attentions of merchants offering the finer things in life, from perfumes to precious stones.

Egypt's agricultural surpluses were the driving force behind her international trade, whose volume rose enormously under Ptolemy II. But the state also maintained tight control of all of Egypt's manufacturing industries, either through direct ownership or through highly regulated private enterprise—the nation had a world monopoly on the manufacture of papyrus paper, for example, and was not above manipulating the market. When rivalry between the great libraries in Alexandria and Pergamum reached a peak, Ptolemy II reportedly stopped the export of Egyptian paper in an attempt to stifle the academic work at Pergamum and attract its best scholars to Egypt. Legend has it that the scheme failed, as the ever resourceful scholars of Pergamum began experimenting with writing on fine animal skins, and in the process invented something even better than papyrus—parchment, which gets its name from the Latin word for the city, Pergaminus. It is a fitting though probably apocryphal story, as parchment scrolls from elsewhere are known to have existed before this time.

The center for this thriving economy was Alexandria, where all the grain surpluses and all the money from all the markets across Egypt eventually returned. The city was becoming famous as a home for far more than the necessities of life. Besides papyrus, oil, and linen production, Alexandria itself was becoming renowned for the production of books for export and for works of art. Her glassware, perfumes, and jewelry were especially sought after, as were her superb (Hellenistic) sculptures and mosaics. Even beyond the Necropic Gate in the City of the Dead, art was flourishing in a unique fusion of Greek and Egyptian traditions. Here the wealthy were choosing to be buried in that most Egyptian of ways, mummified, wrapped in elaborate bandages, and placed in a series of brilliantly painted sarcophagi. But there was a difference. Not for these Greco-Egyptian merchants the old formal mummy masks with their stiff features. These are faces full of life and character, individuals who wanted to be remembered as themselves and who now, over two millennia later, still smile out at us with wry amusement from the museum cases that have become their homes.

Nor did Ptolemy II have to depend solely on locally produced materials to fuel his economy. Alexandria was already a major shipbuilding center, and the pharaoh maintained fleets for commerce as well as defense in both the Mediterranean and the Red Sea, linking the two with a canal that ran via the Nile to Alexandria itself. Down that canal came exotic perfumes from Arabia and spices from India. Across the Mediterranean came timber, olive oil, and wine. From the upper Nile came gold, ivory, slaves, ebony, and a steady flow of exotic wildlife from the African interior. From caravan routes that stretched across the Western Desert came Saharan commodities, including valuable salt from the legendary mines of Mali. In Alexandria all these goods could be bought and sold. It was the entrepôt of the world, where leopard skins and the perfumes of Punt could be exchanged for Afghan lapis lazuli and Indian cinnamon, and where warehouses stood piled to their roofs with the fragrant cedarwood of Lebanon, and locked ebony boxes held fortunes in frankincense and myrrh.

Many of these riches were reserved exclusively for royal use. What then did Ptolemy II spend his massive wealth on? Naturally the humdrum expenses of the court, the museum and its state-sponsored scholars, the books and the ever-growing library, all ate into the royal purse. The maintenance of an enormous civil service was essential to administer and regulate the planned economy, but this still left the pharaoh with substantial surpluses, and these he spent on incredibly ostentatious displays and festivals.

For Ptolemy such festivals were more than simply an opportunity to spend money, however. Although he was an Egyptian ruler—a pharaoh—he was also a Greek king—a basileus—and from a Greek perspective a basileus must demonstrate his power and success through lavish displays which often bordered on megalomania. And in Egypt there were the appetite and the money to take this to new extremes.

When Ptolemy II became king he celebrated his accession with an enormous festival in Alexandria. In instituting the "Ptolemaieia," in honor of his family and in particular his father, Ptolemy II devised an enormously elaborate pageant, deliberately designed to rival the other great four-yearly event in the Mediterranean world, the Olympic Games. An observer named Callixeinus of Rhodes made a detailed account of the procession.

Some 485 years later, the writer Athenaeus of Naucratis produced a book called *The Learned Banquet,* probably for his patron, a Roman called Larensis. The book describes a party lasting several days, during which the guests discussed law, medicine, literature, and philosophy with Larensis. During this time the guests remembered other famous celebrations from the past, quoting from some 1,250 authors. This is the real value of the work, a gold mine of quotations from plays and books most of which are now lost, and among them is the description of Ptolemy's procession.

The parade was a celebration of the Greek god Dionysus, whom the Ptolemies had elegantly associated with their new Egyptian deity, Serapis. At its center came "a four-wheeled wagon fourteen cubits [twenty-one feet] high and eight cubits [twelve feet] wide[;] it was drawn by one hundred and eighty men. On it was the image of Dionysus—ten cubits [fifteen feet] high" (Athenaeus of Naucratis, *Deipnosophists, or The Learned Banquet,* book 5).

If the sheer scale of this statue were not impressive enough, it also appeared to the crowd to be magical, moving of its own accord:

> *He was pouring libations from a golden goblet and had a purple tunic reaching to his feet. . . . In front of him lay a Lacedaemonian goblet of gold holding fifteen measures of wine, and a golden tripod, in which was a golden incense burner, and two golden bowls full of cassia and saffron, and a shade covered it round adorned with ivy and vine leaves and all other kinds of greenery.*

> Athenaeus of Naucratis, *Deipnosophists,*
> *or The Learned Banquet,* book 5

More wagons laden with gilded bowls and tripods followed, along with a display from the royal menagerie consisting of twenty-four chariots drawn by four elephants each, twelve chariots drawn by antelopes, fifteen by buffaloes, eight by pairs of ostriches, eight by zebras, and twenty-four by lions. There was also one final scene of conspicuous consumption. A wagon forty feet long and fifteen feet wide trundled down the granite road drawn by six hundred men:

On this wagon was a sack, holding three thousand measures of wine
and consisting of leopards' skins sewn together. This sack allowed its
liquor to escape, and it gradually flowed over the whole road. . . . The
cost of this great occasion was 2,239 talents and 50 minae.

Athenaeus of Naucratis, *Deipnosophists,*
or The Learned Banquet, book 5

At the time of the above translation in 1998 that quantity of gold would have cost the modern equivalent of roughly $35 million—a sizable amount to spend on a single parade.

These parades also carried political messages—in this case Ptolemaic solidarity with the Grecian city-states of the Corinthian League—and were deliberately designed to impress the local diplomatic corps as well as visiting delegations with the raw wealth and power of the new rulers of Egypt. In all this they were highly successful, and Ptolemy II, with his immaculately harnessed economic machine, could well afford them. He seems not to have recognized, however, that such ostentatious displays have a certain addictive quality—once you've done a few, everybody expects the delightful new tradition to continue indefinitely, with disastrous consequences for later, less financially adroit Ptolemies and their decadent, pleasure-addicted courts.

A further pull on the royal purse strings came from the priests and temples of the Egyptian state religion. The Egyptians in Ptolemy's kingdom did not require him simply to put on impressive shows, however much they may have enjoyed them. For them their ruler had a far more spiritual role, mediating between the gods and men. A pharaoh had to perform the vital religious rituals which ensured that maat—harmony or stability—remained in Egypt, so one of his greatest financial obligations was toward the temples.

But maintaining buildings was never enough for true Egyptian pharaohs. Egypt was a country defined by its monumental buildings, where kings had turned whole cliff faces into statues, where the Great Pyramid still remained far and away the largest and to many the most mysterious structure on earth. If the Ptolemies wanted to rule this country in a way that inspired Egyptians and overawed Greeks, they would have to build temples.

Building temples was also about building bridges. The introduction of the Serapis cult had ushered in a small reformation in Egyptian religion, which must have left many temple priests on edge. The government's shift from Memphis to Alexandria must also have rankled. But like Alexander before them, both Ptolemy I and his son knew that their positions ultimately depended on retaining harmonious relations with the Egyptian priesthood, as the priests influenced the will of the people. Temple building eased this pressure by investing state funds in the priestly caste and by reminding the guardians of Egyptian religion that their new Greek masters respected and needed them.

Little wonder then that all the Ptolemies were powerful supporters of religious institutions, right through to the great Cleopatra VII, whose image, along with that of her son by Julius Caesar, appears carved in bas-relief on one of the pylons of the temple of Hathor at Dendera. In fact, their programs of temple building and restoration were so extensive throughout Egypt that most of the buildings which tourists visit today and assume to be of "ancient" Egypt were either built or restored under the Ptolemies. When walking through the almost perfectly preserved first pylon of the temple of Horus at Edfu, we are not walking into the world of Rameses and Tutankhamen, but into a creation of Ptolemy II's son. The temple of Isis at Philae, so spectacularly saved by UNESCO from the rising waters of Lake Nasser, stands on remains from more ancient times but is itself a work of the later Ptolemies and was decorated in the time of Roman rule. The temples at Esna and Kom Ombo likewise were not even thought of when Ptolemy II paraded through the streets of Alexandria. Although these buildings have become our image of ancient Egypt, they are themselves just a dream—imaginings by Greek rulers of what were already the long-lost days of the pyramid builders.

But if the new temples springing up across Egypt in Ptolemy II's reign were simply harking back to older times, they were certainly not without value to their native audience. In preserving and developing their religious patronage, these places also kept indigenous art traditions and scholarship alive. All over Egypt today you can see pharaohs and their queens, carved in traditional stances, wearing traditional Egyptian clothing and jewelry, brandishing traditional weapons and adornments and "smiting the enemy" in entirely traditional manners. They might in fact be images of

Greek-speaking Macedonians, but to the ultraconservative Egyptians they were good enough, reminding them of their illustrious past and offering the tantalizing possibility that those days had now returned.

This extensive investment in Egyptian culture had other benefits beyond simply keeping the priesthood and peasantry happy. Under Ptolemaic patronage Egyptian intellectual life flourished. Not just the spoken word but both hieroglyphic and demotic writing blossomed, while the need for translation gave rise to perhaps the most important surviving object from ancient Egypt, the Rosetta stone, whose parallel texts in hieroglyphics, demotic (another, more cursive, Egyptian script), and Greek provided the key to the decoding of the hieroglyphs. And with new styles of writing came new subject matters, including a new Egyptian literary style of romantic tales told in story cycles and featuring the gods, royalty, magic, romance, and the mighty deeds of their warrior heroes.

Even in this halcyon period there was a much darker undercurrent flowing through the Ptolemaic family arteries. The rule of the Ptolemies, like those in the other successor states to Alexander's empire, was a family affair, and within that tortuously intermarried and interbred family deadly rivalries were already brewing.

Around 300 BC Ptolemy I had arranged for his sixteen-year-old daughter Arsinoe to marry King Lysimachos of Thrace, who had also been in the entourage of Alexander the Great; a clever tactical move, as, after 285 BC, Lysimachos also became king of Macedonia. Now the Ptolemies could hold out the prospect of inheriting Alexander's original patrimony, for if Lysimachos and Arsinoe had a son, then Ptolemaic blood would run through the veins of the next ruler of Macedon. There was a problem, however. The king already had an heir, Agathocles, by a previous wife. So Arsinoe, with characteristic Ptolemaic ruthlessness, quickly set about arranging his death. But in the highly interrelated families of the Mediterranean, things were never so simple, and after his murder Agathocles' widow fled the country and managed to raise a war against Lysimachos in which the king was eventually killed (281 BC).

It was a disaster for Arsinoe, and in the ensuing confusion, Lysimachos's Thracian throne was seized by Arsinoe's half brother, who demanded that she marry him. If on the surface this looked like another triumph for the Ptolemies, however, the truth was very different. The marriage to Arsinoe had nothing to do with family beyond gaining access to her children, who the usurper knew were the rightful heirs to Macedon and Thrace. But escaping the marriage proved impossible, and not long after the ceremony, her sons by Lysimachos were duly murdered. With no further need for her, she was expelled from the kingdom. Her half brother had only wanted her hand in marriage so he could kill her children.

This then was the brutalized and vengeful woman who a few months later arrived back at her brother Ptolemy II's court in Alexandria, around 279 BC. Here she continued to intrigue, this time aiming her venom at the king's wife, also confusingly called Arsinoe (I). Arsinoe I was, incidentally, the daughter of Lysimachos and thus theoretically Arsinoe II's stepdaughter-in-law. She had soon arranged for the queen to be accused of plotting to kill the king, and Arsinoe I was sent into exile at Coptos in Upper Egypt. Here a memorial built by an Egyptian called Sennukhrud who was once her steward calls the fallen queen "the king's wife, the grand, filling the palace with her beauties, giving repose to the heart of King Ptolemy." But such titles were now just memories for her. Even her loyal steward couldn't help but give away her true position in society when it came to writing her name, which he wrote without the royal cartouche surrounding it. She might still have called herself queen in far-off Coptos, but in Alexandria she was nothing.

This clinical excision cleared the way for Arsinoe II to take a step that would outrage Greek society but which, to the Greeks' great surprise no doubt, ingratiated her with the native Egyptian population. Seeking a throne for the third time, she proposed marriage to Ptolemy, her full brother. Ptolemy now had to choose. Stay true to his Greek roots and shy away from what any Macedonian would certainly have considered incest, or take the opportunity to consolidate his power, free from the influence of alien wives or suitors, and make Ptolemaic rule an entirely family affair. Fortunately for both of them, they lived in a country with a two-thousand-year precedent for this. Egyptians not only approved of incestuous royal marriages, they preferred them. Royal incest fitted into their religious cosmology and had been widely practiced by pharaohs at the height of Egypt's power. Though her motives were Greek, Arsinoe could not have made a more Egyptian move, so she took a throne for the third time as wife and queen to her brother, the couple taking the epithet "Philadelphus" (brother-loving).

On her death at the age of fifty-four, in July 270 BC, she was deified by her husband, but she bore him no children during their marriage, so Ptolemy had his children by Arsinoe I declared as children of his second, divine wife and heirs to the throne.

Reaction in the museum to the announcement of the two Ptolemies' incestuous marriage must have been mixed. It was an idea that sat very uneasily in Greek minds, as did many aspects of this Greco-Egyptian rule. Yet clearly ruling in a manner that to Egyptians at least seemed correct was working, and most Greeks could be practical enough to turn a blind eye to something they might consider unsavory but could see was profitable. As such the museum trod carefully, its members rarely explicitly commenting on this alien custom.

Indeed, the interest of the museum's scholars was by now, perhaps deliberately, drifting away from the bloody cut and thrust of politics toward the more uplifting arena of poetry. The leading intellectual figure at the time was Theocritus (c. 300–c. 260 BC), an extremely important and influential poet who was the originator of a new form of poetry known as the "pastoral idyll." Greek poets preceding him were mostly interested in storytelling, in character and action, not in the intrinsic beauty of nature. Theocritus totally altered that by creating little pictures of rustic life cast in dramatic form. These could be very naïve:

> Sweeter, shepherd, and more subtle is your song
> Than the tuneful splashing of that waterfall
> Among the rocks. If the Muses pick the ewe
> As their reward, you'll win the hand-raised lamb;
> If they prefer the lamb, the ewe is yours.

Theocritus, *Idylls* 7

Theocritus's idylls and bucolics were immensely influential, right through to the eighteenth century AD and beyond, forming the basis for works like Milton's *Lycidas*, Shelley's *Adonais*, and Matthew Arnold's *Thyrsis*. He also wrote extensively about love, often taking up the quintessentially Greek theme of the love of an older man for a youth:

> *Art come, dear youth? Two nights and days away!*
> *(Who burn with love, grow aged in a day.)*
> *As much as apples sweet the damson crude*
> *Excel; the blooming spring, the winter rude;*
> *In fleece the sheep her lamb, the maiden in sweetness*
> *The thrice-wed dame; the fawn the calf in fleetness;*
> *The nightingale in song all feathered kind—*
> *So much thy longed-for presence cheers my mind.*
> *To thee I hasten, as to shady beech,*
> *The traveller, when from heaven's reach*
> *The sun fierce blazes. May our love be strong,*
> *To all hereafter times the theme of song!*
> *Two men each other loved to that degree,*
> *That either friend did in the other see*
> *A dearer than himself. They loved of old*
> *Both golden natures in an age of gold.*

Theocritus, *Idylls* 12

Whether Theocritus's brief mention of the "thrice-wed dame" could possibly be an aspersion on Arsinoe II is unclear, but we do know that Theocritus was shrewd enough to write openly only in fulsome praise of the incestuous royal marriage, and cast it as the act of divine siblings like Isis and Osiris, which won him much praise and doubtless handsome rewards from his royal patrons.

Another court poet was not so prudent, however. Sotades was also in Alexandria at the time, but his was a very different reputation. Known as "Sotades the Obscene," he is remembered for having invented his own meter for the obscene subject matter of his poetry. Sotades is sometimes credited with inventing the palindrome, where a phrase reads the same both forward and backward, and a Sotadic verse has the opposite meaning when read backward. Almost none of the work of this colorful character has survived, though both Plutarch and Athenaeus noted one line from the satirical poem he wrote about the royal marriage. They said it read: "You are pushing the peg into an unholy hole." It did not amuse his royal patron. According to Plutarch, Ptolemy had Sotades the Obscene thrown into jail. According to Athenaeus, however, Sotades escaped from prison and fled, but he was eventually caught by Ptolemy's admiral Patroclus on the island of Caunus. Patroclus did not bother returning him to his master for punishment but simply had him sealed up in a lead coffin and tossed into the sea.

A third scholar at the museum at the time was Lycophron. He was a tragedian and the only member whose name has survived from a group of seven (sometimes eight) tragic poets of the time known as the Pleiades. However, Ptolemy chose to give him the task of arranging and cataloging all the comedies in the library. This he dutifully did, and he subsequently produced a tract on the subject, *On Comedy*, which is now lost. In fact, only one of his works has survived, a poem in 1,474 iambic lines entitled *Alexandra or Cassandra*, which deals with the fortunes of Troy and the Trojan and Greek heroes after the war, ending, appropriately enough for his audience, with a reference to Alexander the Great. It is so riddled with bizarre, little-used words and words invented by Lycophron himself that even in his own lifetime he became known as "Lycophron the Obscure." Being hard to understand can be a blessing in a violent and highly charged court, however, and Lycophron the Obscure lived to tell more of his enigmatic tales, which became immensely popular in court during the Byzantine period.

But even as his obsequious court poets sought to immortalize their sovereign in verse, Ptolemy II set his sights on more concrete edifices to his glorious reign. His three greatest Alexandrian commissions began with the rebuilding of the museum, which had expanded piecemeal under his father's rule but had long since outgrown its original premises. In place of the old dormitories and assembly halls, he commissioned a magnificent range of buildings right alongside the royal palace on the waterfront, with expansive lecture theaters, the library and great assembly halls, observatories, and plant and animal collections. Finished in white marble and designed to harmonize with the royal palace, it must have been the envy of all the other princes of the time. At this complex's heart stood the museum itself, where the greatest minds in the world could meet and talk and think and write, the first integrated scientific research complex in the world.

To provide fuel for their thoughts, there was the great library—a place where all the works of the ancient world could be stored and ordered, available to any of the scholars to consult, provided of course they had royal permission. Constructed on the waterfront in the royal district known as the Brucheum, it quite early on became known as the "mother library" whose "daughter" was to be found in the Serapeum. Linked to the museum by a white marble colonnade, the mother library contained at least ten large interconnecting rooms or halls, each dedicated to a specific area of learning, such as rhetoric, theater, poetry, astronomy, and mathematics. The walls of each hall were broken up by series of alcoves where the papyrus scrolls were stored. Off the main rooms were smaller ones where scholars could read, write, or discuss their work, and participate in special studies. It was to be a sanctuary for thought in a violent age, and carved over its entrance was a simple inscription: "A Sanatorium for the Mind."

Ptolemy's third great building project may also have been conceived in his father's time but only came to fruition now. If the museum and library stand as testament to the father, it is perhaps this most practical of buildings that should stand as a tribute to the son—the great lighthouse on the island of Pharos. Ptolemy II would no doubt have also been delighted to find that it was this, rather than his father's library or museum, that would go down in history as one of the Seven Wonders of the Ancient World and become Alexandria's most illustrious icon.

The man credited with building the lighthouse (although we are not sure if he was the donor or the architect) was Sostratus the Cnidian, a famed architect and builder who is also credited with having constructed a "hanging garden" in his hometown of Cnidus in Caria and a clubhouse in Delphi where his fellow citizens could meet. The task Ptolemy now set him was to solve one of Alexandria's most persistent problems. Built on an almost totally flat coastline, the harbor at Alexandria was hard to locate from vessels several miles out to sea. And there was a further danger. Those ships unwise enough to stray too close to the shore searching for the anchorage would find themselves in dangerous shoal waters, studded with reefs and sandbanks where all but the most skillful captain might founder. Even with the harbor in sight, the most dangerous reef lay hidden across the entrance itself. Those ships might find themselves wrecked on the shores of Pharos, where the notorious inhabitants of the Port of Pirates could easily pick them off.

There was thus a pressing need to construct some sort of navigational mark that sailors approaching the city could use as a guide, preferably both day and night. In short—a lighthouse. It seems likely that this solution had already been agreed to when Sostratus was summoned by Ptolemy, but aided by the mathematicians of the museum and works from the library, Sostratus was able to propose a structure on a scale that even a Ptolemy could not have expected.

The great lighthouse was to be constructed in granite and limestone blocks faced with white marble. Its total height would be at least 400 feet—that is, about the height of a modern forty-floor skyscraper. Erected on a solid base, it would have three levels. The first level would be square and would house all the workers needed to fuel and operate the great light. The second floor would be octagonal in shape, decorated with exquisite statuary, which stared out across sea and city and where the people of Alexandria might come to enjoy the breathtaking views. The third level would be circular and crowned with an enormous reflector, quite probably of parabolic shape (another first in scientific design) and made of polished brass. Finally atop this would stand a huge bronze statue of Poseidon, god of the sea, leaning on his trident.

The light was designed to operate both day and night. During the day it was simple enough to just reflect the rays of the sun out to sea, but at night something more was required. For this a circular shaft ran up the center of the entire building, which enclosed the spiral staircase that gave access to the higher floors. Up the middle of this could be winched the piles of resinous acacia and tamarisk wood that provided the fuel for a great bonfire whose light was reflected far out to sea each evening by the great mirror.

Though wildly exaggerated claims have been made for both the height of the lighthouse (1,500 feet!) and the visibility of the light (500 miles!) the consensus is that it was visible from about thirty miles out to sea. The location for the lighthouse was obvious, on the island whose name would come to stand for lighthouses everywhere—Pharos. Here it would be most conspicuous, not least to the wreckers and pirates who called the island home. Strabo, who saw the lighthouse in the late first century BC, gives us its location:

> Pharos is an oblong island, very close to the mainland. The [eastern] extremity of the isle is a rock, which is washed all round by the sea and has upon it a tower constructed of white marble with many stories and bears the same name as the island. This was an offering by Sostratus of Cnidus, a friend of the king's, for the safety of mariners, as the inscription says: for since the coast was harbourless and low on either side and also had reefs and shallows, those who were sailing from the open sea thither needed some lofty and conspicuous sign to enable them to direct their course aright to the entrance of the harbour.

> Strabo, *Geography*, book 17, chapter 1

The building project took twelve years to complete and was said to have cost Ptolemy about eight hundred talents, approximately $3 million at today's gold rates. A story, which may be apocryphal, attaches to its dedication. It's said that when it came to placing a dedicatory inscription at its entrance, Sostratus knew he would have to dedicate it to Ptolemy and his wife, but was determined that he would not be forgotten himself. So he had his inscription engraved in the stone, then had it plastered over and the dedication to the Ptolemies etched into the plaster. In time, and hopefully long after Ptolemy's death, the plaster would then eventually decay and fall away, revealing his words: "Sostratus, son of Dexiphanes the Cnidian, dedicated this to the Saviour Gods, on behalf of all those who sail the seas" (recorded in Lucian of Samosata, *How to Write History*).

Certainly this is the inscription that Strabo and other classical authors record as being carved into the lighthouse. Whether or not it was what Ptolemy saw at its dedication will forever remain unknown.

And Sostratus certainly built the lighthouse to last. Surviving several tsunamis and a devastating succession of earthquake swarms, it was still working when the Arabs took the city in AD 642, though about fifty years later the reflector was damaged by an earthquake. Around AD 1165

the Moorish traveler Yusuf Ibn al-Shaikh saw that the building was still
in use and confirmed its construction in three levels, adding that the base
was constructed of massive red granite blocks, joined with molten lead
rather than mortar to strengthen it against the pounding waves. He also
gives us a rare glimpse inside the building, describing how at that time the
first section housed government offices and a military barracks together
with stabling for at least three hundred horses. Above this in the octagonal section, refreshment stalls sold fruit and roasted meats to tourists who
had climbed the tower to marvel at the statues that decorated the balco-
nies. Above these a higher balcony gave visitors a panoramic view over
the city and the sea beyond.

The third section had changed its use by al-Shaikh's day. The cylin-
drical tower no longer contained the cresset for the beacon fire, but a
small mosque now took its place. Perhaps above this, and crowning the
whole structure, the colossal statue of Poseidon, god of the sea, leaning on
his trident, still looked down on the tourists crowding around his feet.

However, by the time the fourteenth-century Arab voyager Ibn
Battuta, on his way to China, reached Alexandria, the Pharos was in its
death throes:

> At length we reached Alexandria [on April 5, 1326]. . . . I went to
> see the lighthouse on this occasion and found one of its faces in ruins.
> It is a very high square building. . . . It is situated on a mound and
> lies three miles from the city on a long tongue of land which juts out
> into the sea from close by the city wall, so that the lighthouse cannot
> be reached by land except from the city. On my return to the city in
> 1349 I visited the lighthouse again and found that it had fallen into
> so ruinous a condition that it was not possible to enter it.

Ibn Battuta, *Travels in Asia and Africa*, p. 47

A sad end for such an extraordinary monument, yet for a building of
forty stories' height to survive for more than fifteen hundred years in an
active seismic zone was little short of miraculous. And way back in those
heady days when Ptolemy and Sostratus saw their colossal dream rising
on the tiny barren island, they must surely have realized that now Alexandria truly was "the Light of the World."

CHAPTER SEVEN

THE MUSIC OF THE SPHERES

I saw Eternity the other night,
Like a great ring of pure and endless light,
All calm, as it was bright;
And round beneath it, Time in hours, days, years
Driv'n by the spheres
Like a vast shadow, moved; in which the world
And all her train were hurled.

Henry Vaughan, "The World," in *Silex Scintillans*

The beacon on Pharos that now drew the traders of the Mediterranean to the world's greatest emporium was also attracting other travelers. Among the scholars of the Aegean, word was out that Alexandria offered an environment where it was possible to think the unthinkable—to challenge the fundamental and apparently self-evident certainties of the world. The museum and library were fast becoming a new type of institution: a community of the world's thinkers, working together to decipher the mysteries of the universe—the first true university.

The grain pouring out of Alexandria's port continued to fund the work of the scholars now pouring in, giving Ptolemy II the pick of the most brilliant scholars of the age to tutor his son and heir, Ptolemy III. He in turn demonstrated as he grew up that, if anything, he was even more passionate about collecting, copying, and archiving books than his father and grandfather.

Strangely, it would not be philosophy that provided the foundation for Ptolemy III's own rule, but war and tragedy. Following the death of his father in 246 BC, Ptolemy III succeeded to the kingdom without opposition, but the death of the old monarch had been seized on elsewhere to foment trouble. As part of a peace treaty between the Ptolemies and the rulers of the Seleucid dynasty of Syria, Ptolemy II's daughter Berenice had been married to Antiochus II Theos, who had agreed to repudiate his previous wife, Laodice. When news of the pharaoh's death reached Syria, Antiochus clearly considered himself no longer bound by that peace treaty and returned to his former wife. It was a deadly mistake, as Laodice immediately poisoned her former husband and declared her son the new king. Berenice and her son were bound to oppose this, and called on her brother Ptolemy III for help. War was inevitable.

By the time Ptolemy had raised an army and stormed across Egypt and up into the Middle East, news was emerging that Laodice had arranged the murder of Berenice and her son. Infuriated, the pharaoh raged through the region in a campaign that left the whole area stunned. One inscription from Adulis in Eritrea proudly compares this to the magnificent Middle Eastern exploits of the great Rameses II. When Ptolemy returned to Egypt his baggage train was laden with spoils, enough to comfortably support even the most lavish basileus. So rich was he that he offered to pay for the rebuilding of the Colossus of Rhodes. The 160-foot-tall statue (including pedestal) of the god Helios had stood at or near the harbor entrance to the island since its dedication fifty-six years earlier in thanks for Ptolemy I's assistance in the wars of Alexander's successors. The statue—as high as the Statue of Liberty—had recently collapsed following an earthquake, but the Rhodians, fearful they had offended the god, refused the offer to rebuild. The statue then spent another eight hundred years lying broken on the shore, although even fallen it was still a major tourist attraction, Pliny the Elder noting that few people could manage to reach their arms around the thumb.

But Ptolemy did not need the Colossus. He had other, more important statues in his baggage train. The wagons that rolled back into Alexandria brought with them the two thousand statues of Egyptian gods that the hated Persian king Cambyses had removed from Egypt. For this the people loved him and gave him the title "Euergetes"—"the Benefactor." With Ptolemy having this title and more money than he could spend, the rest of his reign was both peaceful and prosperous. Patronizing the great-

est minds of his age was thus both pleasurable and affordable, and Alexandrians could turn their minds from war to contemplating far greater
things.

During the war a legend emerged which perhaps hints at the growing
importance of one particular new area of science in the city. After Ptolemy left for his campaign, his wife, a Cyrenian also called Berenice, went
to the temple of Aphrodite to pray for her husband. Here she promised
to sacrifice her famous long hair to the goddess if Ptolemy returned safely.
When he did she duly honored the pledge and cut off her hair, having it
placed in the temple. The next day the offering was found to be missing,
leaving the king and queen furious. Only one man could calm them, an
astronomer called Conon. He told the queen that the hair had not been
stolen but that the gift had so pleased the gods that they had taken it up
into heaven. That night he proved it to her, showing her a small group
of stars which he called "Coma Berenices"—"Berenice's Hair"—and the
constellation retains that name to this day.

By this time another astronomer and mathematician, Aristarchus of Samos,
who had arrived in the city as a young man sometime before 281 BC,
was also enjoying Ptolemy and Berenice's largesse. He had turned his
extraordinary mind away from the earth to contemplate the heavens, not
simply to interpret signs of the zodiac so beloved by the ever-nervous
rulers of the ancient world, but to understand the mechanisms of the
universe itself. What he would see in the heavens was far removed from
the theological ideas of gods and creation prevalent in his day, far removed even from the concepts of the universe discussed in the museum.
He had brought to Alexandria a unique heritage, and to look into his
world is to look into the very dawn of science.

Aristarchus came from Samos, birthplace of perhaps the most famous
philosopher, mathematician, and astronomer of all time—Pythagoras.
Pythagoras, who lived from around 580 BC to about 500 BC, stands
almost at the dawn of rational philosophy, that is, at the point where
reasoning began to supplant faith as a means of understanding how the
universe, and everything in it, works. But he had one predecessor, a man
who many classical writers assert actually met and taught the young Py-

thagoras when he was about seventy years old. His name was Thales of Miletus, and he was known throughout the classical period as "the First of the Seven Sages of Ancient Greece."

Before Thales, those seeking answers as to how or why things occurred in the universe invariably referred to the gods. Divine interventions caused earthquakes, changed the seasons, played with the lives and health of puny mortals, and so on ad infinitum. People had only a hazy idea of the shape of the earth and the surrounding cosmos. Many believed the earth was flat and round, floating boatlike on an all-encircling ocean. They then added to the disk of earth sitting in its ocean-saucer some form of pillars or supports (the Egyptians placed them at the cardinal points and anthropomorphized them as the arms and legs of the sky goddess Nut), holding up the dome of the heavenly firmament which sun, moon, and stars traversed in a regular manner. Outside this cosmic eggshell some placed water, which could descend from above in the form of rain and snow or well up from below in springs, lakes, and wells.

But what was all this actually composed of? What was the fundamental matter? Before Thales, and for many after him, the answer to this question was invariably divinity. Call it soul, spirit, or god, the fundamental matter was divine, untouchable, metaphysical.

Thales, however, preferred water. Water is, after all, fundamental: It can be solid, liquid, or gaseous, and without it there can be no life. Right up until the nineteenth century AD scholars believed that life could generate itself spontaneously in water. As the early metallurgists had discovered, even metals could be reduced to liquids with sufficient heat. And with the seasonal inundations of the great rivers of the ancient world—the Nile, Tigris, and Euphrates—water created earth in revitalizing silt deposits and islands in the deltas of these great rivers.

But this is where Thales made his great leap. He asserted that earthquakes were the result of waves, disturbances in the water on which the earth floated, and not the acts of irate gods. This was one of the greatest revolutionary ideas of all time.

Of course today we know that earthquakes are not caused by ripples on a cosmic ocean, but it is Thales' idea, not his conclusion, that matters. In attributing a natural phenomenon to mechanics and not gods, he took the universe out of the hands of divinities and claimed, extraordinarily, that everything was understandable, knowable. The furious sea god Po-seidon was no longer shaking the planet as he strode across it. Something physical was making the world shake. This idea alone marks the beginnings of science.

Thales is credited by all the great masters—Plato and Aristotle among them—with being the founder of natural philosophy, Aristotle reporting simply that Thales considered that he had found the "originating principle." "Thales says it is water," he proclaimed.

Though his own writings are lost, stories about his life and thoughts were widely reported in classical times, particularly his musings on astronomy. Diogenes Laertius devotes his first book in *The Lives and Opinions of Eminent Philosophers* to Thales:

> *After having been immersed in state affairs he applied himself to speculations in natural philosophy, though, as some people state, he left no writing behind him. For the book on Naval Astronomy, which is attributed to him, is said in reality to be the work of Phocus the Samian. But Callimachus was aware that he was the discoverer of the Lesser Bear [Ursa Minor]; for in his Iambics he speaks of him thus:*

> *And he, 'tis said, did first compute the stars*
> *Which beam in Charles' wain, and guide the bark*
> *Of the Phoenician sailor o'er the sea.*

> Diogenes Laertius, *The Lives and Opinions*
> *of Eminent Philosophers*, book 1

Diogenes goes on to report that other people claimed that Thales did write two books, one on the solstice and the other on the equinox, thinking that everything else would easily be explained. Both Herodotus and Xenophanes are said to have praised him for being the first person able to predict the eclipses and motions of the sun and to have really studied astronomy—a slightly dubious claim, as the Chaldean Babylonian astronomers were considerably further advanced than the Greeks in charting the movements of the celestial bodies. Diogenes also attributes to Thales numerous other advances, all of which flowed out of his realization that the universe was rational and could be understood. He tells us that Thales affirmed the path (known as the ecliptic) along which the sun appears to move during the day, calculated the size of the sun, and was even the first person to call the last day of each month the "thirtieth," presumably implying that he devised a new calendar. He also considered more intangible things, and we are told that

> some again (one of whom is Choerilus the poet) say that he was the
> first person who affirmed that the souls of men were immortal. . . . But
> Aristotle and Hippias say he attributed souls also to lifeless things,
> forming his conjecture from the nature of the magnet and of amber.

> Diogenes Laertius, *The Lives and Opinions*
> *of Eminent Philosophers,* book 1

It was Thales' method rather than his results that had begun a revolution, and he believed that with that method he could understand everything. Plato even credits him with being the first absentminded professor in history. He tells us that the philosopher would wander at night, gazing up at the stars and not looking where he was going. On one occasion this led him to fall into a ditch, where a pretty young girl found him and teased him, saying "that he was so eager to know what was going on in heaven, that he could not see what was before his feet," before wryly adding, "This is applicable to all philosophers" (Plato, *Theaetetus,* 174A).

The heir to Thales' innovative view of the world was a man whose name stills strikes fear into the hearts of schoolchildren—Pythagoras. Like that of Thales, none of Pythagoras's own work has survived. In fact, the cult which he led—half religious, half scientific—followed such a tight code of secrecy that it may well be that they forbade the writing of their secret formulas and discoveries. But even in his lifetime Pythagoras was such a towering figure that his biographical details were written down by others, and some of these accounts have survived.

Many busts of the great mathematician also survive, although none are contemporary, so they probably bear little relation to what he actually looked like. The only physical feature we do know about is a striking birthmark on his thigh. His father was a merchant from Tyre (in Syria) who was granted citizenship in Samos after he donated grain to the island in a time of famine. His mother was a native of Samos. Pythagoras grew up on the small island but also traveled extensively with his father, visiting Tyre, where he was taught by Chaldean magi from Babylonia, renowned for their knowledge of astronomy and astrology, and other learned Syrians. His educators also taught him to play the lyre and to recite Homer and other poetry.

It was on his travels, the sources tell us, that he encountered both Thales and his pupil Anaximander and attended the latter's lectures on geometry and cosmology. It is also said that Thales advised the young man to travel to Egypt to study with the priests there, just as Thales himself had done fifty years previously.

Pythagoras took the old man's advice. At that time Samos was allied to Egypt, which apparently gave Pythagoras access to the temples and their scholar-priests, who accepted him among them. There are so many close parallels between the society which Pythagoras later set up in Italy and the operation of the Egyptian priesthood that we can assume that it was in Egypt that he developed his ideas for his own school. This would explain his cult's emphasis on secrecy, the striving for purity, and even the refusal to eat beans or wear any sort of animal skins, all of which were Egyptian priestly taboos.

Ten years after he arrived in Egypt, the country was invaded by Cambyses II, king of Persia, and Pythagoras was captured and sent to Babylon. There, we are told by the philosopher Iamblichus,

> he gladly associated with the Magi . . . and was instructed in their sacred rites and learnt about a very mystical worship of the gods. He also reached the height of perfection in arithmetic and music and the other mathematical sciences taught by the Chaldeans.

Iamblichus, *The Life of Pythagoras*

Around 530 BC or earlier Pythagoras left Babylon and made his way back to Samos, where he founded his school, which he called the Semicircle. There all manner of philosophical issues were discussed, his pupils sitting in a semicircle around the master. But back at his birthplace Pythagoras was again drawn into the political and diplomatic life of his people, which greatly distracted him from his philosophical work. It is also said that the local people disliked his Egyptian style of symbolic teaching, and he used this as an excuse to move the school to the Greek city-state of Croton (now Crotone) in present-day southern Italy. Here he reestablished the school with an inner circle known as the Mathematikoi who lived in the school, had no possessions, were vegetarians, and lived according to the strict regime prescribed by the master.

The members of the Semicircle were required to live by a set of tenets which stated that

- ◇ At its deepest level reality is mathematical in nature.
- ◇ Philosophy can be used for spiritual purification.
- ◇ The soul can ascend to union with the divine.
- ◇ Certain symbols have special, mystical significance.
- ◇ All brothers and sisters of the order must observe strict loyalty and secrecy.

Following the strictures of the group, Pythagoreans were hence the first to devise a consistent cosmos, based on pure numbers. By associating a point with 1, a line with 2, a surface with 3, and a solid with 4, they arrived at the sacred and omnipotent total number of 10. They believed that 10 would also be the key to understanding the structure of the cosmos.

A new element in this cosmic glass-bead game of mathematics and astronomy which Pythagoras introduced was music. Noting that vibrating strings produce harmonious tones when the ratios of their lengths are whole numbers, he went on to arrange the universe into similarly harmonic groups of spheres, even claiming that the Music of the Spheres really existed, though we have lost the ability to hear this background noise. According to Pliny, Pythagoras thought the musical interval between the earth and the moon was a tone, the moon to Mercury a semitone, Venus to the sun a minor third, Mars to Jupiter a semitone, and so on, so that the heavenly bodies actually played tunes as they waltzed past each other.

The Pythagoreans' universe was one of absolute mathematical perfection. All heavenly bodies were, for them, perfectly spherical and moved in perfectly spherical orbits. At the center of the universe Pythagoras placed the earth, then the moon, then the sun, and next the planets. The whole universe was finally wrapped in an outer sphere of the fixed stars.

Arthur Koestler catches the essence of the structure perfectly: "The Pythagorean world resembles a cosmic musical box playing the same Bach prelude from eternity to eternity" (Arthur Koestler, *The Sleepwalkers,* p. 33).

Having turned the universe from a whim of the gods into a mathematical machine, Pythagoras set the stage for the objective study of astronomy. It was a pupil of Pythagoras, named Philolaus, who would first suggest that the reason for the rising and setting of the sun, moon, and stars might not be that these celestial bodies moved across the sky but that the earth itself was spinning. Sadly, he went on to obscure this brilliant and counterintuitive revelation by inventing two new astral bodies apparently invisible to the human eye. First he had the earth spinning around the "cosmic hearth," an invisible fire at the center of the universe. On the same sphere there was another invisible object, a counterearth responsible for generating certain eclipses. The next sphere was our earth, then the moon, the sun, the five known planets, and finally the sphere carrying all the fixed stars, bringing the total number of celestial spheres up to the desired mystical number ten. Pythagoras would have been proud of him, had it not been such a cumbersome and fanciful creation!

The idea of a rotating earth would only be taken up again some centuries later, in Plato's lifetime, by an astronomer named Heraclitus, who first proposed that the earth rotated once each day on its own axis. This mortally offended Plato, who still insisted that while the earth remained perfectly still at the center of the universe, every other celestial body rotated dutifully round it, and us. But this troubled Heraclitus. He had observed how some of the planets, in particular Venus, do not move smoothly through space as the perfect Pythagorean model insisted; rather, for some nights they advance, but then they stop and appear to go back on their own course for a few days. What, he asked, could make the planets wander so? It was a pressing problem, and one which even echoes into our language today, the word "planet" deriving from the Greek word for "wanderer." For Heraclitus the solution was obvious: At least two of the planets, the so-called inner planets Venus and Mercury, must orbit around the sun, not the earth, and it was this complex movement that, viewed from the earth, seemed to make them wander. This astute model quickly caught on and became known as the "Egyptian System." Its only flaw was that it didn't go far enough—it still had the earth at the center of the universe, and the sun, now with its two "moons" of Venus and Mercury, obediently circling it.

This then was the confusing view of the universe that Aristarchus of Samos brought with him to Alexandria. But under her clear skies and aided by the new facilities of the museum's observatory, that fog of confusion was about to lift, leading to one of the greatest scientific discoveries of all time.

Aristarchus had studied with Ptolemy II's tutor, Strato of Lampsacus, a man whose devotion to the study of nature earned him the label "the Physicist." Trained in Aristotle's Lyceum in Athens, Strato took his master's passion for the rational study of nature a step further by claiming that there was no need for any divine explanation of the universe. He declared that there was just nature, and that all things natural could be subjected to observation, measurement, and experimentation. In this respect he is considered the first atheist philosopher, but more important for our story, he essentially saw the universe as a mechanism which operated without the need for transcendental, divine forces. It was this idea that he impressed on the young Aristarchus, and which gave his pupil the confidence to ask a previously unasked question: If the universe is simply a machine, how does it work?

That we know the answer he devised in Alexandria is thanks only to a near fluke of history. Only one of Aristarchus's works has come down to us, known as *On the Sizes and Distances of the Sun and Moon*. At first this seems disappointing, as it is largely assumed to be an early work, in which Aristarchus appears to accept the predominant, geocentric universe of those times. But on closer scrutiny even this early, fragmentary work is very revealing. First, the very notion that we can attempt to measure the size and relative positioning of the three largest-seeming celestial bodies—earth, sun, and moon—is a very bold opening gambit. It assumes that these are free-standing entities in stable relations with each other and of calculable dimensions.

It must be said that the figures he derived for the sizes of these bodies are wildly inaccurate. His own calculations led him to believe that the sun was about 20 times the size of the moon and 18 to 20 times as distant from the earth as the moon was. In fact the sun is about 450 times as far away from us as the moon is. He also calculated the diameter of the sun as about 7 times that of the earth, and therefore estimated that the sun's volume was about 300 times the volume of the earth. In fact, the diameter of the sun is about 300 times that of the earth, its volume about 1.3 million times that of the earth. However, modern mathematicians have examined his propositions in great detail and find that effectively Aristarchus was not let down by his math (drawn from the ever-reliable Euclid) but by his observational data. So although Aristarchus was enormously wide of the mark, he hit the bull's-eye in a far more crucial way. What he established, at least to his own satisfaction, was that the moon was the runt of the litter and that the sun was vastly bigger, more voluminous, and presumably heavier than the little earth. So why then should this huge celestial titan, at least 300 times the volume of the earth, be dutifully pirouetting around so small a planet every day? For the priests the answer had been simple: because that was how the gods had ordained it. But there were no gods in Aristarchus's universe, so he had to seek answers elsewhere.

But at this point, just as he was about to make his great discovery, his trail appears to have gone cold. None of Aristarchus's other work survives, and his brilliant idea might have remained unknown in the modern world were it not for a small aside in a book by another great mathematician: Archimedes.

In his book *The Sand Reckoner,* Archimedes set out to demonstrate methods for dealing mathematically with extremely large numbers, such as the number of grains of sand which would fill the universe (hence the title of his book). Of course to arrive at the largest number possible, he had to find a description of the largest theoretical universe known in which to place his grains, and for that he turned to Aristarchus. Having explained to his patron, King Gelon, that most astronomers believed the earth to be the center of the universe, around which everything else rotated, he added almost as an aside:

> But Aristarchus has brought out a book consisting of certain hypotheses, wherein it appears, as a consequence of the assumptions made, that the universe is many times greater than the "universe" just men-

tioned. His hypotheses are that the fixed stars and the sun remain
unmoved, that the earth revolves about the sun on the circumference of
a circle, the sun lying in the middle of the orbit, and that the sphere
of fixed stars, situated about the same centre as the sun, is so great
that the circle in which he supposes the earth to revolve bears such a
proportion to the distance of the fixed stars as the centre of the sphere
bears to its surface.

Archimedes, *The Sand Reckoner*, chapter 1:4–5

Here then was Aristarchus's great thought, preserved only as a reference
in another book. Archimedes for his part did not even believe it to be true,
only being interested in the sheer scale of the model he proposed.

The response to Aristarchus's hypothesis of a heliocentric solar system
was perhaps to be predicted and may in itself help to explain why so few
of his own works survive. Contemporaries were horror-struck by the new
role this Alexandrian astronomer gave to the earth and, by implication,
to the people on it. How dare he take away their special position at the
very heart of creation? One of them, by the name of Cleanthes, wrote a
treatise entitled simply *Against Aristarchus*. This has since been lost, so we
don't know on what grounds he attacked Aristarchus, but Plutarch would
later comment that Cleanthes

> *thought it was the duty of the Greeks to indict Aristarchus of Samos*
> *on charges of impiety for putting in motion the Hearth of the Universe*
> *(i.e. the Earth), this being the effect of his attempt to save the phe-*
> *nomena by supposing heaven to remain at rest and the Earth to re-*
> *volve in an oblique circle, while it rotates at the same time, about its*
> *own axis.*

Plutarch, *On the Face Which Appears on the Orb of the Moon*, book 6

We don't know if Aristarchus was ever indicted, or whether a trial
ensued; it would perhaps seem unlikely in the liberal atmosphere of Alexandria, though we should not forget Socrates' fate and the threats laid
upon both Plato and Aristotle. But at the very least this bold new theory
provoked a reassertion of the official orthodoxy from several scholars,

including Dercyllides, who argued somewhat pompously the need to assert that the Platonic model of a fixed earth with its "Hearth of the house of the gods" countered by moving planets and the rest of the heavens was correct. He claimed that it was essential to reject those who brought to rest the things that move and set in motion the things that by their nature and position are unmoved, insisting that such a supposition was contrary to the theories of mathematicians.

In the end these reactionary responses held sway. Aristarchus had no significant followers in his own generation or the following ones, and his only known disciple was a Chaldean named Seleucus who lived by the Tigris River and adopted Aristarchus's teachings around 150 BC. Why this rejection of Aristarchus should happen is one of the greatest riddles of the ancient world. Aristarchus's heliocentric universe seems so clearly true to us, who have the benefit of modern science and space travel to help our imaginations, that it's hard to envisage what it must have been like to be committed to an earth-centered view of the cosmos. Yet that was the view that prevailed for thousands of years throughout antiquity, and which would continue as the only acceptable model of the solar system until the sixteenth century AD.

But there are two other profound reasons why Aristarchus's beautifully mathematical, mechanical universe was too far ahead of its time to be acceptable, even to the scholars at the museum in Alexandria. First, we need to return to the age-old dichotomy between faith and reason, or religion and rationality. Even the great Plato had comparatively recently insisted that while our fallen, corrupted world may be analyzable using rationality, the really pure, uncontaminated cosmic bodies were to be found in the skies, or rather the heavens. Here were the seats of pure spirituality, divine beings if you like. To reduce these heavenly spheres to mere lumps of rock shunting around an infinitely huge void was tantamount to heresy: hence Cleanthes' determination to indict Aristarchus for *impiety*—godlessness—not bad science.

But at an even more profound level, great minds like Archimedes balked at the idea of a sun-centered universe because it took the spotlight off us humans. An earth-centered universe is also an ego-centered universe. Why should the gods create the universe at all if not to give us humans somewhere to play, and to puzzle about? Plato had already decreed that humans were at the very zenith of creation, and that we had already gone through five phases of evolution, the last, most elevated phase being that of the philosopher—the lover of wisdom. Aristarchus's universe was a vast and lonely place, where the earth was relegated to the role of just another planet circling around a fixed sun, shrouded in a vault of impossibly distant stars. No god marked out this earth as special—it had become just another wanderer. To demote the earth to this was to deny that the universe was built *by* the gods, *for* us. That was like denying both our descent and our ascent. Most preferred a more comfortable, human-centered universe, and this conception would survive right down to Darwin, when he scandalized Victorian society with his notion that people might be descended not from God but from mere apes.

So the cometlike genius of Aristarchus flared across the Alexandrian skies, then vanished. But not forever. In AD 1543 Copernicus published his revolutionary heliocentric model of the universe just before his death, which possibly occurred only hours after he received the first printed copy of the book. It has even been argued that Copernicus may have died of fear—fear of the wrath of the Catholic Church at a man of the cloth daring to suggest that the earth goes around the sun and not vice versa. Certainly we know that he sat upon his manuscript for decades, steadfastly refusing to publish it.

More recent research reveals, however, that his anxieties may have been driven by guilt as much as by fear. For in the original handwritten manuscript there were several references to Archimedes' *The Sand Reckoner*, which of course contained his summary of Aristarchus's book on the heliocentric universe. These references have, however, been systematically removed from the printed version of the text, and no mention is made either of Archimedes' book or of Aristarchus. And still today nearly all of us credit Copernicus with the "discovery" of the true nature of our planet's motion around the sun. It's particularly ironic that Aristarchus is sometimes referred to as the "Greek Copernicus" when in fact it is Copernicus who should be referred to as the "Polish Aristarchus."

Aristarchus's books, including his work on the sun-centered universe, were of course lodged in the great library in Alexandria, which is very probably where Archimedes read them (he was about twenty-five years younger than Aristarchus). While Aristarchus's great ideas never caught on in his lifetime, his work was known and read, proving that from just a small observatory on the grounds of a temple, Alexandria was already turning the universe—and the world with it—on its head. The gods had begun to release their grip, leaving humans to stagger into the daylight and begin to explore their world.

CHAPTER EIGHT

THE LITTLE O

His face was as the heav'ns, and therein stuck
A sun and moon, which kept their course and lighted
The little O, the earth.

William Shakespeare, *Antony and Cleopatra*

While Aristarchus put the earth and heavens in motion, it would fall to another Alexandrian to attempt the seemingly impossible and actually measure them. In the process he would transform disciplines as diverse as mathematics, astronomy, and geography forever. Aristarchus had told the Alexandrians we lived on a planet ceaselessly circling our sun, but it would be Eratosthenes who would describe the nature of the craft on which he traveled.

Eratosthenes, son of Aglaus, was born around 275 BC in the city-state of Cyrene (now Shahat) in present-day Libya. It was a city firmly bound into the Alexandrian world, having been conquered by Ptolemy I, but one with a reputation for freethinking, encouraged by the liberal constitution that the first Greek pharaoh had granted it. Even in Eratosthenes' youth the city already had many famous institutions, including a medical school, and many famous sons, among them the philologist Lysanias and the great Callimachus himself, both of whom personally tutored the young man. Some years before it had also nurtured one of the more individual thinkers of the day, Aristippus, a companion of Socrates, and his grandson (also called Aristippus), who had founded his own Cyrenaic school of philosophy. Here it was taught that only the present moment exists and that immediate pleasure is the only purpose of any action.

It was to Athens, however, that Eratosthenes was soon drawn, to the places where Plato and Aristotle had taught, and here he came under the influence of the Skeptics. At the Academy the young Cyrenian met the greatest philosopher of his day and the institution's *scholarch* (or director). Arcesilaus was a man famed for his wide circle of friends and correspondents across the Mediterranean; his quick wit; his broad interests; his love of wine (one source reports he died during a drinking bout when seventy-five years old); and, according to some sources, his harsh teaching methods. As a Skeptic, Arcesilaus taught his pupils to argue both sides of a question, to see a problem from other angles, and then to remain "skeptical," that is, to withhold judgment. In arguing against the Stoics, some of whom Eratosthenes also counted among his friends and tutors, the Skeptics proposed that one cannot rely entirely upon one's senses and that the Stoical view that truth came from clear perception followed by certainty was wrong. It was a philosophy that would have a profound impact on Eratosthenes, not merely in his philosophical musings but in the actual practical business of his life.

Clearly during his time in Athens the members of the Academy had already noted something special in Eratosthenes, and he had soon joined the international network of thinkers, which led him inexorably toward the Ptolemaic court, Alexandria, and the great library. His Athenian master had after all been a pupil of Aristotle's friend and successor, Theophrastus, and the Alexandrian project must already have been well known to him. He was also becoming known to the Ptolemies. For all the peace and glamour of Ptolemy III's court, one problem did play on the pharaoh's mind: Who would tutor his son? For every Ptolemy this was a matter of vital importance, as over the preceding three generations they had each, in turn, benefited from the most privileged education available. Ptolemy I had learned from Aristotle, his son had been taught by Strato of Lampsacus, and his son by Apollonius of Rhodes, author of *Jason and the Argonauts*. When news reached Alexandria of this bright new star at the Academy, Ptolemy III knew he had found his man, and the invitation was duly issued.

At the moment Eratosthenes stepped ashore in the Great Harbor of Alexandria, one of the brightest periods in the city's history began. Yet with a certain irony, even as he climbed the marble steps to the palace to meet his new charge, he was approaching the little boy who, years later, would begin to bring the whole Ptolemaic edifice tumbling down.

For now, however, this was the greatest opportunity of the young philosopher's life. He was under the protection and patronage of one of the wealthiest and most liberal rulers of his day, and before him lay the full resources of the museum and library, where he could explore the entirety of the knowledge of the world. And that is exactly what Eratosthenes wanted to do—he wanted to know everything.

Court life must have been tiresome for the young tutor as he struggled to instruct the self-indulgent young Ptolemy IV, who, unlike his forefathers, seems to have taken little interest in learning any of the skills that had created his dynasty. But there was a greater reward for a patient tutor close at hand. It was not long after arriving in Alexandria that Eratosthenes became not only a member of the museum, but the librarian of the great library, following the death (or possibly the retirement) of Apollonius of Rhodes.

Now began an explosion of work in a huge range of fields. The scholars in the pharaoh's pay were not, like modern academics, required to become specialists in one subject. There were certainly some, the physicians and mathematicians among them, who were highly focused on a single area, but the work of a philosopher in Alexandria was generally considered to include the exploration of all fields of knowledge and thought. The boundaries of art and science had not yet been fenced off, and a great mind could wander freely. Men such as Eratosthenes might write about mathematics and poetry, astronomy and literary criticism, comedy and geography. And that is exactly what he did.

The curse of Alexandria is also Eratosthenes' curse, and today almost none of his original works survive, but their impact was such that we still have glimpses, caught in references and quotes in later works. We know that at this time he produced twelve books entitled *On Ancient Comedy*, dealing with the history, language, and authorship of Greek comic plays. He also compiled a star catalog of 675 stars and books on the constellations and the mythology surrounding them. Having compiled a list of Olympic victors, he went on to write his *Chronology*, the first scientific attempt to fix the major dates of political and literary history from the siege of Troy, through the Dorian migration and the first Olympiad, up to his own time. And to ensure that no future scholar had such trouble calculating the dates for ancient events, he drew up a sophisticated calendar, complete with leap years, a system Julius Caesar would later "borrow" and claim as his own—the Julian calendar.

Meanwhile he still found time to write on pure philosophy, mainly ethics, and we can still hear an echo of his liberal attitudes in Strabo's *Geography*, which quotes extensively from Eratosthenes' lost works:

> Now, towards the end of his treatise—after withholding praise from those who divide the whole multitude of mankind into two groups, namely, Greeks and Barbarians, and also from those who advised Alexander to treat the Greeks as friends but the Barbarians as enemies—Eratosthenes goes on to say that it would be better to make such divisions according to good qualities and bad qualities; for not only are many of the Greeks bad, but many of the Barbarians are refined—Indians and Arians, for example, and, further, Romans and Carthaginians, who carry on their governments so admirably. And this, he says, is the reason why Alexander, disregarding his advisers, welcomed as many as he could of the men of fair repute.

Strabo, *Geography*, book 1, chapter 49

Here then was a man who had seen beyond the artificial boundaries of race and discovered good in the many foreign works found in his precious library and among the foreign scholars who thronged her halls, and who reminded his fellow Greeks that superiority came not from being Greek but from doing something worthwhile.

Eratosthenes also found time to create his own poetry, including the short epics *Hesiod* and *Hermes* and the elegy *Erigone*. The *Hesiod* (or *Anerinys* as it is sometimes called) deals with the death of the great Greek poet Hesiod, who, having been warned by the Delphic oracle that the "issue of death should overtake him in the fair grove of Nemean Zeus" (Thucydides, *The History of the Peloponnesian Wars*, book 3, chapter 11), retired from Nemea to Oenoe in Locris only to discover that this site was also sacred to Nemean Zeus. Here his hosts, the brothers Amphiphanes and Ganyetor, began to suspect Hesiod of seducing their sister and murdered him. In the end Hesiod was revenged when his body, cast into the sea to hide the crime, was brought ashore by dolphins. The brothers tried to escape by sea but perished in a storm.

The *Hermes* and the *Erigone* have themes we might perhaps associate more with Eratosthenes, as both are bound up with tales of the stars. In his *Hermes* he tells us of the birth of the messenger god, his miraculous infancy (he invented the lyre on the first day of his life), and his ascent to the planets. The *Erigone* tells the tragic tale of the daughter of Icarius. The latter had been given the first vine by Dionysus and made wine from it, but when he had given this to his neighbors to drink, the effects of the alcohol made them believe they were being poisoned, and they killed him. His daughter Erigone was guided by their dog, Maera, to the body and was so overcome with grief that she hanged herself on the spot. All the other virgins of Athens then began to follow suit until her ghost was appeased and she, her father, and her dog were taken up into the heavens to form the constellations Boötes (Icarius), Virgo (Erigone), and Canicula (Maera).

But it was in the realms of mathematics and science that this most versatile of Alexandrian librarians really shone. In his *Platonicus* Eratosthenes set out the whole mathematical system that, as he saw it, underlay Plato's philosophy. This included not only basic definitions of geometry, as first propounded by Euclid, but also the nature of arithmetic, and even the meaning and construction of music. He also produced practical tools for understanding some of the more arcane areas of mathematics, some of which are still used today. Among these is "Eratosthenes' sieve," a reiterative method of calculating prime numbers that is still used by mathematicians who study the branch of the subject known as number theory.

Strangely enough, what made Eratosthenes most famous in his own day was a mechanical solution to a problem we would today consider ethereal: the Delian problem, or the "doubling of the cube." This was one of three mathematical problems that deeply concerned ancient Greek mathematicians, the other two being "trisecting the angle" and "squaring the circle." Although we have so little of Eratosthenes' original work surviving, we do have his own explanation of this problem, preserved in a forged letter (nominally from himself to Ptolemy III Euergetes) cobbled together sometime after his death from pieces of his own writing. Here then we can just briefly hear the voice of an Alexandrian librarian:

> When the god proclaimed to the Delians through the oracle that, in order to get rid of a plague, they should construct an altar double that of the existing one, their craftsmen fell into great perplexity in their efforts to discover how a solid could be made the double of a similar solid; they therefore went to ask Plato about it, and he replied that the oracle meant, not that the god wanted an altar of double the size, but that he wished, in setting them the task, to shame the Greeks for their neglect of mathematics and their contempt of geometry.
>
> Quoted in Theon of Smyrna, *On Mathematics Useful for the Understanding of Plato*

So pleased was Eratosthenes with his own solution to this problem that he set up a column in Alexandria inscribed with an epigram explaining how he'd done it. It ends, however, with a wry comment on his work teaching the recalcitrant Ptolemy IV:

> Happy art thou, Ptolemy, in that, as a father the equal of his son in youthful vigour, thou hast thyself given him all that is dear to muses and Kings, and may he in the future, O Zeus, god of heaven, also receive the sceptre at thy hands. Thus may it be, and let any one who sees this offering say "This is the gift of Eratosthenes of Cyrene."
>
> Quoted in T. Heath, *A History of Greek Mathematics*

If it was mathematics that made Eratosthenes' name in his own day, it is an entirely different area of study that makes it still stand out today—geography, a subject which on his arrival in the city barely existed. There had of course been travelers throughout the ancient world for many centuries before. Herodotus had extensively explored Egypt, Babylon, and the Aegean and left books detailing what he had seen, but these were more travelers' tales, more anthropology with a sprinkling of mythology, than geography. Equally, traders and merchants had traveled long distances over established trade routes, but these had been arrived at by trial and error rather than cartography, local guides covering each part of the route but none truly knowing it in its entirety. Aristarchus may have set this earth in motion, but no one yet knew exactly what it was that we were traveling on. With Eratosthenes that changed forever.

For him the fundamental question was: What was the shape and size of the earth? Was it, as Thales had claimed, just a flat disk floating in an infinite ocean? Did it have an edge? What happened if one continued walking forever in one direction? Where and how did it end? Until this time these questions may have seemed purely academic or perhaps more a matter of faith than observation, but Eratosthenes knew there were clues to the answers, and clues that lay not at the far ends of the earth, but on his doorstep in Alexandria.

From the top of the forty-story Pharos lighthouse, where, no doubt, the philosophers of the museum sometimes gathered to gaze across the vastness of the sea and debate the nature of the world, a number of strange phenomena were visible, phenomena that would make any Skeptic question his senses. On extremely clear days, as they watched ships sail north from the harbor across the Mediterranean, they would have seen that the hull of the ship would slip beneath the horizon before the mast. Likewise when ships were first spotted heading toward the beacon of the Pharos, their masts were the first things to appear, and only later could the hull be made out. A similar problem faced those energetic enough to run up the Pharos after first spotting a ship traveling along the horizon, for it was clear that a ship that appeared little more than a mast top from the base of the lighthouse appeared as a complete vessel from the top. Somehow, between the top and bottom of the lighthouse, something was getting in the way of the view. Could that obstruction be the curvature of the earth itself? In the night sky astronomers had also seen a further clue in the form of lunar eclipses. When the earth was between the sun and the moon and cast her shadow across it, the encroaching dark red gloom was clearly curved at its edge, implying that the shadow of the earth was curved. That, and the observations from the Pharos, could mean only that the earth itself was a sphere. The later geographer Strabo, drawing on Eratosthenes' work, thought the explanation was obvious:

> It is obviously the curvature of the sea that prevents sailors from seeing distant lights at an elevation equal to that of the eye; however, if they

are at a higher elevation than that of the eye, they become visible, even
though they be at a greater distance from the eyes; and similarly if the
eyes themselves are elevated, they see what was before invisible. This
fact is noted by Homer, also, for such is the meaning of the words:
"With a quick glance ahead, being upborne on a great wave [he saw
the land very near]." So, also, when sailors are approaching land, the
different parts of the shore become revealed progressively, more and
more, and what at first appeared to be low-lying land grows gradually
higher and higher.

Strabo, *Geography*, book 1, chapter 20

Of course the idea that the earth was a globe had profound implications. It implied that there was something that made us, and everything else on the planet, stick to its surface—something we now call gravity. It also implied that there were two ways of getting from any one place to another—by going in opposite directions—and this meant that the whole nature of geography had to be changed. And the man to start that ball rolling was Eratosthenes.

The problem that Eratosthenes set himself was one which even today seems impressive. If the earth was a sphere, then he wanted to know just how big that globe was. And he set out to measure it without the help of artificial satellites, laser range finders, Global Positioning Systems, or even a theodolite. Instead, without ever leaving Egypt, he measured the earth by applying simple logic to careful observation, aided only by a stick and a well.

Eratosthenes' solution was as stunning as it was simple. He had heard among travelers' tales that there was a deep well at Syene (modern Aswan), far to the south on the very edge of Ptolemy's Egypt, near the first cataract of the Nile. The well, or at least an ancient well, is still there, just a short felucca trip from Aswan itself across to Elephantine Island. Here a wide stone-lined shaft, lined with spiral stairs, plunges down to the water table. On just one day of the year, at midday, the sun shines directly down this well, illuminating the bottom. As water always lies flat, Eratosthenes knew that for the sun to be reflected back required it to be directly overhead, its rays hitting the surface of the earth there at 90 degrees at just that moment. Now all he had to know was the distance from Syene to Alexandria.

We do not know whether the librarian personally made the six-hundred-mile journey up the Nile in the blazing midsummer sun to see for himself if the story was true. However, for a man taught to take nothing as read but to observe and question everything, it seems highly likely that he did. Having ascertained that the story was true, Eratosthenes then dispatched a royal official to begin the laborious job of making the next calculation he needed. Among Ptolemy II's huge civil service staff were the royal pacers, men trained to walk, or run, with exactly even, measured steps, so that large distances could be accurately measured. At Syene one of these men now began the long walk back to Alexandria while Eratosthenes, as royal tutor and librarian, no doubt enjoyed a more leisurely journey home down the Nile on one of Ptolemy's barges.

Eventually the royal pacer returned to Alexandria, carrying in his head the number of paces he had taken from the well to the place in a royal park where Eratosthenes had asked him to stop. This place was then marked and the distance recorded. The librarian knew that all he had to do now was wait.

The following summer on the very same day—the summer solstice—when the sun was directly overhead at midday on the Tropic of Cancer, and at the very time when its rays penetrated the bottom of the well at Syene, Eratosthenes returned to the point he had marked in the Alexandrian park. Removing a small stick from his clothing, he placed it vertically at the point. This stick, or gnomon (itself an invention of Thales'), cast a shadow, just as the vane on a sundial does, and he simply measured the length of the shadow it cast on the ground. Happy with the result, he now returned to the museum knowing he had everything he needed to calculate the circumference of the earth.

He made two assumptions: first, that Alexandria was due north of Syene, and second, that the sun was so far away from the earth that its rays were effectively parallel. Hence on that summer's day when a ray fell vertically at Syene, the fact that it cast a shadow in Alexandria meant the earth was angled away from it at that point. Having measured this angle (which he could do using Pythagoras's theorem, since he knew the height of the gnomon and the length of the shadow), and knowing the distance between the two cities, he could then turn to the works of Euclid in the library and find the method to calculate the circumference of the sphere.

Of course there was plenty of room for errors in his calculation. Syene was not exactly on the Tropic of Cancer, so at the summer solstice the sun was not exactly overhead at midday. However, the well was quite wide, allowing some of the sun's rays to pierce to the bottom even though it was not exactly overhead. A further problem lay with the question of how accurately the distance from Alexandria had been measured, although knowing the Ptolemies' love of bureaucracy, we might imagine that the royal pacers were startlingly accurate. Finally, there was the fact that Alexandria was not quite due north of Syene but on a more westerly longitude. Compared with the size of the earth, however, these errors were trifling, and his result was still extraordinary.

The angle of the shadow in Alexandria had been 7 degrees, so Eratosthenes calculated that the distance between Syene and his point must be 7/360th of the circumference of the earth. As he knew that distance was 4,900 stadia, he calculated that 1 degree was 700 stadia and hence that the circumference of the world was 700 × 360, or 252,000 stadia. Sadly we do not now know exactly which measurement of a stadion he used (there were several), but the "walking" stadion which we might imagine a royal pacer to use was about 516.8 feet. This would give a circumference for the earth of 24,662 miles. The circumference around the poles is now known to be 40,008 kilometers (24,860 miles). Using just a stick, a well, and a royal pacer, he had proved the earth was a globe and measured its circumference to within 318 kilometers (198 miles) of its true diameter while never leaving Egypt.

But Eratosthenes had only just started. Having noted that the sun reached the zenith at Syene on the summer solstice but on no other day, he calculated that the earth's axis must be tilted toward the sun. This would explain how at different times of year the sun rose to a different height above the horizon. To measure this he also created another first in the history of science, the armillary sphere—a model of the celestial globe constructed from a skeleton of graduated metal rings (or *armillae*), linking the poles and representing the equator, ecliptic, meridians, and parallels, with a ball representing the earth at its center. So pleased was he with this device that he was said to have set one up in "that place which is called the square porch" (quoted in Charles Kingsley, *Alexandria and Her Schools*, lecture 1), almost certainly the portico of the museum, and it was here that he then used it to calculate the angle of the earth's tilt at 23 degrees 51 minutes. Its true value is 23 degrees 46 minutes. He was just a twelfth of a degree off. His proof provided the first scientific explanation of a phenomenon that every Greek and Egyptian experienced: the seasons. When the Northern Hemisphere is tilted away from the sun, it is winter there; when it is tilted toward the sun, it is summer.

Emboldened by the success of these measurements, he now went on to attempt to span truly astronomical distances. Using the same lunar eclipses which had first hinted at the shape of the earth, he first calculated the distance between the earth and the moon and then the distance now known as the astronomical unit, between the earth and the sun. Sadly, due to mistakes in his understanding of how large the sun and moon were relative to the earth—something even Aristarchus had had trouble calculating—these figures were somewhat less accurate. His distance from the earth to the moon came out at 122,300 kilometers (76,437.5 miles), as opposed to the real figure of approximately 384,600 kilometers (240,375 miles), and his calculation of the astronomical unit was, somewhat more accurately, 125.5 million kilometers (78,437,500 miles) as opposed to the true figure of about 150 million kilometers (93,750,000 miles).

Inspired by his new understanding of the shape of the world on which he lived, Eratosthenes now turned his attention to mapping it, creating a detailed drawing of Egypt as far south as Khartoum and correctly hypothesizing that the annual Nile flood was caused by rains in unknown hills far to the south where the Nile had its source. Previously it had been believed that the flood was caused by the Etesian winds blowing water up the delta and preventing the Nile from draining into the Mediterranean. Eratosthenes' correct hypothesis would not finally be proved until the eighteenth and nineteenth centuries AD, when the sources of the Blue and White Nile were finally discovered by Speke, Burton, and Bruce.

But for a man who had measured the world, mapping Egypt alone would never be enough, so he set out, with his usual breathtaking self-confidence, to draw up something even more impressive. He had measured the world; now he intended to map it. This lost masterpiece was a landmark in both mapmaking and geography. Covering the world from Iceland and the British Isles to Sri Lanka and from the Caspian Sea to Ethiopia, it was built around a daring new concept of prime meridians and their offsets, or what we would call longitude and latitude. For his prime line of longitude he chose his own city, drawing the north–south line from the mouth of the Borysthenes (Dnieper River) south through the Euxine (Black) Sea, through Rhodes and Alexandria, down to Syene. Had his map and his prime meridian survived, perhaps we would today use Alexandrian mean time rather than Greenwich mean time as the world's chronological baseline.

For his prime meridian of latitude, Strabo tells us, Eratosthenes takes the world and

> divides it into two parts by a line drawn from west to east, parallel to the equatorial line; and as ends of this line he takes, on the west, the Pillars of Heracles [Straits of Gibraltar], on the east, the most remote peaks of the mountain-children that form the northern boundary of India. He draws the line from the Pillar through the Strait of Sicily and also through the southern capes both of the Peloponnesus and of Attica, and as far as Rhodes and the Gulf of Issus. Up to this point, then, he says, the said line turns through the sea and the adjacent continents (and indeed our whole Mediterranean Sea itself extends, lengthwise, along this line as far as Cilicia); then the line is produced in an approximately straight course again for the whole Taurus Range as far as India, for the Taurus stretches in a straight course with the sea that begins at the Pillars, and divides all Asia lengthwise into two parts, thus making one part of it northern, the other southern; so that in like manner both the Taurus and the Sea from the Pillars up to the Taurus lie on the parallel of Athens.

Strabo, *Geography*, book 2, chapter 1:1

And he had a new word for this new work, a new description of what it was to understand the nature of the world and where things are placed upon it. This idea he called "geography"—the first time the term had ever been used.

While his own maps would later be surpassed by those of Hipparchus, Strabo, and Ptolemy, his understanding of the nature and measurements of the earth as recorded in his *Geographica* would remain unrivaled in the ancient world. Following the destruction of the library where it was stored, this knowledge would lie in abeyance for 1,700 years. Only in AD 1491 would Martin Behaim dare to commission a terrestrial globe, and twenty-three years more would pass before Copernicus reinstated the heliocentric solar system. Eratosthenes was the first to assert that it would be possible to reach India by sailing west from Spain—something that Christopher Columbus had difficulty persuading the Spanish monarch of 1,800 years later. He also maintained that Africa could be circumnavigated, something not proven until Bartholomeu Dias's voyage of 1488. As for the measurement of the circumference of the earth? That wouldn't be superseded until Jean Piccard published his new calculations in AD 1671.

Despite these achievements Eratosthenes was not destined for the universal fame that he deserved. To his fellow philosophers in Alexandria he was known as *beta* or *pentathlos*. Yet to him, and indeed any librarian in Alexandria, this was, in its way, the greatest of compliments. By "beta" his contemporaries weren't accusing him of being second best but saying that, behind the specialists, he was the finest mind in each subject. Likewise to call him "pentathlos," the pentathlete, was to imply that while there were specialists who might outclass him within a field, Eratosthenes knew all the fields and was almost as good as the best in each of them. He was a jack-of-all-trades, but he was also a master of all of them—one of the greatest polymaths of all time.

With what many modern scientists would consider a lifetime of achievement already behind him, Eratosthenes returned to his duties at the library. He reorganized the entire institution's five hundred thousand volumes before adding further to that tally by writing yet more on geography, mathematics, grammar, and literary criticism, and even penning a history of philosophy. None of these has survived complete and many are known only by their name or vague references in later works by other authors. Bearing in mind what these casual asides tell us of the man, we can only guess at what we have lost.

The end of Eratosthenes was as tragic as the loss of his books, though in his mind at least, it was perhaps fitting and right. Having discovered in 194 BC that he was beginning to lose his sight, this visionary thinker realized that he would soon no longer be able to read the collections in the library he had tended and enriched. Without this there was nothing. Unable to continue his work, he chose to starve himself to death. He was around eighty-one years old. He was buried in his adopted home of Alexandria, and his epitaph, written by Dionysius of Cyzicus, states simply:

A gentler old age and no dulling disease quenched thee, and thou didst
fall asleep in the slumber to which all must come, O Eratosthenes,
after pondering over high matters; nor did Cyrene where thou sawest
the light receive thee within the tomb of thy fathers, O son of
Aglaus; yet dear even in a foreign land art thou buried here, by the
edge of the beach of Proteus.

Dionysius of Cyzicus, "Peace in the End,"
epigram 5, in *Palatine Anthology*

It is doubtful that Eratosthenes himself would have worried overly much about being buried far from home in the sands of Alexandria, or as Dionysius more poetically puts it, "by the edge of the beach of Proteus"—Proteus being a mythical king of Egypt. He had compassed the world, had been the first to really see and describe the globe we all now know we live on. This was his idea, and therefore anywhere on its surface could be said to be his home.

CHAPTER NINE

THE "EUREKA" FACTOR

*Give me but one firm spot of land on which to stand, and I will move
the earth.*

Archimedes, quoted in Pappus, *Synagoge*, book 8

Eratosthenes lived at the high noon of the Ptolemaic Empire, at a
moment when the academic star of the Hellenes shone at its brightest, and this star attracted still greater minds from across the Mediterranean. Of those other students in Alexandria, one brilliant light
eclipsed all others, a man whom Eratosthenes had met when he was
young, who would become perhaps his closest friend and correspondent,
and whose life would mark a profound turning point in the fortunes of
the philosophers of Alexander's city.

Archimedes, son of Phidias the astronomer, was born around 287 BC
in the city of Syracuse in Sicily. At the time the island was not yet a part
of the ever-expanding Roman world but was still made up of Greek city-
states whose independence had fluctuated, depending on the degree of intervention from the great trading nation of Carthage across the sea in North
Africa and the power and stability of the greatest state among them, Syracuse itself. Since its foundation by Corinthian colonists around 734 BC,
the city's fortunes had risen and fallen many times over, and they had sunk
rather low by the time of Archimedes' childhood, the city having been
sacked by the Carthaginians and then having suffered under a series of
ineffectual tyrants. This does not of course mean that it was not still a very
civilized place to grow up, connected as it was to the international Hellenistic world and peopled with Greek descendants who kept in close
contact with developments in the mainland Greek states and Alexandria.

And it was to Alexandria that the young Archimedes was drawn, to the Pharos shining out across the water and to the museum and library where the ideas planted in his Sicilian childhood could flower. We do not know the exact date when Archimedes came to Alexandria; indeed, we have no formal proof that he came here at all, other than his lifelong friendships with men like Eratosthenes and the astronomer Conon, which can have developed only through meeting them in person. That, and one mechanical legacy that remains in use to this day.

Archimedes was an engineer and an inventor, though he would not have thanked any of his contemporaries for saying so. In his mind all that mattered was the beauty of mathematics and the exploration of pure thought. To him the mechanical marvels for which he is still famous were just toys, demonstrations of principles. To us today they seem almost miraculous, the first real applications of the discoveries made in the library at Alexandria to the world outside its porticoes.

One of the most famous of these can still be seen in Egyptian fields in the delta today. The "Archimedean screw" consists of a spiral inside a hollow pipe, the bottom end of which lies in an irrigation ditch by the edge of the fields, and the top of which is over the field. When the screw is turned it captures a puddle of water in the bottom end of the tube and, as it spins, carries it up the length of the tube, ejecting it at the top, in effect making a smooth, perpetual pump. Had this been Euclid studying spirals, the Archimedean screw would have remained a geometrical idea; thanks to Archimedes it became a practical tool that has survived over two thousand years intact. But that same genius that turned abstract thought into practical devices would prove to be a double-edged sword.

It is unlikely, however, that at the time Archimedes was walking in the gardens of the museum with Eratosthenes and Conon, he was discussing engineering problems. His surviving works, of which thankfully there are many, show a mind electrified by the abstractions of mathematics, and particularly geometry: how to calculate the volume of a sphere, how to estimate the number of grains of sand in the universe, how to construct a regular heptagon, the operation of mirrors and levers. It was the source of this pure theory at Alexandria that must have attracted Archimedes here in the first place, where he first held and read the original works of Euclid and Aristarchus, which in later life he would recall, not always favorably, in his own books. Indeed, without his fame and the survival of so many of his works, there are many names from Alexandria and many wonderful books that we might not know of at all.

It was only when Archimedes finally left Alexandria and returned to Syracuse that he found the opportunity to exploit practically the knowledge he had gained in Egypt. Only back home, in the relative backwater of Sicily, was there time and reason to apply the knowledge he had won to the business of everyday life.

That is not to say that Archimedes' life was "everyday" by the standards of an ordinary citizen of Syracuse. He seems early on to have become a close friend (and may even, according to Plutarch, have been a relation) of Hiero II, a commander in the wars against Carthage who had managed to seize power in Syracuse around 270 BC and whose rule would grant his city one last Indian summer of peace and freedom before it lost its independence forever.

Syracuse was then, for a while, an Alexandria in miniature, where state and philosophers relied upon each other for support and protection. Just as the Ptolemies had their scholars, so Hiero had Archimedes, who through his correspondence with Eratosthenes and Conon remained in touch with the heart of the Hellenistic intellectual world. But Syracuse and Hiero had need of practical things, far removed from the ethereal abstractions of the great library, and it was in his brilliant adaptation of pure theory to practical advantage that Archimedes would now make his name.

Of all the stories told about this greatest of thinkers perhaps the most famous derives from this time, and it is one in which we see both how the state and academia could become co-dependent and how a moment of genius could become enshrined in legend.

The story goes that Hiero invited Archimedes to the palace to present a problem to him. He had decided to order a precious votive crown made for a temple in the city as thanks for his victories in war. He had chosen the maker and sent from the treasury a large quantity of gold with which to manufacture it. In time the beautifully wrought crown had been returned to him and he had dedicated it in the temple. But now a rumor had come to his ears that the maker, for all his craft, was a cheat and had kept some of the gold for himself. Of course the first thing palace officials would have done on receiving the crown was to weigh it to confirm that it weighed the same as the quantity of gold the craftsman had been given. This had indeed been done and the weight was correct, but the rumor suggested he had achieved this by alloying the gold with extra, cheaper silver, something not only offensive to Hiero but no doubt in his mind very offensive to the gods to whom the crown had been dedicated. So the ruler summoned Archimedes, who was asked to discover a solution. He did, and in the process invented the whole field of hydrostatics.

Exactly what provided the inspiration for the solution may never now be known, but the story, and it is a famous one, was already current in the lifetime of the first-century BC Roman architect Vitruvius, who recounts the story:

> He by chance went to a bath, and being in the vessel, perceived that, as his body became immersed, the water ran out of the vessel. Whence, catching at the method to be adopted for the solution of the proposition, he immediately followed it up, leapt out of the vessel in joy, and, returning home naked, cried out with a loud voice that he had found that of which he was in search, for he continued exclaiming, in Greek, Eureka! (I have found it out).

> Marcus Vitruvius Pollio, *Architecture,* book 9, chapter 10

The method he had discovered was simple but revolutionary. In the bath he had realized that the volume of water displaced by the immersion of his own body was equal to the volume of his body. So now he filled a bowl to the brim, placed in it a piece of gold that weighed the same as the crown, and noted how much water spilled over the brim. He then repeated the experiment with a piece of silver of the same weight. This time it displaced more water than had the gold—because gold is far more dense, so a piece of any given weight has a much lower volume. Finally he filled the pot once again to the brim and then placed in it the crown itself. This displaced a quantity of water somewhere between the volumes displaced by the lumps of gold and silver. It contained some gold but was not pure. From this Archimedes could then work out exactly how much silver the craftsman had surreptitiously alloyed with the gold as a ratio of the displaced volumes of water. It was a brilliant experiment, using just water and logic to untangle the proportions of two metals bound tightly together in alloy. Hiero was rightly impressed. Although we never hear of him again, the craftsman, we might imagine, was less so.

Of course, the exact details of the story, and in particular the running through the streets naked shouting "Eureka!" are really not provable. Indeed, we know from Plutarch that Archimedes didn't really like taking baths anyway and that

> *oftimes Archimedes' servants got him against his will to the baths, to wash and anoint him, and yet being there, he would ever be drawing out of the geometrical figures, even in the very embers of the chimney. And while they were anointing of him with oils and sweet savours, with his fingers he drew lines upon his naked body, so far was he taken from himself, and brought into ecstasy or trance, with the delight he had in the study of geometry.*

> Plutarch, *Life of Marcellus*, in *Parallel Lives*, 17

This glimpse of a disconnected genius, churlish and difficult with his servants, reluctant to engage in the everyday world but retaining an almost childlike delight in the purity of geometry and mathematics, the perfection of shapes and form, is perhaps a truer view of the man. But for all his delight in the abstract, the practical world was catching up with the great thinkers of the third century BC, and what Archimedes was developing in Syracuse would soon come back to haunt both his physical home there and his intellectual home across the Mediterranean in Alexandria.

Contemporary heads of state were especially keen to make practical use of his discoveries. This was not of course a new idea; the foundation of the library had been part of Ptolemy I's plan to secure his hard-won empire, an empire where his patronage of academia gave him not simply kudos but real power. It was to this end that his grandson Ptolemy III had begun his somewhat unscrupulous and manic collection policy, which included seizing all books arriving in the port of Alexandria for compulsory copying. Usual policy was to return the copy and keep the original—in case anything had been missed. These originals were then marked "from the ships" and placed in the library. For those attempting to remove books from the city, harsh penalties existed. All ships leaving the two harbors were searched, and any books found on board which had not been surrendered for copying were confiscated. Nobody removed information from Alexandria.

Foreign libraries were treated with the same acquisitive contempt. Ptolemy III had, according to Galen (17.1, in Kühn, pp. 601ff), set out his desire to copy every book in the known world in a letter entitled "To All the World's Sovereigns." However, these rulers' libraries proved reluctant to lend their precious volumes, no doubt aware of the fate of the books "from the ships." The libraries in Athens were no exception. Indeed, it was only after years of pressure and the payment of a hefty deposit of fifteen talents (enough to pay an Alexandrian workman's salary for over 120 years) that the Athenians finally relented and released their manuscripts of the complete works of Aeschylus, Euripides, and Sophocles for copying. They never received their copies or saw the originals again. When they protested, Ptolemy told them they could keep the fifteen talents. In his view he had a bargain.

But a new force was rising in the Mediterranean. The Roman Republic also knew all about power, including that held in books, but it took a more selective and practical approach to collecting knowledge. The Romans would use the tools of Hellenistic thought not to delight in geometry or astronomy but to conquer the world, and in the process Archimedes, the Ptolemies, and many Alexandrians would lose their lives.

By the time Archimedes heard that a Roman army was marching on his home city he'd already had plenty of exposure to their methods; indeed, he may already have been partly responsible for them. One of the devices described by Vitruvius is the innocuous-sounding "odometer," a machine for measuring large distances—in principle like that on an automobile. It was based on a wooden cart with a series of gears connecting the axle to a hopper of pebbles, one of which dropped into a collecting bowl with each full turn of the gears. As the distance it took for the gears to make one full turn could easily be measured, by counting the pebbles in the bowl at the end of a journey and multiplying that number by the basic unit of distance, the total length of the journey could be calculated. If, as some modern commentators have suggested, this was invented by

Archimedes, he would soon have reason to regret their practical applications of his theoretical knowledge. Archimedes himself typically didn't consider such trifles of any real importance, as Plutarch once again tells us:

> *Archimedes possessed so high a spirit, so profound a soul, and such treasures of scientific knowledge, that though these inventions had now obtained him the renown of more than human sagacity, he yet would not deign to leave behind him any commentary or writing on such subjects; but, repudiating as sordid and ignoble the whole trade of engineering, and every sort of art that lends itself to mere use and profit, he placed his whole affection and ambition in those purer speculations where there can be no reference to the vulgar needs of life.*

> Plutarch, *Life of Marcellus,* in *Parallel Lives,* 17

The Roman army did not share his noble sentiments. For them the odometer wasn't a vulgar toy but a device for laying out Roman milestones, which meant they knew how far one place was from another, which in turn meant they knew how long it would take to get an army from one place to another. This enabled them to plan military campaigns over wide areas with great precision, and they were planning one right now—against Syracuse and Archimedes' old friend Hiero.

The Roman army was marching toward Archimedes and Syracuse for a very good reason. The politics of the Mediterranean had swung around again, and Hiero's former enemies, the Carthaginians, were now his friends. Syracuse was offering help to this great trading nation, and that in turn antagonized the Romans. They, under the guise of improving the security of both themselves and their allies, had decided to confront the competition. But Sicily stood between the two powers and would now feel the force of their first great clash in what became known as the Punic Wars. This was all about the practical politics of power. The Romans weren't particularly interested in philosophy or geometry unless it gave them an advantage in trade and war, two areas of life quickly merging in the Roman mind.

What we know of Archimedes' last days are sketchy but indicative of how one worldview was replacing another. Plutarch tells us it all began when Archimedes developed the compound pulley, not for practical purposes but as a way of explaining a mathematical problem to his king. He then demonstrated its efficacy by pulling a laden ship from its dock single-handed, using a complex series of ropes and pulleys.

As the Roman siege tightened, it was these mechanical skills that Hiero called on Archimedes to use against his enemy. Plutarch tells us that Archimedes turned his mind to creating wonderful siege engines which employed the mathematics he so loved to perform similar apparently superhuman acts. Great catapults were designed to rain stones upon the legions who foolishly believed themselves to be out of range. When Roman ships approached the harbor walls, cranes were swung out which either dropped huge rocks on their ships to sink them or hooked them out of the water, dumping their crews in the sea before overturning them and consigning them to the depths. Plutarch provides a vivid description of the result on the Roman soldiers' psyches:

> *Such terror had seized upon the Romans, that, if they did but see a little rope or a piece of wood from the wall, instantly crying out that there it was again, Archimedes was about to let fly some engine at them, they turned their backs and fled.*

Plutarch, Life of Marcellus, in Parallel Lives, 17

Of course, these tales had probably been greatly embellished over the centuries between the siege of Syracuse and Plutarch's day, but they contain at least an echo of what was clearly a gargantuan struggle and a glimpse into the difference in mind-set between Greeks and Romans. Romans could terrify Greeks with numbers and brutality—their strength was their army; Greeks, however, could panic Romans with their minds. Their strength was in books—their arsenal, a library in Alexandria.

In the end, however, the relentless might of the Roman army triumphed, and thought gave way to force. As the Roman army flooded into the town, the Roman general Marcellus sent out orders to fetch Archimedes for him. But somehow things went wrong and Archimedes was killed. But Plutarch cannot leave it so baldly writ and gives us instead one last glimpse of the great man, still the disconnected theoretician, still more in love with ethereal mathematical ideas than reality, still more concerned with universal constants than the value of his own life:

> *Archimedes . . . was . . . as fate would have it, intent upon working*
> *out some problem by a diagram, and having fixed his mind alike and*
> *his eyes upon the subject of his speculation, he never noticed the incur-*
> *sion of the Romans, nor that the city was taken. In this transport of*
> *study and contemplation, a soldier, unexpectedly coming up to him,*
> *commanded him to follow him to Marcellus; which he declining to do*
> *before he had worked out his problem to a demonstration, the soldier,*
> *enraged, drew his sword and ran him through.*

Plutarch, Life of Marcellus, in Parallel Lives, 19

This is probably Plutarch's own romantic notion of the great man's death. He also records two other versions, the last of which may perhaps hold more of a glimmer of the truth:

> *As Archimedes was carrying to Marcellus mathematical instruments,*
> *dials, spheres, and angles, by which the magnitude of the sun might*
> *be measured to the sight, some soldiers seeing him, and thinking that*
> *he carried gold in a vessel, slew him.*

Plutarch, Life of Marcellus, in Parallel Lives, 19

Death at the hands of a looting soldier searching for gold would not be a surprising end for a Syracusan captured by the Romans. But what is intriguing is the mention of what Archimedes was actually carrying, which was likely worth more than gold. These strange devices created by Archimedes for predicting the movement of the heavens, or marking time, or estimating location may have been what Marcellus was really after. They were certainly within Archimedes' scope. We know he wrote a book on the construction of planetaria, although tragically this is lost, and in his long friendship with Eratosthenes he must have spoken of, and had probably seen, the armillary spheres constructed by his friend in the great porticoes of the museum. Furthermore, his creation of mechanical planetaria is hinted at by the Roman statesman Cicero in his *Tusculan Disputations* (book 1, chapter 25). We also have another tantalizing quote by the fourth-century AD poet Claudian, suggesting that Archimedes took the theoretical models of the universe he had read of in Alexandria and, through his engineering genius, made them into real devices:

Look! By his skill an old man of Syracuse has copied the laws of the heavens. . . . An animate force within attends the different stars and moves along the living mechanism with its regulated motions. A pretend zodiac runs through its own private year and the simulated moon waxes with the new month.

Claudian, *Archimedes' Sphere*, in *Epigrams*

But even more extraordinary than this, we may actually have an ancient example of one of Archimedes' machines. Thanks to a chance discovery in 1900 and the work of another Alexandrian, we might even be able to reconstruct one of these devices, perhaps the most exotic mechanism from the ancient world: not a clock or a planetarium, but a computer.

The story of Archimedes' computer begins, appropriately enough, in Egypt. Since its invention there sometime in the fourteenth century BC, a device known as the clepsydra, or "water thief," had been used for marking out time.

Improved on by the Greeks, it was a simple but very effective timer consisting of a metal sphere with a tube sticking out of the top and small holes drilled in the bottom. The container was filled with water and the tube was stopped up. When you wanted to begin timing something, you'd take the stopper out and let the water slowly drain out of the tiny holes in the bottom. Every time it was filled with the same amount of water it took the same time to empty.

The clepsydra was an ideal timer, often used in courts to time the speeches for the defense and prosecution so lawyers and clients had equal time and didn't drone on too long. When the bung was taken out, you started pleading your case. When the water ran out, you stopped—time up! The system had an added advantage. Should your great speech be interrupted, you could put the bung back in and put everything on hold. And so in Greek courts began our obsession with, and indeed enslavement to, time. Plato became one of the earliest writers to complain about the relentless pace of life when he said, "Lawyers are driven by the clepsydra—never at leisure" (Plato, *Theaetetus*, Introduction and Analysis, part 2).

But the problem with this device is that it wasn't a clock, just a timer. When it was full, water rushed out quickly, slowing as the head pressure reduced. This made it a very uneven way to measure time even if it was refilled as soon at it emptied. The people of Alexandria were used to uneven time. Each day was divided into twelve "hours" not of a fixed length but simply one-twelfth of the time between dawn and dusk. Confusingly, this meant that an hour in summer was a lot longer than an hour in winter.

Then around 270 BC a barber in Alexandria had a simple but brilliant idea that would change time forever. Ctesibius worked in his father's barbershop but was something of an amateur inventor as well. Visitors to the shop could have seen his ingenuity in the angle-poise mirror he invented to assist his father, but it was when he turned his mind to time measurement that he made his greatest breakthrough. Ctesibius realized that if the clepsydra was always full, then the water pressure would always be the same and the water would flow out at the same speed. So he added another water tank above the clepsydra. This poured water into the top faster than it could flow out the bottom. That meant the clepsydra was always full and any excess water just overflowed. Then he put another tank below the outflow to catch the water coming out of the clepsydra. That tank now filled up at a constant speed, so if a scale was put on the tank and a pointer was floated in it, then he could measure time constantly. Ctesibius's water clock made him justly famous. In 270 BC he had created not only the first mechanical clock but one so accurate it wouldn't be bettered for another 1,800 years.

Using the knowledge he had gained from his days of experimenting in his father's barbershop, Ctesibius was now inventing a whole new subject: hydraulics. He realized that the constant dripping of water could do more than tell the time. Soon Ctesibius's clocks were smothered in stopcocks and valves, controlling a host of devices from bells and puppets to mechanical doves that sang to mark the passing of each hour—the very first cuckoo clock! Having mastered the hours, Ctesibius now found time to invent the organ and build singing statues for the Ptolemaic pharaohs.

Mechanical marvels like these must have come to Archimedes' attention when he first arrived in Alexandria, since they'd first been constructed only twenty years or so before. Indeed, Ctesibius may still have been alive when the young philosopher first stepped ashore at the Great Harbor.

Just where these devices were set up is unclear from what we can recover of the city plan of ancient Alexandria, but across the Mediterranean in Athens a nearly contemporary device does survive which may fill in a missing link in the story of Archimedes' "spheres."

If you walk through the Plaka district of Athens that skirts the foot of the Acropolis, you come eventually to the Roman marketplace, or agora. Here amid the ruins a strange little octagonal building, constructed in white Pentelic marble, still stands. Known today as the Tower of the Winds, after the weather-beaten figures of the winds carved onto its faces, it has survived only because it was thought to be the tomb of Socrates and Plato and was later converted into a small Christian church or baptistery. Long before that, however, it was known as the Horologion of Andronicus and was the municipal clock of ancient Athens, built by the astronomer Andronicus of Cyrrhus in the first century BC. On the sides facing the sun were sundials for telling the time on sunny days, while on the top a weather vane indicated the wind direction.

But inside, through one of the two Corinthian doorways, was Ctesibius's legacy: a mechanical device for telling the time on cloudy days or at night when a sundial wouldn't work—a mechanical water clock. The sockets and scars that line the walls of this peculiar marble tower can still be made out today. These once held the mechanism for one of the water clocks invented by Ctesibius, and inside the drip, drip, drip of his clepsydra beat out the rhythm of the classical world.

But the Tower of the Winds may have held a device even more extraordinary than a water clock—indeed, Ctesibius's device may simply have provided the steady power for a yet more groundbreaking ancient discovery, one that contemporary sources hint may have been invented by Archimedes, inspired by the astronomical work of his friend Eratosthenes and the hydraulic genius of Ctesibius. And we can conjecture this because we have one of these machines, thanks to a storm in the Aegean Sea.

Spring weather on the seas off Greece is notoriously changeable, and it was with some annoyance but little surprise that Captain Dimitrios Kondos and his group of Greek sponge divers found themselves sheltering from a storm, miles off course, by an isolated island known as Antikythera, between Kythera and Crete in the Ionian Sea, just before Easter in AD 1900.

As the weather cleared, the men decided to make the most of their unplanned trip by diving in the deep, clear waters off the island. After all, even the great Greek philosopher Aristotle had said that the best, softest sponges lie in the deepest waters. The first man down was Elias Stadiatos. It was a dangerous dive of some two hundred feet to the seafloor: There was always the chance that the divers might return to the surface with nitrogen narcosis—the notorious "rapture of the deep."

When Elias broke the surface again that was exactly what his crewmates thought had happened to him. The man was shouting incoherently. As they dragged him out of the water and unscrewed his heavy helmet, he clutched at Captain Kondos and began jabbering about a pile of dead women on the seafloor—everywhere dead women.

His friends tried to calm him, thinking nitrogen narcosis had driven him mad. But Elias Stadiatos wasn't mad, and, disturbed but intrigued by his diver's words, the captain ordered another dive later that day to discover exactly what it was he had seen. Better prepared than his comrade for what lay beneath, this diver returned to the surface with a very different story. There were indeed human bodies littering the seafloor, but they were not corpses—they were ancient statues from a long-lost wreck, surrounded by a treasure the likes of which had never been seen.

Overnight the wreck became one of the most celebrated finds from ancient history, and when Captain Kondos returned the following year, this time with Greek archaeologists, it was to salvage Elias's "dead women" from the greatest ancient treasure ship ever found. Over the summer of 1901 thousands of priceless items were winched from the Antikythera wreck. Huge boulders scattered across the site proved to be rare bronze statues, covered with two thousand years of encrustation. Marble statues also reappeared, along with coins, beautifully decorated Greek vases, jewelry, and lavish tableware. Everything fine and rare from the ancient world seemed to be there.

But there was something else besides the obvious treasure. Divers that summer had recovered a lump of thick bronze corrosion with traces of wooden panels clinging to the outside. It certainly wasn't a bronze statue, so no one took much interest. But it would prove to be the most extraordinary object to have survived from the ancient world. By 1902 this corroded lump had still not been properly examined, but a lot more was known about the Antikythera wreck. Pottery on board had been identi-

fied and dated. The wreck was of a merchant ship that had sailed sometime in the first century BC from the Greek islands of Rhodes and Cos
to Rome with a priceless cargo of Greek art no doubt destined for the
home of a wealthy Roman.

Like the sponge divers some two thousand years later, this ship too
seems to have been caught out by a storm and driven toward the remote
little island of Antikythera. But its captain hadn't been as lucky as Captain
Kondos. The wealthy buyer who sat in Rome all those centuries ago
waited in vain for his shipment of Greek wonders, as the ship carrying
them had disappeared beneath the waves.

It was sometime in 1902 that an archaeologist at the National Museum of Greece, Valerios Staïs, decided to have another look at the mysterious lump. When he looked carefully he saw there was something
among all the corrosion—metal plates covered with writing. He got a
specialist in Greek inscriptions to check it out, and sure enough it was
ancient writing—from the first century BC. All the words on it that were
legible also seemed to refer to astronomical or zodiacal terms.

But there was more to come. Since its removal from the water the
wooden panels that had encased the object had begun to dry and crumble
away. As Staïs gently removed them he made another discovery—layers
of carefully interlaced cogs and wheels. Whatever was in this lump was
some kind of ancient machine.

Initially there were two schools of thought. One said that it was clearly
too complicated to be ancient and must have been dropped overboard
onto the wreck centuries later. The other said it was just an astrolabe, a
type of navigational device known from the seventh century BC onward.
But it was in fact neither. The writing on the plates was clearly ancient
Greek of the same period as the wreck, so it had to be contemporary, and
it was obviously much more complicated than any ancient astrolabe. It
would take more than another fifty years for the answer to be found, and
then not by an archaeologist but by an English physicist.

Derek de Solla Price was in a unique position to tackle the problem
of what was by then known as the "Antikythera mechanism." Holding
PhDs in both experimental physics and the history of science, he had
been trying to understand the mechanism since the early 1950s, when the
first X-ray images of the still only partially inspected device had been

taken. In 1959 he published his initial findings in *Scientific American*, suggesting that the device was far more complex than previously thought, but this paper was met with disbelief by classicists, who considered such a thing impossible for the date.

It was only in the early 1970s that gamma ray images of the machine, taken by the Greek atomic energy authority, came into his hands and he could finally announce to the world what lay behind the corrosion and concretions: a computer.

Price's meticulous study of the cogs, gear ratios, and inscriptions enabled him to put together a model of how the Antikythera mechanism worked and what it did. The mechanism was a hugely sophisticated analog computer for calculating the movements of the planets, the rising and setting times of stars and constellations, and the phases and movements of the moon—a complete mechanical calendar and model solar system in a box. By turning a crank handle that would have been on the outside of the wooden box it was possible to calculate the time, day, month, season, and year. It even corrected for errors in the old Egyptian calendar, which, without leap years, lost a quarter of a day each year. The Antikythera mechanism had a special "slip dial" that could be adjusted for that. By looking at how this dial was set, modern computers have calculated when the mechanism was last set and hence the date of the wreck: 80 BC.

So sometime in 80 BC the proud owners must have set the correction dial on this incredible device for the last time. Perhaps they had just sold it to a wealthy Roman and were shipping it off, along with numerous other Greek treasures, from Rhodes or Cos. The new owner must have been looking forward to its arrival—perhaps more so than all the other treasures on board. With this machine he could calculate exact dates and times, make corrections for the notoriously inaccurate official calendars—in short, be master of time itself.

This, then, was the successor to the spheres and planetaria that we know Archimedes wrote about theoretically and that Plutarch places in his arms at the moment of his death. But where had this device come from? And who built it? The answer perhaps lies in the one surviving book by a Greek called Geminus. In this almost unknown work he describes a mechanism he says was built in 87 BC. There are three extraordinary things about this description. First, he appears to be describing a machine like the Antikythera mechanism. Second, the wording he uses is repeated almost exactly on the inscribed plates of the mechanism itself. Finally, Geminus was from Rhodes, where another great philosopher, possibly even his tutor, lived; Poseidonius, who according to Cicero, had made a "sphere . . . the regular revolutions of which show the course of the sun, moon, and five wandering stars, as it is every day and night performed" (Cicero, *On the Nature of the Gods*, book 2, chapter 34). Rhodes was also of course probably the starting point of the mechanism's fateful last journey, some five years after Geminus had written.

Some have suggested that the mechanism was Geminus's very own. Certainly the discovery in the cold waters off Antikythera proved he was not just being fanciful in his description. Others have even claimed the mechanism may have been built by the great Archimedes himself, who is recorded in antiquity as having built a model for "imitating the motions of the heavenly bodies."

One final suggestion takes us back to Athens and the Tower of the Winds. No crank handle was ever found with the Antikythera mechanism, and Derek de Solla Price suggested it may have even been automatic rather than hand turned. If so, it is not taking a great step to imagine Ctesibius's water clock dripping away at the top of this tower providing the constant power to turn the mysterious, miraculous wheels of the Antikythera mechanism, whirring quietly away below, beautifully mimicking the movements of the heavens so Athenians could tell the time, and know the date and the positions of all the heavenly bodies at that moment.

But if such a miraculous device did grace the Tower of the Winds, it was marking out the last days of its inventor's world. In Alexandria the political climate was changing, and a series of immature and ineffectual royal Ptolemies would prove unable to protect themselves, their city, their country, or the scholars who succeeded Archimedes and Ctesibius. The life of Archimedes epitomizes the dichotomy of academic life in the Hellenistic world. Under the patronage of Hiero, king of Syracuse, Archimedes found the time and money to turn his supremely brilliant mathematical mind to questions of pure theory, but only in between solving the more practical problems of his employer. The emergent world order—that of the Romans—had even less time for theory. They had demonstrated this fatally when they encountered the engrossed theorist Archimedes somewhere in a street in Syracuse in 212. There Rome triumphed, and Archimedes' last problem was solved not with mathematics but with the point of a sword.

Archimedes' last wish was upheld by the Romans, however, and he was buried in his home city in a tomb bearing the epitaph he had himself chosen. It was not the list of conquests favored by Roman generals, nor the hereditary titles on the graves of kings. Instead, Archimedes chose a diagram of a cylinder circumscribing a sphere with a note describing how the sphere would be exactly two-thirds of the circumscribing cylinder in both area and volume. It was a proof Archimedes had discovered himself and, in his view, vastly more important than odometers, siege engines, and even mechanical computers. It was what his life work had been for—a very Alexandrian epitaph. To the Romans, and indeed even the Romanized Greeks of Syracuse of later years, however, it must have seemed strangely irrelevant. Their age was one of practical action, in which the theories devised in the library of Alexandria had little place. Even Archimedes' tomb was left to fall into ruins and become overgrown and forgotten, along with his name. In fact it would only be the idle curiosity of the Roman orator Cicero that would eventually bring it back to light, as Cicero himself describes. He tells us that while he was quaestor of Syracuse in 75 BC (some 137 years after the philosopher's death) he sought out the tomb of an "obscure little man" called Archimedes, but the native population, either still terrified of their Roman masters or simply forgetful, knew nothing about it. Eventually he found his way to an old cemetery by one of the city gates, choked with brambles and thorns, where he remembered

having heard of some simple lines of verse which had been inscribed on his tomb, referring to a sphere and cylinder modelled in stone on top of the grave. And so I took a good look round all the numerous tombs that stand beside the Agrigentine Gate. Finally I noted a little column just visible above the scrub: it was surmounted by a sphere and a cylinder. I immediately said to the Syracusans, some of whose leading

citizens were with me at the time, that I believed this was the very
object I had been looking for. Men were sent in with sickles to clear the
site, and when a path to the monument had been opened we walked
right up to it. And the verses were still visible, though approximately
the second half of each line had been worn away.

Cicero, *Tusculan Disputations*, book 5, chapter 23

So one of the most famous cities in the Greek world, and in former days a great center of learning as well, would have remained in total ignorance of the tomb of its most brilliant citizen, had a man from Arpinum not come and pointed it out. Roman rule had changed Syracuse and its people, and that process of change was now rippling across the Mediterranean.

If even the great Archimedes could be all but forgotten in just over a century in his physical home, what of the fate of his fellow philosophers at his spiritual home, the great library? Dangerous times were coming to Alexandria, and neither books nor their authors would be spared.

CHAPTER TEN

A GREEK TRAGEDY

Slowly the poison the whole blood stream fills.
It is not the effort nor the failure tires.
The waste remains, the waste remains and kills.

Sir William Empson, "Missing Dates"

Ptolemy III's successor was not the new Rameses his father had hoped for. By the time he came to the throne at about twenty years old in 222 BC, it was clear that he had neither the military genius of a Macedonian king nor the mental sophistication of an Egyptian pharaoh.

This alone was no reason to fear for Egypt's future. The new pharaoh had inherited a stable administration and stable borders. Provided he could maintain this balance—the Egyptians' beloved maat—and avoid external trouble, there was reason to think that Ptolemaic rule would continue at least to appear glorious. But what made Ptolemy IV's succession different was not the usual threats and maneuvers from abroad, but something much closer to home. When the young pharaoh took the Egyptian throne he was not alone. Standing in the shadows was another man, a man who was not simply the king's adviser but his puppeteer.

The man in the shadows was a court official called Sosibius, and the classical historian Polybius is quite blunt about his role in what was about to unfold: "Sosibius . . . appears to have been a dextrous instrument of evil who remained long in power and did much mischief in the kingdom" (Polybius, *Histories*, book 15, chapter 25).

The problem had begun long before Ptolemy IV took the throne, when it became clear that he would rely on favorites for everything, being unable or unwilling to take any role in the running of his household or the state himself. Many previous pharaohs had of course relied upon court officials to administer the country on their behalf, but all had at least the knowledge and instincts to choose their proxies well. Ptolemy IV was inexperienced, lazy, and a very poor judge of character, and the result was that on his taking the throne Sosibius became Egypt's first minister. Ptolemy, convinced that the running of the state was now in hand, then retired to indulge in the lavish festivities of the court and the pleasures of the royal bedchamber.

Sosibius kept a tight exclusion zone around the pharaoh, ensuring that all the information he got from the outside world came through him. In doing so he carefully created an atmosphere of suspicion and fear in which those who threatened him or his control over the pharaoh could be denounced and neutralized in a moment. The cull had begun, as in so many previous Ptolemaic reigns, with the death of the new king's immediate family—those best placed to challenge his rule. Within months of his accession, his uncle (his father's brother) was dead, then his younger brother was "accidentally" scalded to death with boiling water while taking a bath, and finally his mother perished, most probably poisoned. Sosibius had a hand in all these killings, and the move served him well. Not only could he claim to have removed those who might envy the king his throne, he had in the process left Ptolemy alone, without friends or family for support or advice. Ptolemy was now entirely under Sosibius's spell. "The murdered is well disposed" (Zenobius, *Proverbs,* book 3, no. 94) became a saying in Alexandria at the time. While stripping away Ptolemy's support, Sosibius was also careful to build his own. Aiding and abetting him was a courtier called Agathocles, who was probably a boyhood friend of the young king's, and who cemented his hold on the king by way of his sister, Agathoclea, who became the royal mistress.

Hearing only the whispers of his ministers and mistress, Ptolemy began his reign confident of his own security. He flattered himself that his summary action against his relatives had secured his throne, while news from the Near East that two of his main foreign enemies, Antigonus and Seleucus, had died, leaving children on their thrones, further boosted his sense of invulnerability. The result, as Polybius tells us, was predictable:

*Secure therefore in his present good fortune, he began to conduct him-
self as if his chief concern were the idle pomp of royalty, showing
himself as regards the members of his court and the officials who administered Egypt inattentive to business and difficult of approach, and
treating with entire negligence and indifference the agents charged with
the conduct of affairs outside Egypt, to which the former kings had paid
much more attention than to the government of Egypt itself. . . . This
new king, neglecting to control all these matters owing to his shameful
amours and senseless and constant drunkenness, found, as was to be
expected, in a very short time both his life and his throne threatened
by more than one conspiracy.*

Polybius, *The Histories*, book 5, chapter 34

The first signs of trouble seemed relatively unimportant. During the
reign of Ptolemy III an exiled Spartan king by the name of Cleomenes III
had taken asylum in Alexandria, where he continued to make a nuisance
of himself, constantly plaguing the new king with requests for a ship
and a small army so that he could retake his native land. But Ptolemy IV,
who on his accession took the almost ironic name Philopator ("he who
loves his father"), refused to assist. Cleomenes was not a man to be rebuffed, however, and he began attempting to recruit an army in the city
himself. At this news Sosibius panicked, suspecting that the Spartan king
might turn the mercenaries currently employed by the Egyptian state
against him, so he had Cleomenes imprisoned. In sheer desperation, when
Philopator was visiting the delta town of Canopus, Cleomenes and his
colleagues managed to escape and, running through the streets of Alexandria, tried to incite the mob to turn against the pharaoh. But despite
their shouts that they had evidence that the king had murdered his
mother, a very popular woman in the city, and despite the fact that the
claim was probably true, the usually restive city mob failed to rise up. In
despair Cleomenes and his men took the Spartan way out of what was
becoming an impossible situation and killed themselves with their own
knives. The Spartan's wife and children, entrusted to the care of Ptolemy,
fared equally poorly and were soon put to death on Sosibius's orders.

If Ptolemy and Sosibius had been wrong in thinking they could keep
their private affairs from the Alexandrian public and men like Cleomenes,

they were also mistaken in their assessment of their foreign rivals. A far more serious threat was now emerging in the form of the young Antiochus III, ruler of the Seleucid Empire. Unlike his counterpart in Alexandria, this young man kept himself fully informed of all the news from his rival kingdoms, and so soon realized that the young Ptolemy was both weak and ensnared by a corrupt and self-serving court. He wasted no time. Gathering a strong army, he invaded Syria, rolling up the Ptolemaic possessions in the Near East almost a far as Palestine, Egypt's front doorstep, before the Egyptian army could muster. In the blink of an eye the conquests of Philopator's father were lost and the way to Egypt looked open.

Fortunately for Ptolemy Philopator, Antiochus's campaign encountered much stiffer resistance as it moved south toward Egypt proper, with several cities withstanding his sieges for months. As Antiochus's army got bogged down, Sosibius called for and got a cease-fire for four months. It was a desperate gamble but it worked, buying time so that he and Agathocles could gather an army to resist the invasion of Egypt itself.

In an attempt to fool Antiochus into believing he would sue for peace, Sosibius built up Egypt's army secretly at Alexandria. Negotiations for the cease-fire and all other diplomatic traffic were rerouted from the capital to Memphis during the winter of 219–218 BC as recruits from all over the Mediterranean were gathered, drilled, and formed into fighting units in Alexandria. Paying for this huge mercenary army naturally put a heavy burden on the Egyptian peasantry, but Sosibius planned to utilize his own population in another, entirely novel way. Whereas in the past the Ptolemies had fought their wars with local and imported Macedonian and other foreign troops, this time Sosibius decided to recruit and train a local phalanx of Egyptian troops, armed and drilled in Macedonian style. The twenty-thousand Egyptians of the phalanx would be led personally by Sosibius and would play a decisive role in the forthcoming battle, and beyond.

At the end of the cease-fire in 218 BC, Antiochus resumed his conquest of southern Syria, but the revitalized Egyptians put up sufficient resistance to check him in the Bekaa Valley, in what is now Lebanon, and to hold on to Damascus and Sidon. This bought enough time for Sosibius to bring his new weapon into play.

By the spring of 217 BC the Ptolemaic secret army was ready and was led to battle by Ptolemy IV. According to Polybius the army included

70,000 infantry, 5,000 cavalry, and 73 African elephants. Against him Antiochus fielded 62,000 infantry, 6,000 cavalry, and 102 Indian elephants.

The two armies met outside the small town of Raphia, modern-day Rafah near Gaza, setting up camp opposite each other, where they sized each other up for five days. On the fifth day, June 22, 217 BC, Ptolemy moved his troops out of camp to take up battle positions, and Antiochus immediately followed suit. Both sides placed their strongest, handpicked phalanxes in the center, with elephants and cavalry on each wing. Ptolemy, his sister Arsinoe, and their retinue took a place on the left flank, opposite Antiochus and his horse guards on their extreme right. At the same moment, Ptolemy and Antiochus gave the signal for their elephants to charge, and the battle began. According to Polybius, Antiochus's Indian elephants outweighed and outfought the smaller African forest elephants of Ptolemy's army, and many of the latter turned and fled into their own ranks, breaking the line of Ptolemy's left wing and causing enormous confusion. Still the forces facing each other on Ptolemy's right wing held back, waiting. Polybius tells us:

> When he [Echecrates, Ptolemy's general] saw the cloud of dust being carried in his direction, and their own elephants not even daring to approach those of the enemy, he ordered Phoxidas with the mercenaries from Greece to attack the hostile force in the front, while he himself with his cavalry and the division immediately behind the elephants moving off the field and round the enemy's flank, avoided the onset of the animals and speedily put to flight the cavalry of the enemy, charging them both in flank and rear. Phoxidas and his men met with the same success; for charging the Arabs and Medes they forced them to headlong flight. Antiochus' right wing then was victorious, while his left wing was being worsted in the manner I have described. Meanwhile the phalanxes, stripped of both their wings, remained intact in the middle of the plain, swayed alternately by hope and fear.

> Polybius, *The Histories*, book 5, chapter 85

An overconfident Antiochus now pressed home his advantage on the right wing, assuming that both the center ground held by the phalanxes and the left wing were as victorious as he had been, and hence believing that the battle was as good as won. But at that moment Ptolemy, who had taken shelter within his own phalanx, suddenly rode forward, urging his men on. This stunned the enemy and rallied Ptolemy's own troops in the center. Lowering their *sarissas*—eighteen-foot-long double-pointed pikes—the phalanx under Ptolemy's general Andromachus and the Egyptian phalanx under Sosibius advanced together in full charge. The Syrians facing them resisted briefly, but soon crumbled under the overwhelming pressure and turned and fled. Antiochus, not yet the great general he would one day become, was forced to dash for cover behind the walls of Raphia and console himself with the solace of all bad workmen who blame their tools rather than themselves: "He retired to Raphia, in the confident belief that as far as it depended on himself he had won the battle, but had suffered this disaster owing to the base cowardice of the rest" (Polybius, *The Histories,* book 5, chapter 85).

Polybius reports that Antiochus left behind on the battlefield more than 10,000 infantry dead and 300 cavalry also killed, with a further 4,000 men taken prisoner. Ptolemy had lost about 1,500 foot and 700 horse, as well as 16 elephants dead and most of the rest captured. Ptolemy, so it seemed, was as victorious as his father had been. But this would be the last time Asia would see a pharaoh ride out to battle in person.

The next few, heady months were spent reoccupying Syria, after sending Sosibius to Antioch to negotiate punitive peace terms with Antiochus. In the meantime the young Ptolemy occasionally laid siege to or sacked a town to keep up the pressure on the negotiations. Finally, on October 12, 217 BC, Philopator returned in triumph to Egypt, rewarding his victorious army with three hundred thousand pieces of gold and sending abundant gifts to the temples of Egypt, to thank the gods for his great victory. On the face of it, he seemed to be repeating the pattern of all his ancestors, setting off while still young to score a resounding victory in Asia and reestablishing the Near Eastern buffer zone. Surely now he was entitled to the abundant leisure he so craved. Unfortunately for the Ptolemies, back in Alexandria, the perfect setting for his decadence had already been created, ironically enough, in the halls of the museum.

The literary scene that would provide the backdrop to Philopator's disastrous reign had been created during his father's lifetime, and it had begun with a new emphasis in the institution on literature rather than science. Ptolemy III had given his most gifted scholar-writer, Callimachus of Cyrene, the immense task of cataloging the ever-increasing mountain of books accruing in the library. This he began at the height of his powers around 250 BC when he embarked on his *Pinakes* (literally, "Lists"), whose full title translates as "List of Those Who Distinguished Themselves in All Branches of Learning, and Their Writings." As the full title suggests, this was no mere catalog. Running to 120 separate books, it was a comprehensive survey of all the books held in the great library, along with biographical and bibliographical details of the authors—in short, a survey of all known classical literature up to the time of its compilation.

In this work he also introduced the notion of a library classification system—the forerunner of our Dewey decimal system—in which all books were classified as written by (1) dramatists, (2) epic and lyric poets, (3) legislators, (4) philosophers, (5) historians, (6) orators, (7) rhetoricians, or (8) miscellaneous writers. Not that this impressed everyone; one of the first new tomes Callimachus had to catalog with his system was Aristophanes of Byzantium's highly critical *Against Callimachus's Library Lists*. History does not record which number he chose for it.

Besides the mammoth task of the *Pinakes*, Callimachus also wrote his own poetry. His longest work, the *Aitia* ("Causes"), is a narrative elegy in four parts, one of which, *The Lock of Berenice*, records the story of the constellation Coma Berenice. This poem was freely copied by Catullus and subsequently became the model for Alexander Pope's 1712 poem *The Rape of the Lock*.

Callimachus was above all a stylist, famed for his conciseness, precision, and artistry, a great master of the finely turned phrase, often in epigrammatic form. Even when he tackled enormous subjects like the *Pinakes* or Homer's *Iliad* and *Odyssey*, his method was to break up the longest works by having them copied into shorter sections. He is said to have maintained that all big books were boring books.

For all his love of brevity, Callimachus was a prolific writer, credited with producing about seven hundred works in all, and he became hugely famous in his day and in the succeeding centuries. In fact no other Greek poet except Homer is so often quoted by the grammarians of late antiquity. He was best known for his epigrams, of which sixty-three have survived. Epigram 31, an epitaph, displays his wit and elegance superbly. It takes the form of a dialogue:

> Tell me, is Charidas buried here?
> "If it's the son of Arimmas you mean, he's here."
> Charidas, how is it down there?
> "Darkness."
> What of Return?
> "A lie."
> And Pluto?
> "A myth."
> We're done for, then.
> "I've given you the truth. If you prefer
> a pleasantry, beef's a penny a pound in Hades."

Callimachus's insistence on brevity put him somewhat at odds with his most famous pupil, Apollonius of Rhodes, whose lifetime ambition had been to set down in verse the epic adventures of Jason and the Argonauts. But Apollonius's epic chimed with the times: an adventure tale of brave Greek warriors who journeyed (like Alexander) to the edges of the known world, visiting en route Cyrenaica, the Aegean Islands, and the Black Sea, all places of considerable interest to the Ptolemies and their trading, seafaring nation. The heroes are portrayed in overtly Homeric style, and the boat itself and accompanying technology are deliberately set in an archaic context, but Apollonius weaves into the text all sorts of "modern" scientific (and geographical) ideas and knowledge along with the more traditional fabulous geography of clashing rocks, sirens, and mythical beasts.

Into this admixture of modern science within the traditional setting, Apollonius introduces an innovation of his own, a running commentary on his own narrative, as Richard Hunter explains in the introduction to his 1993 translation of the *Argonautica*:

A particular mode for the expression of this textual self-consciousness is irony and humour; where the poet is constantly also a commentator on his poetry, the anticipation of reading and reception is inscribed in the text itself, and the poet becomes not just a creator but also a reader, himself surprised by his own creation. . . . When, for example, Medea puts the evil eye on Talos, Apollonius reacts as a particular type of reader of the Argonautica *might react:*

"Father Zeus, my mind is all aflutter with amazement, if it is true that death comes to us not only from disease and wounds, but someone far off can harm us, as that man, bronze though he was, yielded to destruction through the grim powers of Medea, mistress of drugs."

—Apollonius, *Jason and the Golden Fleece*
[*The Argonautica*], trans. R. L. Hunter

The poet stands outside his poem and contemplates it, almost as though he had nothing to do with it.

This dreamlike, wistful mythmaking was now the setting for Ptolemy IV's return from the wars. The revival in heroic literature gave him the perfect foil for his own reign, the perfect opportunity to revel in his own position as a hero-god to his people; but in this, as with so much, he was gravely mistaken.

Taking the sister who had accompanied him to war as his wife, although still entirely under the sway of his mistress Agathoclea, he now lost himself in romantic reveries of heroic tales. The future seemed bright. His father had fought a great war at the beginning of his reign and then retired, safe, to live out his years among his scholars and courtiers. Why shouldn't the son do exactly the same? But Ptolemy was no returning Jason, and his Argonauts were no more than a gaggle of sycophants. Back at court the king and his favorites became ever more detached from the reality of life in Egypt and the political situation outside. The young king duly set about building his own literary court, but even here something was clearly different from his father's day. In the place of the Aristarchus and Eratosthenes of previous years the court now, according to an early-twentieth-century biographer of the Ptolemies, "swarmed with literary pretenders, poets, grammarians, whores, buffoons, philosophers" (Edwyn R. Bevan, *The House of Ptolemy*, chapter 7).

It seems Ptolemy Philopator was not content simply to fund the museum; he intended to be its greatest star as well, and as such gathered around him a multitude of favorites to praise his own work. When he wrote his own, terrible play, an erotic idyll called *Adonis*, the obsequious Agathocles immediately produced a laudatory commentary on it. One story from the time tells how the king arranged a poetry competition where the entries were judged on the amount of applause each rendition received. However, one judge, Aristophanes of Byzantium, chose the poem that received the least applause. When asked why, he went to the great library and produced texts that proved that only the poem he had chosen was actually original. All the others were simply copied from earlier works. Ptolemy's court had pretensions to be the museum, but in fact it was a mockery.

But far more serious than the pharaoh's personal delusions was the situation in his country. The great victory Sosibius had orchestrated contained a poisonous seed.

That seed lay in the heart of Sosibius's greatest achievement, among the native Egyptian troops he had raised and trained to fight for their pharaoh. They had seen the magnificence of the Greek Ptolemaic court, they had seen the plunder, and now they had returned to the reality of life in their country. Many of these highly trained warriors made their way back to the heartland of the ancient capital of Thebes (modern Luxor), only to find their families in extreme poverty and much of the land in disrepair. Native Egyptians had always known they were an underclass under Greek rule, but while the Ptolemies made Egypt great again, they had kept their silence. Now the administration was in the hands of corrupt favorites, taxes were exorbitant, and their sacrifice in the Middle East seemed to have benefited everyone except themselves.

There was only one conclusion: Ptolemy IV Philopator was not a god-king, he was a foreign impostor; and when the situation in the countryside failed to improve, a full-scale rebellion broke out in Thebes in 206 BC against the "false gods" of the Alexandrians. This immediately struck chords with the Egyptian peasantry, who had been taxed to the breaking point to finance Ptolemy's war. In fact many had fled to remote areas in the desert or in the marshy Nile Delta, where they had become outlaws, roaming the countryside and ravaging small villages and temple complexes, rather than working themselves to the bone for next to no reward. This process, known as *anachoresis* (literally, "to go up-country"), had occurred quite frequently in pharaonic times of famine, crop failure, or acute economic pressure. This time, however, it was spearheaded by fully trained, battle-hardened troops, troops who had seen how the other half lived in Alexandria.

The rebellion soon spread to the delta, where a vicious twenty-one-year guerrilla war broke out; but if it was bad in the delta, it was far worse farther up the Nile. Around the old Egyptian city of Thebes, just across the river from the resting places of the greatest native Egyptian pharaohs in the Valley of the Kings, nationalism was rife. Upper Egypt, backed by the kings of Nubia, now effectively seceded from the north, and the rebels declared their leader, an Egyptian named Herwennefer, their pharaoh in 206 BC.

Though Ptolemy had retrieved his territories in Syria, he had almost simultaneously lost more than half of Egypt, and his lifeblood: her grain. The Nile Valley and the Fayyum were the great breadbaskets of Egypt, and with them in rebel hands the Ptolemies', and Alexandria's, revenues plummeted. So severe was the economic crisis that at one point Ptolemy had to abandon the use of silver coinage and introduce a worthless bronze currency instead. The need to retain a large standing army to oppose the rebels further increased the burden on the economy. Egypt could no longer pay her bills.

At the very center of the maelstrom stood the temples. The early Ptolemies had always been extremely careful to cultivate the temple priests, whose institutions not only nominally owned much of the land but also collected the taxes on behalf of the crown. Traditionally the temples had also been a way for these foreign pharaohs to demonstrate their credentials for ruling Egypt.

As the revolt gained momentum, many of these institutions fell into rebel hands, including the vast new complex begun under Ptolemy III at Edfu, the temple of Horus. This magnificent building, measuring 448 feet in length and 246 feet in breadth, would become a monument to Philopator's increasingly unsustainable belief that he could live as a Greek basileus but rule Egypt as a divine pharaoh.

Perhaps the most striking aspect of the temple is how this huge monument—the pylons at the entrance are nearly 130 feet tall—and all its architecture and decoration are executed entirely in the pharaonic tradition. Great bas-relief carvings depict the (Greek) pharaohs in battle, and specific mythological tales relating to the patron god, Horus, the falcon-headed son of Isis and Osiris, are all depicted in traditional fashion. The temple itself was said to be built on the site of the mythic battle between Horus and his deadly enemy Seth, god of chaos and murderer of Osiris. And it was doubtless to Philopator's taste that the great temple was also the scene of a love match. Every year, at the Feast of the Beautiful Meeting, a statue of Horus's wife, Hathor, traveled by river from her temple at Dendera to be brought together with her husband, arriving at the full moon and spending their nights in the *mamissi,* or birthing house. Reliefs at the entrance to the mamissi, some still retaining their colored paint, portray the ritual of the birth of Harsomtus, Horus and Hathor's son, and symbolically represent the fertility of the gods, their royal descendants, and the nation as a whole.

Yet the inscriptions on the temple itself show that from the beginning of the troubles, no further work was carried out on the building, and therefore, we must assume, no revenues from the temple's estates were returned to Alexandria until long after the king's death.

> Then trouble arose, because ignorant rebels interrupted in the South the works on the Throne-of-the-gods [i.e., the temple of Edfu]. The rebellion raged in the South until year 19 of the king of Upper and Lower Egypt, "the heir of the gods Philopatores," the son of Re "Ptolemy, loved by Ptah," now deceased, the god Epiphanes, the strong one, the king who chased disorder out of the country.

Inscription from the Naos, temple of Edfu

It was ironic that after the outrageous success at Raphia, it would be his own Egyptians, those "ignorant rebels," who would humble the all-conquering pharaoh and bring his most Egyptian work—the building of the temple of Horus at Edfu—to a halt. After his victory in Palestine, Ptolemy IV had chosen to return to Egypt on that god's birthday, traveling like the new Horus downstream by ship from Memphis to Alexandria at the inception of the annual flooding (and symbolic rebirth) of the Nile. To honor him and his sister-wife it was decreed that statues of the king and queen be placed in the largest courts of all the major temples in Egypt; Ptolemy Horus, it was declared, was his father's protector and his victory at Raphia was "beautiful." In this way the polite fiction of the divinity of Ptolemy Philopator was at least maintained in his own mind. In truth the victory was not beautiful but hollow.

In 204 BC, still in the midst of the native rebellion and just forty years old, Philopator departed to join the gods. The circumstances surrounding his death are shrouded in mystery. There was no formal announcement of his death from Sosibius or Agathocles; he simply wasn't seen for several months. Then, mysteriously, his wife-sister, Arsinoe, who would certainly have taken the role of regent, disappeared too. Finally, Sosibius summoned the court and announced that both king and queen were dead. He then proceeded to read out a forged royal will appointing himself and Agathocles guardians of the new king. There were few tears shed for the death of the king, but the people were immediately suspicious about Arsinoe's death. How had she come to die simultaneously with her husband, and what, or who, had killed her? Polybius tells us that on receiving the news of her unhappy death "the people fell into such a state of distraction and affliction that the town was full of groans, tears and ceaseless lamentation, a testimony, in the opinion of those who judged correctly, not so much of affection for Arsinoe as of hatred for Agathocles" (Polybius, *The Histories*, book 15, chapter 25).

Sosibius escaped the backlash, dying a few months later, but Agathocles was determined to continue as sole guardian of the new king and proxy ruler of the nation. His first acts were to send away from Alexandria all the most able and influential people at court, on diplomatic missions, so that he gained absolute ascendancy there. Having secured his own position, he began to revel in it, living a life of constant drunkenness and debauchery, "sparing neither women in the flower of their age nor brides nor virgins, and all this he did with the most odious ostentation" (Polybius, *The Histories*, book 15, chapter 25).

Loathing of Agathocles had spread throughout the streets of Alexandria and among the Macedonian soldiers quartered there, and when Agathocles attempted to torture and execute some soldiers he thought were plotting against him, word spread around the garrison and among the townsfolk that revolt was imminent. At the same time, Agathocles was engrossed, as Polybius would have it, in his nightly banquet and orgy, after which he fell into a drunken sleep. He was aroused from this by a party of furious soldiers demanding that the king be surrendered to them. Realizing that he and his sister were trapped, Agathocles eventually surrendered the boy with his bodyguard to the soldiers, who took him on horseback to the stadium, where crowds of citizens and soldiers had assembled.

The crowds were elated to see the king freed but bayed for the blood of the tyrant Agathocles and his harlot sister. At that moment Sosibius's son, who had remained in the background since his father's death, saw an opportunity to betray his father's old colleague and perhaps improve his own standing. Approaching the king, he asked his assent for the crowd to be given satisfaction. The pharaoh apparently nodded, and the crowd roared its approval as soldiers set off to the houses of Agathocles and his sister. In due course they, their attendants, and all their families were brought shackled to the stadium, the women naked, where they were stabbed, bitten, and mutilated until they were all dead. "For terrible is the cruelty of the Egyptians when their anger is aroused," notes Polybius (*The Histories*, book 15, chapter 33). The younger Sosibius meanwhile slipped away with the young king, eager to protect him from the sight of the mob at work.

Polybius is equally merciless in his final assessment of Agathocles, damning his memory as formidably as the Alexandrians had damned the man:

> Agathocles displayed neither courage in war nor conspicuous ability, nor was he fortunate and exemplary in his management of his affairs, nor, finally, had he that acuteness and mischievous address which serve a courtier's ends and which made Sosibius and several others so successful until the ends of their lives in their management of king after king. On the contrary it was quite different with Agathocles. Owing to Philopator's incapacity as a ruler he attained an exceptionally high position; and in this position finding himself after the king's death

most favourably circumstanced to maintain his power, he lost both his
control and his life through his own cowardice and indolence.

Polybius, *The Histories,* book 15, chapter 34

The key phrase here, however, is not about Agathocles, it's about Ptolemy IV: "Owing to Philopator's incapacity as a ruler . . ." And there lies the rub. Ptolemy's failings had sadly not died with him; indeed, his legacy was only just beginning to bear its bitter fruits. Yet from the inscriptions surviving from the early reign of his son, Ptolemy V, one could be forgiven for thinking that another renaissance was in the air.

From this date come a number of apparently upbeat reports. The uprising in the delta was finally brought under control by a ruse. Well protected in the same papyrus marshlands that had harbored the Egyptian resistance to the Persians, the leaders of the revolt had proved impossible to capture until an offer of a peace was made. When the leaders finally emerged to sign the peace declaration they were promptly arrested, harnessed to carts, and forced to drag them, like animals, through the streets. They were then publicly tortured to death. But Ptolemy V proved merciful, if we are to believe one famous, laudatory inscription that dates from this time—the Rosetta stone, whose fame as a key to translating hieroglyphics has rather overshadowed its actual contents. It deals with the aftermath of the delta rebellion, restoring lands and rights and making concessions, particularly to the temples. When it comes to the rebels themselves it also treads a cautious but clearly victorious line, saying the king had "ordained that those who return of the warrior class, and of others who were unfavourably disposed in the days of the disturbances, should, on their return, be allowed to occupy their old possessions."

The news from Upper Egypt seemed positive as well, if we can rely on the inscriptions at Edfu that marked the restoration of the temple after the rebellion and spoke of the new Ptolemy as the king who "chased disorder out of the country."

But in these inscriptions rests the lie. Ptolemy V was king in name only. He hadn't chased anyone or anything out of the country, nor had he magnanimously pardoned the rebels; he was just a boy growing up in a court of murderous "favorites." On his death, still young, there were no brothers to succeed him, no adult kings-in-waiting who might take the court in hand and reassert royal power. They had all been killed on Ptolemy V's succession, and the only real achievement of his short life was the siring of a son of his own, another child pharaoh to take on the mantle of political impotence on his death and continue the cycle of manipulation and murder.

While court factions squabbled for control of the boy pharaoh, real political power was slipping away. Few rulers of the Near East believed any pharaoh would last long, and without a real leader in Egypt they grabbed every opportunity to erode his empire. The descendants of Alexander's other generals—the Seleucids in Persia and Syria, and the kings of Macedonia—took back all of Egypt's territories in the Aegean, Asia Minor, and Palestine. And there was little danger of revenge.

But while the court bewailed the loss of empire and the Alexandrian merchants the loss of trading influence, both would have done well to look across the Mediterranean to a far greater threat looming on the horizon.

CHAPTER ELEVEN

THE LAST PHARAOH

For Rome, who had never condescended to fear any nation or people, did in her time fear two human beings; one was Hannibal, and the other was a woman.

Mary R. Lefkowitz and Maureen B. Fant,
Women in Greece and Rome

Three things would bring down the Ptolemaic dynasty and bring to a close the three-millennia-old rule of the pharaohs. The first was the huge success of the early Ptolemies, whose radical reinvention of the Egyptian state made the nation once again a treasure worth fighting for. The second was the failure of their heirs to resist being seduced by the wealth and power they inherited. The third did not come from within Egypt but, in the summer of 48 BC, was already traveling across the sea toward Egypt and Alexandria. On the deck of that ship stood the leader of an aggressive Italian people who was writing himself into world history as the greatest general since Alexander. What and whom he found there would set the scene for perhaps the most famous series of romances in history, later immortalized by William Shakespeare. And their results would be no less deadly to all concerned than fate was to Shakespeare's other star-crossed lovers, Romeo and Juliet.

Since Alexander's death in 323 BC the eastern Mediterranean had been involved in an almost continuous struggle among the descendants of his heirs for control of an empire that had always been more myth than reality. But while Macedonians, Seleucids, and Ptolemies fought, another power had been growing in the west which would come to dominate them all—Rome.

The warning signs had been there since the First Punic War, when Rome decided to clip the wings of the rival trading empire of Carthage. Archimedes had actually seen it in the eyes of the Roman soldiers besieging his city of Syracuse and felt it in his last moments on the point of a Roman sword. Rome was not a state to countenance other empires when it had it in its power to bring them down. Carthage had come back for more, keen to stand up to the cold, unblinking expansionism of Rome, and had been defeated again. Finally, after the Third Punic War, Carthage was not only defeated but erased from the face of the earth. The Roman orator Cato had first found expression for what was clearly now Rome's policy when he exhorted the senate with the words *"Carthago delenda est"*—Carthage must be destroyed. And it was. The city of Carthage itself was demolished, its inhabitants were massacred, and the fields around it were, according to legend, sown with salt so nothing and no one could live there. There could be no clearer statement of the Romans' overall intent. They would never be content with being players in the game of ruling the Mediterranean world—they planned to be the victors.

That their attention would turn to Alexandria was inevitable. Between the death of Ptolemy IV and the accession of Ptolemy IX the Roman state had patiently watched 150 years of Egyptian economic decline. Rome had no need to humble Egypt as it had Carthage—Egypt was doing that on her own. When most of the work of conquest had been done, Rome finally chose to act, drawn to the Alexandrian flame by Egypt's two remaining treasures: her potential to grow grain, and the greatest library and museum in the world.

If it was grain that actually brought the Romans to Alexandria, that was not its only attraction for her generals. Despite their republican protestations it was clear that some of the military leaders of the late republic—men like Julius Caesar and Mark Antony—craved a place in history alongside that greatest conqueror of them all: Alexander. To them the journey to Alexandria was as much pilgrimage as diplomatic mission, even if the tomb of Alexander himself was now closed, supposedly to protect the bodies of the Ptolemaic pharaohs who now rested alongside him. In truth, as the Romans probably well knew, it was to disguise the fact that the bankrupt Ptolemy IV had pawned Alexander's golden coffin.

But Alexandria held one other attraction for the men of this new world power. By the Great Harbor, in a palace flanked with ancient obelisks, a new pharaoh ruled. She would be Egypt's last and perhaps the most famous: Cleopatra.

The reign of Cleopatra will always be remembered for drawing the curtain on the Ptolemaic world, but in truth, by the time she ascended to the throne in 51 BC, Egypt was already lost. As far back as 80 BC her father, Ptolemy XII, had been little more than a puppet of the Roman dictator Sulla, having formally allied himself with Rome. Egypt's ancient name had then been inscribed on the Roman "list of allies and friends," the *amici et socii populi Romani* which proved to be the death warrant of so many independent states. Roman friendships were very one-way affairs, and despite Egypt's paying a sizable tribute for the "privilege" of friendship, this formal alliance had not prevented Rome from seizing those Egyptian possessions it felt it needed, including the island of Cyprus, which had been ruled by Ptolemy's brother. For his part, Ptolemy, already overawed by this new world power, sat quietly by and watched until the people of Alexandria, incensed at his inaction, forced him to flee to his friends in Rome. Eventually the Romans reinstalled him in Egypt, their "friendship" extending at least to him personally, but he would enjoy his kingdom for only another four years. In his will he left his country to his daughter Cleopatra and her brother (and husband), the ten-year-old Ptolemy XIII. Tellingly, he chose as his executor the people of Rome.

And so in the spring of 51 BC a succession of grossly corrupt and weak rulers whose lives were defined by little more than assassinations and revolts reached its end, and one last Ptolemy rose to the throne of Egypt. In Cleopatra, however, a free Egypt and a free Alexandria had one final flourish.

Cleopatra was the most remarkable Ptolemy for many generations. Crowned pharaoh while still a teenager, she was the antithesis of the gross caricature that later Romans would draw of her. For many of them, she was a convenient excuse for the bloody civil wars that led to the collapse of their beloved republic and the instigation of totalitarian imperial rule. She was cast as the lascivious temptress, an untrustworthy Eastern woman intent on polluting the moral virtue of Rome and its generals. It was a classic piece of Roman propaganda, and one so successful that it still dogs her memory to this day. The truth was very different.

Cleopatra had been born in Alexandria and, unlike so many of her predecessors, had clearly reveled in the intellectual life that still thrived in what were her dynasty's greatest achievements, the library and museum. As a child she had shown an aptitude for languages, learning Greek, Aramaic, Latin, Ethiopic, and Hebrew—all the main languages of the library—as well as being the first and last Ptolemaic pharaoh ever to learn the native tongue of the country she ruled, Egyptian. She was not, if her coin portraits are to be more trusted than Roman propaganda, the great beauty that later romances and films have made her, but that is perhaps to pay her a compliment. She was no two-dimensional Helen, and her personal magnetism, which even Roman sources are forced to admit, came from a mind and personality molded in what was still the intellectual capital of the world. In fact, even the pro-Roman historian Plutarch concedes that she was much more than simply a beauty:

> For her beauty, as we are told, was in itself not altogether incomparable, nor such as to strike those who saw her; but converse with her had an irresistible charm, and her presence, combined with the persuasiveness of her discourse and the character which was somehow diffused about her behaviour towards others, had something stimulating about it. There was sweetness also in the tones of her voice; and her tongue, like an instrument of many strings, she could readily turn to whatever language she pleased.

Plutarch, *Life of Antony,* in *Parallel Lives,* 27

It was this that marked her out from so many previous Ptolemaic also-rans. Plutarch had no desire to eulogize Cleopatra, but even he could not help but record that her strength came not from her looks but from her mind. It would be another 1,550 years before the English philosopher Sir Francis Bacon would coin the dictum "Knowledge is power" (*Religious Meditations: Of Heresies* [1597]), but already in Caesar's day, Cleopatra was proving it. Sadly, this alone would not be enough to stop Rome from interfering in her rule. Rome chose the stages on which it played out its story, and when it chose wealthy and desirable Egypt, Cleopatra and her people had little choice but to join in the drama.

The endgame of pharaonic Egypt was played out against the backdrop of the bloody struggles among Rome's most powerful generals. In 49 BC, when Julius Caesar's power-sharing arrangement with his ally Pompey collapsed, the seeds of Roman civil war were sown, and Egypt, feeling forced to back one side or the other, had provided ships, grain, and money for Pompey's cause. It proved a mistake, and now, following his defeat at the battle of Pharsalus, the news came that Pompey was fleeing to Egypt. The timing could not have been worse, for there was no peace in Egypt either at that time; indeed, Cleopatra was at war with her brother. A more typical later Ptolemy by far, the young Ptolemy XIII was still under the thrall of three of his ministers: the eunuch Potheinos, Theodotus of Chois (his teacher of rhetoric), and the Egyptian Achillas. These three men had precipitated a split between the co-regents, and Cleopatra had been expelled from Alexandria. Ptolemy was now camped at Pelusium with his army, ready to bring his co-regency, and his sister's life, to a bloody end, when news of Pompey's arrival reached him.

It was an invidious situation for any monarch. With Pompey in Egypt, Julius Caesar could not be far behind. If the pharaoh protected the one, he would become the other's enemy, and in either case he would be an enemy of Rome. And so, according to Plutarch, he, or rather his advisers, took a gamble. With Pompey's trireme riding at anchor off the treacherous shore, Achillas was sent out in a rowboat to bring the Roman over the shoals to shore and into the presence of the king. Pompey himself was nervous, fearing a trap but powerless to resist. As Achillas rowed up he held out a hand to help Pompey into the little tender. The general turned to his wife and son and embraced them, quoting a line of Sophocles:

> He that once enters at a tyrant's door,
> Becomes a slave, though he were free before.

Plutarch, Life of Pompey, in Parallel Lives, 78

He then climbed on board and was rowed silently toward the beach. It was a long row, and during the trip he took out the speech he had prepared for the king and read it through. Then, as the boat grounded and he was being helped to his feet, his assassins struck and he was repeatedly stabbed. To the accompaniment of his wife's screams carrying from the far-off trireme, his head was hacked off and his body unceremoniously dumped in the sea.

It was a bloody murder but of a type in which both Egyptians and Romans occasionally indulged in the name of politics. His head was taken to Ptolemy, who, when Caesar's fleet arrived off Alexandria just two days later, sent a messenger with the gruesome gift.

But if Ptolemy thought that assassinating Caesar's enemy would make him Caesar's friend, or that it would encourage the Romans to fight their civil wars elsewhere, he had seriously misunderstood Roman politics. In fact, he had provided Caesar with the perfect excuse. Had Caesar ordered Pompey killed he would have alienated at least a part of his own people. Now he could portray Pompey as a man whom he had disagreed with but a fellow Roman all the same. It had been the treacherous and untrustworthy Egyptians who had killed him—all the more reason to interfere in and perhaps annex their country. Plutarch describes without a hint of irony the moment when Caesar received Pompey's head, and the crocodile tears began to flow: "From the man who brought him Pompey's head he turned away with loathing, as from an assassin; and on receiving Pompey's seal-ring, he burst into tears" (Plutarch, *Life of Pompey*, in *Parallel Lives*, 80).

Caesar could now play the avenging Roman angel while conveniently ignoring the fact that it had been he who had driven Pompey to his death. Instead of taking the war away from Egypt, as Ptolemy had hoped, Caesar ordered his troops to land and occupy Alexandria.

Caesar quickly sent for reinforcements and meanwhile set up his headquarters in the royal palace and did his best to look like a peaceful visitor. According to Lucan (*Pharsalia*, book 10, line 21), he admired the sights of the city, including the tomb of Alexander, and according to Appian (*The Civil Wars*, book 2, chapter 89), he even joined the crowds listening to the public philosophy lectures given by the scholars of the museum. He also attempted to play the peacemaker between the claimants to the throne, Ptolemy XIII and Cleopatra, whom he asked to appear before him. For Cleopatra it was a risk. Her forces were not in control of Alexandria or Egypt, and she did not have the support of the Alexandrians, or perhaps many Egyptians. Nor could she know what deal, if any, her treacherous brother had struck with the Roman. Her only hope was to use her skills to influence Caesar in private, so she got word to him asking for a secret audience. Smuggled back into the city under a coverlet (or rolled in a carpet, in some versions of the tale), she found herself in the presence of the most powerful man on earth. He was fifty-two years old, she was not yet twenty-two, but in a single night she persuaded him to make her queen again. Lucan in his *Pharsalia,* reveling in his own imaginings of that evening, describes how

> There in her fatal beauty lay the Queen
> Thick daubed with unguents, nor with throne content
> Nor with her brother spouse; laden she lay
> On neck and hair with all the Red Sea spoils,
> And faint beneath the weight of gems and gold.
> Her snowy breast shone through Sidonian lawn
> Which woven close by shuttles of the east
> The art of Nile had loosened.

Lucan, *Pharsalia,* book 10, lines 64–71

It was the beginning of the greatest love story in antiquity but the beginning of the end for a free Alexandria and a free Egypt.

Cleopatra had seen which way the wind was blowing, and during that night she successfully distanced herself from both Pompey and her brother the co regent, so that he would take the full blame for Egypt's ill-considered interference in a Roman civil war. With the deadly calculation and lack of filial love that the Ptolemies were famed for, she now appealed to an unassailable Julius Caesar to reinstall her as pharaoh alongside her truculent brother.

The next day Ptolemy XIII arrived in the palace to find Cleopatra at Caesar's side. In an act almost certainly orchestrated by his adviser Potheinos he then cried out that he was betrayed and ran from the palace, tearing the crown from his head. It was a brilliant move. The people of Alexandria immediately swarmed to the man who appeared to be holding out against Roman occupation, and threatened to storm the palace. Caesar managed on this occasion to calm the Alexandrians, reading Ptolemy XII's will to them and giving his guarantee that it would be fulfilled (i.e., that Ptolemy XIII and Cleopatra would rule), but he decided to take the young Ptolemy XIII into "protective custody" just in case. The scene was now set for the Alexandrine War, a war which would witness the partial destruction of the thing the Ptolemies held most dear: their library.

Caesar had miscalculated. In purely military terms it made a lot more sense to support Ptolemy XIII and his advisers, who still had a sizable army and the support of many in Alexandria. But one night with Cleopatra had changed his mind. Her wit, charm, and political brilliance—the assets of an Alexandrian scholar—had put him in her thrall, and he would pay a high price for it. But while an enchanted Caesar promised the return of Cyprus to Egypt's control and the rebuilding of Cleopatra's power base, he had more immediate problems closer to home. Potheinos had summoned the royal army to besiege Caesar in Alexandria, knowing him to have come to Egypt with only a small force. Unable to field his inferior army in open battle, Caesar was forced to watch from the palace walls as most of Alexandria fell under Potheinos's control and its people, including slaves, were formed into armed militias in protest against what looked to them like Roman military rule.

Caesar had called for reinforcements, but these would take time to arrive. In the meantime he was forced to look for a stronghold that might at least give him control of the Great Harbor. His sights fell on Pharos, and he left us with one of the few eyewitness descriptions of this wonder of the world:

> The Pharos is a tower on an island, of prodigious height, built with amazing works, and takes its name from the island. This island lying over against Alexandria forms a harbour; but on the upper side it is connected with the town by a narrow way eight hundred paces in length, made by piles sunk in the sea, and by a bridge. In this island some of the Egyptians have houses, and a village as large as a town.
>
> Julius Caesar, *Commentary on the Gallic and Civil Wars,*
> book 3, chapter 112

Caesar's interest in the island was purely practical. Even in his day, the island of Pharos was still famous for the pirates who would set upon any ship that accidentally ran aground there or failed to make the harbor entrance. This told him everything he needed to know. As he always did, Caesar reported himself in the third party:

> Without the consent of those who are masters of the Pharos, no vessels can enter the harbour, on account of its narrowness. Caesar being greatly alarmed on this account, while the enemy were engaged in battle, landed his soldiers, seized the Pharos, and placed a garrison in it.
>
> Julius Caesar, *Commentary on the Gallic and Civil Wars,*
> book 3, chapter 112

Whatever Caesar now chose to do, Cleopatra could do little but support him. In a way the people of the city militias were right. It did look like a Roman occupation with her as puppet, and in truth, when reinforcements arrived Caesar might simply have seized Alexandria and made it his. Cleopatra had made her choice, but as Roman troops swarmed over Pharos, she was about to discover its true cost.

The ships remaining in the harbor were an obvious danger for Caesar, and he didn't have to think twice about what to do. He tells us in his own words:

> The enemy endeavored to seize with a strong party the ships of war. . . . They were all of either three or five banks of oars, well equipped and appointed with every necessity for a voyage. Besides these, there were twenty-two vessels with decks, which were usually kept at Alexandria, to guard the port. If they made themselves masters of these, Caesar being deprived of his fleet, they would have the command of the port and whole sea, and could prevent him from procuring provisions and auxiliaries. . . . But Caesar gained the day, and set fire to all those ships, and to others which were in the docks.
>
> Julius Caesar, *Commentary on the Gallic and Civil Wars,*
> book 3, chapter 111

It was summer and the famed Etesian wind was blowing from the north. Normally this brought cool relief to the people of Alexandria, but now, as the ships erupted in flames, burning canvas and rope spiraled into the sky and were blown across the city. First the warehouses on the wharves caught alight, then the dockyards themselves. At this point, Plutarch tells us in a single, bald sentence, "this spread from the dockyards and destroyed the great library" (Plutarch, *Life of Caesar*, in *Parallel Lives*, 49).

There is some confusion among the sources as to whether the great library in the royal quarter itself caught fire, or just the book warehouses on the waterfront, which housed volumes for export and those impounded from the ships. The lack of explicit references to the great library after this date might suggest that this fire was considerably more than a warehouse blaze—it was a disaster. By the time the fire was out, one source reports, some four hundred thousand papyrus scrolls had been lost. It was not the end of Alexandria's library, but the great library itself would never recover its former importance, and the second, or "daughter," library at the Serapeum would now begin to supplant it. The days of Eratosthenes and Archimedes, of Euclid and Callimachus, had passed, and as Cleopatra surveyed the burning city, the works that her ancestors had invested their lives in fluttered in burned ribbons about her.

This was the price of Caesar's support; indeed, some claim the fire in the library was started deliberately on his orders. The library was the Ptolemaic jewel, the last great treasure Rome could not own without first conquering Egypt. Knowledge was Alexandria's strength, and perhaps that made it dangerous in the eyes of the Roman state. But knowledge was as vulnerable and ephemeral as the papyrus on which it was written. What had taken a lifetime to learn, Caesar could destroy in a morning with little more than a torch. The navy could be rebuilt, the houses repaired, but the books in the library could not so easily be replaced.

No records survive to tell us what books were lost that day, but if the damage was extensive it was at least not total, and Alexandria remained a "library city." Of those lost, some could be recopied from other sources and other copies could be bought; but in an age when a book might exist in only a handful of handwritten copies, some of the great works of antiquity may have died forever that day. It had been just a shot across the bow, but the sight of smoke rising over the library or even just the book warehouses marked a change in the life of the library and prefigured its final demise. The library, for all its learning, was vulnerable, and increasingly would now be seen not only as an asset, but as a liability. The pen was perhaps still mightier than the sword, but without soldiers to protect it, the single "barracks" where those words were stored was little more than a tinderbox awaiting a casual spark.

With the burning of the library one era was coming to an end, but on the streets a new one had yet to materialize. The library was certainly the most important casualty in the Alexandrine War, but that war was not yet over, and there was a danger that Caesar might also succumb. At one point he was reportedly set upon when his own ship was stormed by hostile Alexandrians and, despite his years, had to dive into the harbor and swim for the safety of ships moored farther out. Ptolemy's men were now also pumping salt water into the palace's elaborate water system in an attempt to contaminate the water supply—a very early form of chemical warfare. It was a dangerous game of brinkmanship. Would Caesar (and Cleopatra) succumb, or would Roman reinforcements arrive? In a last-ditch effort to stall for time Caesar finally released the hostage Ptolemy XIII, but much to his disappointment, this seems only to have intensified the fighting.

Fortunately for Caesar, Roman political and military might was about to force events. Mithradates of Pergamum, Caesar's general, was now just outside Pelusium, with Cleopatra's own troops and contingents from Judea and Nabatea. Caesar rushed to join them, and in the ensuing battle Ptolemy XIII lost his life, apparently drowned in the Nile. When Caesar returned to Alexandria he was the victor, and the unhappy but pragmatic Alexandrians could do nothing but bow to him and the ruler they had tried to shun, Cleopatra.

When Caesar left Egypt he ordered three legions to stay in the country for the protection of the queen, who was now carrying his son—Caesarion ("son of Caesar," as the Alexandrians called him). Of course few in Alexandria can have doubted that this was not so much an army of protection as one of occupation. With her on the throne he had placed the child king Ptolemy XIV, her younger brother (and new "husband"), as a concession to the supporters of Ptolemy XIII. No one doubted, however, who was in control. Egypt was now, in essence, a Roman protectorate, but while the queen's relationship with Caesar remained close, Egypt was safe, and flourished.

A year later Cleopatra was in Rome with her baby son and her co-ruler. The city was not yet perhaps the city of marble that the emperor Augustus so proudly boasted of (if we believe his own propaganda) but still the city of brick which he would inherit from Caesar. It was also a city of rumor. Cleopatra's influence on Caesar was said to be growing, and was causing much distrust in Rome. For her visit she was staying in Caesar's own house, a scandal in itself, for while what had happened in Egypt was, as the historian and Roman senator Cassius Dio points out, only hearsay, their behavior in Rome was clear for all to see. For many Romans this proved that the great Caesar's head had been turned by a mere girl. They commented that the Alexandrine War, unlike his other victories, was an unnecessary diversion, and one he undertook not for the glory of Rome but out of his love for Cleopatra. There were also in the city those who feared her son would be the heir to Rome, as Caesar had had no children by his wife, Calpurnia, whom he had divorced in 53 BC.

And there were other signs that his time in Alexandria had influenced him. During Cleopatra's visit Caesar introduced the new and more accurate Julian calendar to Rome, which had until that date calculated its years based on a lunar reckoning. This had led, as Cassius Dio puts it, to the days getting "somewhat out of order" (Cassius Dio, *Roman History*, book 43, chapter 26). This new, improved calendar had a 365-day year divided into twelve months, with one extra day added every fourth (leap) year. This exceptionally precise calendar—accurate to one day in 1,461 years—was not of course invented by Caesar, but a product of the mind of Eratosthenes, devised and refined in the museum of Alexandria.

Cleopatra was also having a more direct influence on her lover, playing the game of power politics just as well as he could. On her return to Alexandria her co-ruler was conveniently murdered, so she could now rule jointly with Caesarion. Caesar could content himself with the knowledge that his only son was already a pharaoh, while Cleopatra, sharing a throne with her baby, knew she could in effect rule alone. Despite her political intriguing, however, events were moving too fast even for Cleopatra.

Little did she know that when she left Rome, she would never see her lover again.

The mood in the Roman senate had been turning against Caesar for some time, and the appearance in Rome of his Eastern mistress had done little to improve his standing. Many feared that with Cleopatra's financial aid he would soon dismantle the republic and install himself over them as tyrant. So on the Ides of March, 44 BC, a small group of senatorial conspirators ensured it would never come to pass. Julius Caesar was assassinated in Pompey's theater in Rome, and Cleopatra was once again alone. That year the Nile floods failed and there was famine in Egypt.

The man to whom she now turned for support would prove to be her last ally, and one whose relationship with her has gone down in history as one of the greatest and most tragic romances of all time. Cleopatra was a practical Alexandrian and knew she needed to pick a winner from the civil war into which Rome was diving headlong. There was now a choice of three: Octavian, Julius Caesar's personal heir and effective ruler of the west of the empire; Lepidus, in command in Africa; or Mark Antony in the east. All three "triumvirs" theoretically ruled together, but the time was coming when everyone would have to choose. But in choosing Mark Antony, Cleopatra made more than a simple political decision.

Mark Antony was a natural soldier, with a fine physique and an iron constitution that excesses and hardships alike failed to weaken. His courage, affability, and generosity made him hugely popular with his men, and when he invited Cleopatra to Tarsus in 41 BC even the queen of Egypt could hardly refuse the man who had hunted down and defeated Caesar's murderers. He was clearly the logical as well as the emotional heir to Cleopatra's affections, and in his presence she once again turned around her city's and her country's fortunes in a single night. She arrived in Tarsus displaying all the magnificence and sophistication of an Alexandrian monarch. She was Isis and Aphrodite, the perfect refinement of a Hellenistic ruler and a woman at the height of her powers. Plutarch in his *Life of Antony* describes her arrival

in a barge with gilded poop, its sails spread purple, its rowers urging it on with silver oars to the sound of the flute blended with pipes and lutes. She herself reclined beneath a canopy spangled with gold, adorned like

*Venus in a painting, while boys like Loves in paintings stood on either
side and fanned her. Likewise also the fairest of her serving-maidens,
attired like Nereïds and Graces, were stationed, some at the rudder-
sweeps, and others at the reefing-ropes. Wondrous odours from countless incense-offerings diffused themselves along the river-banks.*

Plutarch, *Life of Antony*, in *Parallel Lives*, 26

After that arrival the meeting could be nothing other than a success.
The first night she banqueted him; the second he tried to respond but
was forced to admit his efforts were "rustic" compared with the magnificence of her meal. But regardless of the food, the bond between them
was already fast. After this brief first meeting Antony returned the compliment by spending the whole of the following winter with her in Alexandria. For a moment it seemed that together they could do more than
save Egypt. For a wonderful, willfully blind moment it seemed they could
inherit Alexander's dream. The Alexandrians loved Antony, saying he
wore a tragic face for the Romans but a comic mask with them (Plutarch,
Life of Antony, in *Parallel Lives*, 29). The two lovers spent days in gilded
games, most famously a fishing trip which Plutarch also describes. Having
gone fishing with Cleopatra, Antony was embarrassed at his lack of luck
and quietly asked one of his fishermen to dive below the boat and attach
to the line a fish they had caught earlier. The trick seemed to work and
Cleopatra appeared impressed by the sudden haul which followed. She
was no fool, however, and had noticed. The next day she gathered large
numbers of courtiers together for another fishing trip so they might witness Antony's prowess. When he dropped his line overboard she signaled
to her fisherman, who dived down and attached a salted herring to his
line. When he pulled it in there was great laughter, and the queen turned
to her champion, saying, "Imperator, hand over thy fishing-rod to the
fishermen of Pharos and Canopus; thy sport is the hunting of cities,
realms, and continents" (Plutarch, *Life of Antony*, in *Parallel Lives*, 29).

Then there were the love tokens. He gave Egypt back its foreign territories in Asia Minor, and in return she directed the vast wealth of Egypt
to his ambition. The following summer, as if to seal the deal, she bore
him twins: Alexander Helios (the sun) and Cleopatra Selene (the moon).
In return he gave her the one present every Ptolemy coveted.

The wealthy kingdom of Pergamum (in what is today Turkey) had recently been acquired by the Roman state, having, rather unusually, been left to Rome in the will of its last king. For the Romans it was a rich trading nation and a welcome source of revenue. But for any Alexandrian it held something worth more than gold—a library of some two hundred thousand volumes, the second largest collection of books on earth. This was Antony's gift to Cleopatra, a suitable recompense for Caesar's damage to the great library and an investment in its future. It was the greatest gift an Alexandrian could receive.

But the heirs of Julius Caesar had no desire to see another Alexander arise in Egypt, and what was more, their leader, Octavian, had personal reasons to distrust Mark Antony, who was still, at least in name, married to his sister. Now Antony was, in Octavian's view, under the control of that evil Eastern temptress who had ruined Julius Caesar. She was everything Rome stood against—a foreigner, a competitor, a political player, and, perhaps worst of all, a woman in an era when Rome viewed women as simply their fathers' or husbands' possessions. Despite several reconciliations, it was clear that Octavian's desire to rule Rome and Mark Antony's dreams of an empire in the East were set to clash head-on. In the end, driven on by Cleopatra, Antony abandoned his wife—in the process snubbing Octavian—and returned to Alexandria to plan one final bid for glory. Together they fueled a propaganda campaign to have themselves associated with Dionysus and Aphrodite—or for their Egyptian subjects, Osiris and Isis. They were to be living gods destined to rule over a new Alexandrian empire. He would provide the military might, she the money, and together they would achieve Alexander's dream and rule an Eastern empire from the city he had founded for that purpose. So enchanted with the prospect was Cleopatra that she instigated a new system for counting dates. This would now be the year 1.

In 36 BC, however, that dream began to crumble. An overconfident Antony suffered a crushing defeat on his expedition against Parthia, leading many of his senior military commanders to doubt both his judgment and his motives. These were Roman troops, after all, and though they had followed Antony across the Middle East, they had done so in the name of Rome, not Alexandria. Many were also aware that his rivalry with Octavian was now beyond reconciliation. Caesar's adopted heir was no fool and clearly saw in Mark Antony's expeditions a personal ambition that far outstripped the orders he received from Rome. He also saw behind him a son of Cleopatra's, Caesarion, a true heir to Julius Caesar.

The excuse for a final war came when Antony made his plans public, in a lavish ceremony in the gymnasium at Alexandria. Here a silver dais was set up with two golden thrones upon it, one for himself and one for Cleopatra, and other seats for Cleopatra's children. Then he declared his lover, who was dressed as Isis, queen of Egypt, Cyprus, Libya, and Coele-Syria, to share that throne with Caesarion, her son by Caesar. He then proclaimed his own son by Cleopatra "king of kings" and allotted to him further territories, including the vast expanses of Armenia, Parthia, Media, Syria, and Phoenicia. In short, he had claimed half the known world.

The resolution of the Roman senate against him and his Egyptian queen (who was now, thanks to Octavian's brilliant propaganda, known in Rome as "the ruinous monster") made war inevitable. The Alexandrian dream had seduced Rome's greatest general, and now he would have to fight for it.

Octavian finally met these would-be Eastern emperors not on land but off the coast of Actium in Greece. The sea battle was brief and bloody, and within a few short hours Antony and Cleopatra were fleeing for the distant safety of Alexandria's walls. Her ships entered the great harbor as tradition dictated, to the strains of victory songs and garlanded with flowers, but not even she could hide this defeat. She had come home for the last time, to the city that had made her, but not in triumph as she had hoped, and she would never leave its walls again. There was to be no sanctuary.

Many of the Roman generals who had supported Antony now began to defect—some no doubt just gauging the way the political wind was blowing, others now overtly opposed to this "un-Roman" dalliance with a woman they considered no more than an unreliable Eastern princess. In their eyes Cleopatra had brought Rome nothing but trouble—trouble for Pompey, trouble for Julius Caesar, trouble for Mark Antony, and now trouble for them.

In the spring of 30 BC Octavian's armies began to march on Alexandria. Antony managed one final victory in the outskirts of the city by the hippodrome, but when he returned to the battlefield the following day, his fleet and cavalry went over to the enemy. On August 1, when Octavian walked into Alexandria, the Ptolemaic kingdom came to an end.

With Octavian on his way to the palace, Cleopatra retired to her mausoleum, sending a note to Antony to say she was already dead. Hearing this, he fell on his sword in despair. The blow was not immediately fatal, however, and he was still writhing in agony when word came that Cleopatra was not dead. In his last moments he asked to be carried into her presence so he might die in her arms. Tied to a cord and hauled up through a high window (for Cleopatra would not open the door for fear of betrayal), he finally gained admittance to the tomb, and that last wish was granted.

Cleopatra did not immediately follow him to the grave. She was flushed out of her mausoleum after Octavian managed to get one of his guards in through the same window as the dying Antony. She immediately tried to stab herself, but Octavian's orders were that she be taken alive, and she was overpowered and brought to him only wounded. Perhaps Cleopatra at least thanked him for being granted the chance to bury Antony with royal honors, but she can have held out little hope that more kindness awaited her than being paraded through the streets of Rome in Octavian's triumph to the jeers and scorn of a crowd he had taught to hate her.

Seeing death as the only noble way out, she then tried to starve herself but was persuaded against this after threats were made against her children. Finally, after a meeting with Octavian on August 10, she persuaded him that she now wished to live, and he dropped his guard. She had bent one last great Roman to her will. Two days later she was dead. Plutarch describes her last moments:

> After her bath, she reclined at table and was making a sumptuous meal. And there came a man from the country carrying a basket; and when the guards asked him what he was bringing there, he opened the basket, took away the leaves, and showed them that the dish inside was full of figs. The guards were amazed at the great size and beauty of the figs, whereupon the man smiled and asked them to take some; so they felt no mistrust and bade him take them in. After her meal, however, Cleopatra took a tablet which was already written upon and

sealed, and sent it to Caesar, and then, sending away all the rest of
the company except her two faithful women, she closed the doors.

Plutarch, *Life of Antony*, in *Parallel Lives*, 85

As soon as Octavian opened the tablet he must have known that it was
too late, for in it she begged the Roman to bury her alongside her beloved Antony. He quickly dispatched messengers to her, but they arrived
to find her lying dead upon a couch, her body carefully arrayed in state
by her two female servants Iras and Charmion. Iras was herself in the last
moments of life as they burst in, while Charmion, also in the throes of
death, was trying to arrange a diadem on her mistress's head. One of the
messengers turned on her: "'A fine deed, this, Charmion!' 'It is indeed
most fine,' she said, 'and befitting the descendant of so many kings.' Not
a word more did she speak, but fell there by the side of the couch" (Plutarch, *Life of Antony,* in *Parallel Lives,* 85).

No one can be sure if Cleopatra died from the bite of an Egyptian asp
in that basket of figs, as was reported at the time, or from some other
poison which, like many rulers of her day, she must have carried about
with her. But the story of the asp provides an appropriate death for a
queen of Egypt and the only Ptolemy ever to have learned Egyptian.

She had been perhaps the most Egyptian ruler of all her dynasty, using
her inquisitive Greek mind to look deep into the past of her adoptive
home for clues to a future free from Roman domination. She had even
beguiled a Roman general into joining her on that journey—an Osiris to
play alongside her tragic Isis. But the great days of Egypt she looked wist-
fully back to had been little more than a memory when Alexandria was
founded, and the Egyptian temples she built along the Nile were more an
homage to the stories of long-dead pharaohs she had read of in the library
than the signs of a resurgent Egypt.

Now at thirty-nine years old she was dead and finally resting next to
her beloved Antony. As for her children, Caesarion, in many ways the
only true heir of Egypt and Rome, was hunted down by Octavian's men
and killed. He was about fourteen years old. Her children with Antony
did survive, although they were forced to walk alongside her picture, in
which she was portrayed with the asp still clinging to her arm, in Octavian's triumph in Rome. Only Cleopatra Selene appears again in the history

books after that, married to King Juba II of Mauritania, where she transformed his minor capital of Caesarea into a little Alexandria, complete with sculptures of her illustrious ancestors and even its own small library.

Back in the real Alexandria that library and the city that held it were now Roman possessions. The Ptolemaic dream was dead, but Alexandria's story was still far from over.

CHAPTER TWELVE

THE CLOCKWORK CITY

Your worship is your furnaces,
Which, like old idols, lost obscenes,
Have molten bowels; your vision is
Machines for making more machines.

Gordon Bottomley, "To Ironfounders and Others"

The Alexandria that awoke the day after Cleopatra's death was changed but not destroyed. Having been defeated in war, the city might have expected to be erased entirely from the face of the ancient world, as Carthage was in 146 BC, as an example to others who might dare to defy Rome.

But this was not to be Alexandria's fate. Octavian limited his revenge to stripping the city of its governing body or senate and founding his own city of Nicopolis (named after a city in Epirus opposite the site of the battle of Actium) in what was then the suburb of Ar Rama. Further humiliation would be unnecessary and, far more important, entirely counterproductive. Egypt was potentially too wealthy, Alexandria was too much of a prize, and what was more, Rome itself was also changing. The Roman province of Egypt—as it now was—had been conquered by a republic, but the general at its head had no intention of maintaining the political traditions of Cicero. He was the first of a new breed of Roman ruler, one who professed republicanism in the name of Octavian, but practiced power as the first emperor—Augustus. Egypt had been where his stepfather, Julius Caesar, and his erstwhile friend, Mark Antony, had looked for the money to conquer the world, and it would be where he would consolidate his rule, taking the Ptolemies' inheritance as his personal fiefdom.

Alexandria fascinated the new emperors of Rome in two ways. Economically, it was the port through which 20 million bushels of wheat were annually exported from the Nile Valley—enough to feed the unemployed and restive city mob back in Rome. More important, it was the center of the intellectual world, an Egyptian city founded on Greek thinking and now ruled by Rome. In its library lay the practical works by men such as Archimedes that had helped Rome build an empire, as well as many others, perhaps yet unread and untapped. And whereas the republic may have had less time for the higher arts, emperors, like pharaohs, could be seduced by their association with the great literary names from history and legend whose works filled the colonnades of the library. That was indeed a prize.

Alexandria was the most extraordinary city on earth, as Julius Caesar and Mark Antony had learned, and as Augustus was now finding out. Around the roads and gates laid out so long ago by Dinocrates, extraordinary buildings now stood. From just south of the Canopic Way the Paneium gave a stunning view across the city. This was itself an astonishing structure, a man-made hill in the shape of a fir cone around which a path spiraled up to a temple dedicated to Pan on the summit. From here the city lay spread out before a visitor. Across the wide granite-paved street lay the Soma, the tomb of Alexander, where the embalmed Conqueror of the World still lay in a crystal coffin (though not the original gold casket, which had been melted down) surrounded by the tombs of the Ptolemies. Through the hazy sides of the sarcophagus one might just have made out the scar where the great man's nose had been recently reattached after Augustus had accidentally broken it off when he demanded to touch this sacred relic. Away to the west, beyond the porticoes of the gymnasium, stood the great temple of the Serapeum, with its own library and stadium where annual games celebrated the power of Ptolemy's invented god.

Off in the distance to the north lay some of the city's most famous buildings, laid out in stately fashion around the harbor. Most impressive of all, after the palaces themselves, were the enormous grounds and buildings of the Sebasteum (or Caesarium), begun by Cleopatra in honor of Mark Antony but finished by Augustus as a celebration of his victory.

Here stood "Cleopatra's Needles"—the three ancient obelisks Augustus
had brought there from Heliopolis, which now stand one on London's
Embankment, one in New York's Central Park, and one in Paris's Place
de la Concorde. Their setting in the Sebasteum is described by Philo, a
Jewish scholar living in the city in the first century AD, as

> *huge and conspicuous, fitted on a scale not found elsewhere with ded-*
> *icated offerings, around it a girdle of pictures and statues in silver and*
> *gold, forming a precinct of vast breadth, embellished with porticoes,*
> *libraries, chambers, groves, gateways and wide open courts and every-*
> *thing which lavish expenditure could produce to beautify it.*

> Philo of Alexandria, *The Embassy to Gaius*, 15

Beyond stood a more sober and sadder sight. By the temple of Poseidon, where arriving sailors gave thanks for their safe passage across the
sea, Mark Antony had built a small promontory out into the harbor. At
the end of this stood the Timonium. This temple, built after Antony's
defeat at Actium, was named after the misanthropic Timon of Athens,
who had been an Athenian lord, wronged and mistreated by his friends,
who henceforth hated and mistrusted all mankind. He had withdrawn
from Athens and lived alone in the wilderness, and Antony, abandoned
by his Roman friends, had wished to imitate him. The depths of such
despair might be gauged from the epitaph on Timon's tomb, which Callimachus, quoted in Plutarch, says read:

> *Timon, hater of men, dwells here; so pass along;*
> *Heap many curses on me, if thou wilt, only pass along.*

> Plutarch, *Life of Antony*, in *Parallel Lives*, 70

Older and happier buildings also crowded around the harbor and
foremost among these was the museum in whose portico Eratosthenes
had placed his astrolabe. This remained a lively and extensive institution,
with its dining halls, colonnades, and gardens, in part of which roamed
the exotic animals of the scholars' private zoo. In the first century AD
there would be a sea change here, inspired not by the pure philosophy of

Greek thought but by practical problems of engineering, which would make this the only modern city in the ancient world.

The fascination with engineering that so failed to impress Archimedes now began to absorb the scholars of the museum. Rome was a physical empire, not an empire of the mind, and it wanted scholars to find practical solutions to their most pressing problems: conquering and ruling the world. The result would be advances in architecture and engineering that would remain unparalleled until the Renaissance: the first use of concrete; concrete that set underwater; aqueducts; metropolitan sewage systems; high-rise buildings; and, in Alexandria, very nearly a revolution.

Among the new breed of inventors who now walked the corridors and gardens of the museum and library, one stood out—Hero—and the revolution he nearly started eighteen hundred years too early was an industrial one. Hero was at one level exactly the type of scholar who had worked at the museum and library for centuries. He was a great geometer; his work *Metrica* (which was lost until 1896) dealt with theoretical problems of geometry, finding the areas and volumes of two- and three-dimensional geometric shapes and reiterating an ancient Babylonian method for estimating square roots which is still used in computing today. But at another level Hero was something new. His purpose in studying at the museum and library was practical. Hero professed none of Archimedes' distaste for engineering but set out to collect the greatest examples from antiquity and add his own to them. For him theory was just a preliminary to practice. Pappus, an Alexandrian mathematician working around AD 320, considered Hero a "mechanician." His school, he tells us, divided mechanics into theory and practice. The theory included the study of geometry, arithmetic, astronomy, and physics, while the practice included metalwork, architecture, carpentry, painting, and any other manual skill. It seems Hero had these skills in perfect balance, and in Pappus's view, that put him among another group—the wonder-workers.

> *The ancients also describe as mechanicians the wonder-workers, of whom*
> *some work by means of pneumatics, as Hero in his* Pneumatica,
> *some by using strings and ropes, thinking to imitate the movements of*
> *living things, as Hero in his* Automata and Balancings, *. . . or by*

using water to tell the time, as Hero in his Hydria, which appears to
have affinities with the science of sundials.

Pappus, *La collection mathématique*, book 8

In fact, in Alexandria in the first century AD, Hero was the greatest of the wonder-workers. He was a designer and builder of automatons—automatically operated machines—with which he delighted and bemused the people of the city. The machines he built used gravity, pressure, heat, and water to power devices that appeared to operate without human intervention. They would have surprised and bewildered an eighteenth-century European as much as they did Romans and Alexandrians. In his great book the *Pneumatica* he explained the purpose of his lifework:

By the union of air, earth, fire and water, and the concurrence of three,
or four elementary principles, various combinations are effected, some
of which supply the most pressing wants of human life, while others
produce amazement and alarm.

Hero of Alexandria, *Pneumatica*, introduction

Simple machines had been a part of Alexandrian life for centuries before, usually seen in the clanking automatons of the great Ptolemaic parades of the early kings. The museum had been collecting peculiar machines, tricks, and unusual natural objects since its very inception. Ever since Alexander ordered his people to send any strange novelty to Aristotle that he might use it in his teaching, the collection of books had gone hand in hand with the collection of "things" in the museum. But before now these were perhaps considered little more than novelties or, at best, talking teaching aids. But in Roman Alexandria, the construction of such novelties now blossomed and expanded. For a moment it looked as though Aristotle's own dream of a mechanized world was about to come true:

For if every tool were able to complete its own task when ordered—or
even anticipate the need—just as the statues of Daedalus supposedly
did, or the tripods of Hephaistus which Homer says "entered of their

*own accord the assembly of the gods"—or shuttles could pass through
the loom by themselves, or plectra play the harp, master craftsmen
would have no need of assistants, and masters no need of slaves.*

Aristotle, *Politics*, book 1, chapter 4

If there was a man to take Aristotle at his word, it was Hero. As with
so many of the great Alexandrians, we know very little about his private
life, but thankfully some of his works survive, either as original texts or as
comments and discussions in the works of later engineers and mathematicians. In these books he describes the machines he built and the practical
skills he learned in the process, and we also gain a sense of his delight at
producing devices which filled their audience with wonder.

The machines that Hero built were the wonders of their age—indeed,
they would have been the wonder of many ages since—and their deploy-
ment about the city made it appear to visitors to be literally a place of miracles. Some were for the home, simply there as entertainments for dinner
parties. Others whirred and clanked away in theaters, producing amazing
special effects. But the most likely place to find one of Hero's machines
was where magic and miracles were only to be expected—in the temples.

Religion in Egypt was a booming business in the early Roman Empire. The Roman view of religion was surprisingly relaxed. Provided that
the imperial cult was acknowledged—more a matter of allegiance than
belief—most Roman citizens and subjects were free to worship whatever
deity they wished. This liberal approach made cities like Alexandria the
home to hundreds of cults, from the traditional Roman and Greek pan-
theons and the worship of the Ptolemaic Serapis, to the uniquely Egyptian mystery cults of Isis and Osiris, to the Mithraism so beloved by the
army officer corps, and even the ecstatic Eastern castration cult of Cy
bele. Within the city, the temples of Isis and Osiris vied with those of the
deified Ptolemies, Zeus, and Jupiter for the devotion (and the money) of
adherents. Attracting enough worshippers to any one, when there were
literally hundreds to choose from, required a miracle, and that's exactly
what Hero could provide.

Hero could build devices which appeared to perform tasks either
without human assistance or through divine intervention. It was the stage
magic of its day, utilizing hidden machinery to make an audience stop in

the street and look in awe at the show being put on by whichever god was worshipped in the temple where Hero had installed his device.

The illusion might begin even before worshippers entered the building, in the form of a machine he describes in *Pneumatica:*

> *Temple Doors opened by Fire on an Altar.*
> *The construction of a small temple such that, on lighting a fire, the doors shall open spontaneously, and shut again when the fire is extinguished. Let the proposed temple stand on a pedestal, A B C D.*

Hero of Alexandria, Pneumatica, machine 37

As the priest and congregation approached they would be faced with the huge, closed doors of the temple. Stepping forward, a priest would light a fire on an altar and, as though the god were pleased with the offering, the doors would swing open of their own accord, accompanied by a fanfare of trumpets. Behind the scenes, where only Hero and the priests ever went, a complex series of air- and water-filled tubes connected the altar to large bucket counterweights attached to the temple doors by pulleys. As the fire heated the air it expanded, forcing water in another tube into the buckets, which would then open the doors when there was enough water to weigh them down and set the pulley train in motion. When the fire was extinguished, the air in the pipes cooled and sucked the water back out of the buckets. As the weight in the buckets lessened, so the doors slowly closed under their own weight. It was all just advanced hydraulics, a subject first studied by another Alexandrian, Ctesibius, whose works Hero must have pored over in the library.

But the mechanical wonders had only begun. Inside temples it was very important for worshippers to purify themselves with holy water before any ritual. Selling this could of course be a useful additional income stream for a temple struggling against the competition, but collecting the money and dispensing the water was a time-consuming and frankly boring job, taking one of the priests away from his other duties. To ease this problem Hero invented a

> *Sacrificial Vessel which flows only when Money is introduced.*
> *If into certain sacrificial vessels a coin of four drachms be thrown,*

> *water shall flow out and surround them. Let ABCD be a sacrificial*
> *vessel or treasure chest, having an opening in its mouth. . . .*

Hero of Alexandria, *Pneumatica*, machine 21

Hero had invented the slot machine. On putting a silver four-drachma coin in the slot, a measured amount of holy water was dispensed—another little miracle for devotees. With ablutions complete, the acolyte could then proceed into the main sanctuary, where Hero could really allow his imagination to run riot with a series of miracle machines:

> *On an Apple being lifted, Hercules shoots a Dragon which then*
> *hisses . . .*
>
> *The World represented in the Centre of the Universe . . .*
>
> *A Fountain which trickles by the Action of the Sun's Rays . . .*
>
> *A Trumpet, in the hands of an Automaton, sounded by compressed*
> *Air . . .*

Hero of Alexandria, *Pneumatica*, machines 40, 46, 47, 49

In one temple a steam boiler was used to create a jet of invisible steam on which a ball floated, apparently defying gravity. Hero also talks of a machine which allowed a group of mechanical songbirds to sing in a tree until a mechanical owl turned around to stare at them, at which point they fell silent in terror. And to complete the effect, in the temple gloom behind the miraculous machines, Hero's moving statues blinked and waved like exotic extras in a Ray Harryhausen movie.

But these devices could also have a more practical use—and raise more money for the temple. Here was a chance for the great engineer to make the gods speak directly to their followers, and like any good showman, he gave them what they wanted. Fortune-telling was a central part of many ancient classical religions, knowledge of the future, or a least a belief in having knowledge of the future, providing some bulwark against the fragility of life. Whole cities and states officially consulted the great oracles such as the Pythia at Delphi. The fabulously wealthy King Croesus of Lydia had many centuries before, according to Herodotus, asked the Pythia whether he should attack Persia. He had received a typically ambiguous response: "If you do, you will destroy a great empire" (Herodotus, *The Histories,* book 1). Heartened by this, he immediately attacked, only to discover that the empire the Pythia was referring to was his own.

Even Alexander had sought the oracle at Siwa to discover if his campaigns would be successful. This may seem like a piece of stage magic today, but the word of the Siwa oracle not only helped Alexander to resolve his course of action, but likely paved the way for his conquests. In the same way, not long after the Chaldean oracles of Babylon began predicting his doom, he did indeed die, and the same doleful prophesying had probably helped to oust Darius before that. Prophecies could be self-fulfilling. Enemies would attack a man marked out for bad luck. A man apparently blessed would be left alone. Oracles, to put it simply, worked, and many of all types and importance vied with each other. At the greatest, such as at Delphi and Siwa, kings themselves might send for answers, receiving back those cryptic messages from the god via a human intermediary, usually a priest or priestess absorbed in an ecstatic trance or under the influence of psychotropic drugs. Romans would seek answers in the entrails of sacrificed animals, as interpreted by their augurs.

Hero was interested in a somewhat more modest scale of fortune-telling, however, and one that could answer a large number of questions quickly and cheaply. So for all those worshippers who wished to know how a love affair might proceed or whether a business transaction would be profitable, he invented an omen machine. The omen machine had to fulfill several requirements. It had to give apparently clear answers, it had to make money for the temple, and, most important of all, it had to give the people the answers they wanted.

A temple equipped with one of these devices would not, of course, expose its mechanism. As a suppliant walked into the gloom of the temple's interior he would see just a mechanical bird and a large wheel. After paying a suitable fee he could ask the god a simple yes-or-no question and turn the wheel, and the bird would either sing or not—the god had spoken.

Singing gave one answer, not singing another, and the priests could choose which was the more appropriate. Inside the mechanism an air pump forced air through a pipe to make the birdsong effect when the wheel was turned. A simple cog attached to the inside of the mechanism could then be disengaged, perhaps by a priest, to silence the bird if the other answer was required.

Hero's machines could also be found in the theaters Alexandrians attended for recreation. Theater was a very big part of life in Alexandria and throughout the ancient Mediterranean world. It was not only where you got to see the latest plays but also a place to be seen. It was the place where politics happened, where great speeches were made, where factions were formed and broken. It had even been the site of Julius Caesar's assassination. In the first century AD all the world really was a stage.

For the wealthy survivors from the old Ptolemaic regime and the new Roman administrators, putting on a big production was a good way to get noticed and hence a good way to make a name for yourself. But standards were high and the Alexandrian audience expected a lot. Just as in our modern city theaters, people wanted more than just brilliant dialogue and acting—they wanted spectacle, effects, something to transport them into the world of the play. Hero himself describes various forms of rotating backdrop for scene changes, flying galleries where gods and heroes could be winched into the air, and even thunder and lightning machines. But Hero wanted to take his audience a step further.

To achieve this he invented a piece of stage machinery with a unique ability to wheel itself on- and offstage of its own accord at a preset time. Even older sources mention such self-propelling devices, although in an entirely mythical context, such as the god Hephaestus's magical tripods, mentioned in Homer's *Iliad:*

> *Thetis of the Silver Feet made her way to the palace of Hephaestus, which the god of the Crooked Feet had built, with his own hands, of imperishable bronze. It shines like a star and stands out among the houses of the gods. She found Hephaestus hard at work and sweating as he bustled about at the bellow in his forge. He was making a set of twenty tripods to stand round the walls of his well-built hall. He had fitted golden wheels to all their legs so that they could run by themselves to a meeting of the gods and amaze the company by running home again.*

> Homer, *Iliad*, book 18

Hero determined to make the myth a reality. The inside of Hero's automatic scenery was, in effect, a giant egg timer. As a huge hopper of sand emptied onto a platform, the weight pulled a cord wound around the axle, pushing the scenery forward. When the cord was fully unwound the scenery stopped—hopefully on the right part of the stage. Sand now continued to pour from one container to the other, marking out a set period of time, and at its conclusion, a lever switched and the scenery trundled back offstage again. Today modern theaters use similar computer-controlled "trucks" to move scenery, but unlike modern versions, Hero's had a problem. Once the machine was put into action there was no way to control it. If the actors spoke too slowly or fast, or if there was some interruption of the play, then the scenery might arrive or leave at the wrong time. A great speech might be rudely interrupted by the untimely departure of the street scene or leafy grove in which it was set. So Hero came up with a solution to this as well—automate the entire play, doing away with human actors altogether.

Attempts at creating robotic theaters had also, perhaps surprisingly, been tried before, notably in the late third century BC by Philo of Byzantium, who was himself an imitator of the Alexandrian Ctesibius. Although Philo's book on automatons is lost, Hero tells us that he proposed mechanical theaters powered by a simple weight on a rope. Unfortunately, this required that the theater be perched on the edge of a cliff for the duration of the action. During these long drops the weights tended to speed up too much, making the final scene more dramatic than intended as wooden actors, scenery, and theater all suddenly hurtled over the cliff edge.

Hero now proposed a much more complex system, and to demonstrate it he chose a play so complicated that it was almost impossible for human theatrical companies to put on. *Nauplius* is a classic Greek tale of tragedy and bloody revenge set just after the Trojan War and centers on King Nauplius, whose son has been stoned to death by Ajax after being falsely accused of treason. Nauplius wants revenge and calls on the goddess Athena to help.

Hero takes up the story:

> At the beginning the curtains open, then in the picture there appear
> twelve figures . . . who are repairing the ship and moving it forward

*to be launched into the sea. These figures move themselves busily: one
is sawing, the others are hammering, while yet others work with drills.
And there is a great noise, as of the sound of actual working.*

Hero of Alexandria, *On Automata*

The curtains then close and open again on another ship being launched.
The scene then changes again and now there is a seascape with the one
ship following the next. For some extra color Hero adds, "Often dolphins swim along with them, which quickly dive into the sea, then become visible, just as they really do. Then the sea becomes stormy" (Hero
of Alexandria, *On Automata*).

When the curtains open again the ships have gone and we see old King
Nauplius, standing next to Athena, who is holding a burning torch. The
curtains then close again and open one final time, where Hero tells us

*there appears the shipwreck of Ajax's boat, and Ajax swimming. A
machine raises Athena above the stage out of view; thunder crashes,
and a bolt of lightning falls directly from above the stage onto Ajax,
who is made to disappear. And in this way the story comes to its
conclusion.*

Hero of Alexandria, *On Automata*

To automate this entire play was a task of breathtaking ambition, but
Hero went on to describe exactly how it could be done. The central
power for all movements came as before from a hopper into which sand
poured, the weight of sand pulling on a rope tied around a drum. As the
rope was pulled down, the drum turned, providing the power. But rather
than just having the drum slowly unwind in one direction, Hero "pro-
grammed" it by placing pegs on the drum's surface; thus the rope could
be wound around in one direction until it reached a peg, then looped
around the peg to run in the other, making the drum reverse. With the
pegs placed correctly, the drum could be made to perform a complex
series of turns and reverses, each one timed to provide the power for one
of the scenes. So when his automatic theater opened its curtains, its audience witnessed the closest thing to a modern movie anyone would see
before the invention of the magic lantern in the seventeenth century.

Nor were Hero's devices restricted to the temple and theater. For the novelty-loving Roman with enough money to spare, Hero also devised mechanical toys for the home. Parties were just as important a part of ancient life as they are today, and then, just as now, it was customary to bring with you something to drink to help break the ice. In Hero's world, that something would probably be wine, and it presented a problem that has remained unchanged for centuries: As host, how do you make sure your guest doesn't bring cheap wine and then just drink your expensive stuff? Or from the guest's point of view, how do you make sure that other people don't drink all the good stuff you were kind enough to bring, leaving you with the dregs? For any party thrower, these were real questions, and Hero had a mechanical answer for them in his *Pneumatica*:

> A *Vessel containing different Wines, any one of which may be liberated by placing a certain Weight in a Cup.*
>
> *If several kinds of wine be poured into a vessel by its mouth, any one of them may be drawn out through the same pipe: so that, if several persons have poured in the several wines, each one may receive his own according to the proportion poured in by him.*

Hero of Alexandria, Pneumatica, machine 32

This was in effect a more elaborate version of the holy water dispenser. Inside the wine jar were three compartments into which each of three guests poured his or her wine. These were all connected to a single outlet which was controlled by a valve. The valve had three open positions, one for each wine, and each weight would set it to one of these. When your guest poured his wine into the top, you handed him the weight that corresponded to the compartment he had filled. When he wanted a drink, he just placed his weight on the dispenser; that action set the valve to his position, and his own wine was then dispensed.

But while Hero's inventions were mechanically ahead of their time, they represent something of a conundrum. Although his work undoubtedly was of practical use to temple priests and he also describes civic projects such as the construction of a fire engine, the vast majority of his work was simply of novelty value. For the Alexandrians of his day, Hero was not a mechanical genius but just another in a long line of toy makers, a gadgeteer. It was this attitude that would lead people to overlook perhaps his greatest invention, one that would eventually change the world forever.

Tucked away in his surviving notes lie his plans for an *aeliopile*. He describes this novelty toy as two copper tubes soldered to the top of a sealed metal container. These passed through two metal sleeves leading into each side of a copper sphere that could rotate between them. From the sphere emerged two outlets facing opposite each other. When water was boiled in the lower sealed compartment, steam would shoot out of the outlets, making the ball spin around, to the delight of the audience. And they should have been delighted and amazed. Spinning at around 1,500 rpm, this was the fastest man-made rotating object in the ancient world.

But it was much more than that. It was the first use of jet power. And more amazing still, it was, of course, a prototype steam engine. Had Hero combined this toy with the piston—something his fellow Alexandrian Ctesibius had invented some three hundred years before—he could have created a working steam engine; but tellingly, he didn't.

To Hero, all these technologies, so similar to those which take pride of place in our modern society, were simply curiosities—the descendants of the first items collected by the museum to help lecturers explain natural philosophy. Of course, even if Hero couldn't see the value of his toys, others could read about them. His extraordinary books continued to fill the shelves of the library: the *Metrica* on measurement of surfaces, the *Stereometrica* on measuring in 3-D, the *Mechanica* on how to move weights with the least effort, the *Automata* on how to build robots, the *Pneumatica* on devices worked by compressed air, the *Dioptra* on taking measurements at a distance, the *Catoptrica* on curved mirrors. Some of them made their way to Greece and Rome, but even there no one realized the potential of these ingenious devices.

There were fundamental problems with his aeliopile design that certainly didn't help. The main problem with it was its efficiency, or lack thereof. To allow the ball to spin freely the joints had to be made quite loose, but if the joints were loose then a lot of the steam escaped through them. Then there was the problem of fuel. In the Roman world the boiler would have to be powered by wood, and that would have to be collected by someone—probably a slave. So if the useful energy gained from burning the wood to make the steam to turn the ball was less than the energy used by the slave to collect the wood, then the efficacy of the device would be lost and the slave might as well be told to do the work himself.

But it's not just efficiency that worked against Hero's steam engine. Those very slaves who would be needed to collect the fuel were themselves an obstacle to there ever being a Roman industrial revolution. The main use of steam engines during our industrial revolution was for producing cheap and readily available power. Hiring people to do jobs by hand was expensive, and it was sometimes difficult to get skilled people when you needed them. Steam engines could work day and night without rest, they were always available, and they were very strong.

The Romans already had a source of cheap and plentiful labor in the form of slaves, and the Ptolemaic administration was particularly well suited to their use. If machines had replaced slaves, where would the slaves have gone? What would they do? No one wanted another Spartacus. For an elite whose wealth was based on land, such a device simply wasn't in their interests.

And so Hero's greatest invention was condemned to be no more than a party novelty, just another description of a marvelous mechanical engine in a book in the vast Alexandrian library. The Romans had no real *need* for his work, so their interest in the contents of the world's greatest library lay not in the abstractions of Plato and Aristotle or in Hero's experimental physics. They were interested in the construction of siege engines and artillery, in the laying out of roads and cities, in harvesting the vast resources of their new conquests. The mechanical delights of wine dispensers and Antikythera mechanisms had their place, but a machine that undermined the whole base of their society—slavery—certainly did not.

Therefore, the complexion of the library and museum was changing. What had been very much a "Royal Society" of selected scholars paid for by the Ptolemaic state was becoming a teaching institution where young nobles might finish their education. More and more it became obsessed with gathering, collating, and revising information rather than speculating and creating new ideas. So the Roman era ushered in a period of decline in the study of pure philosophy and literature. Alexandria would never see another Archimedes or Apollonius; but something new was flowing into the spiritual void left by the seeming prosaism of Roman world domination.

What people on the streets of the city were now talking about was religion, emerging from the museum and combining in the streets with the more personal and powerfully held beliefs of those who now flocked here for education and enlightenment. A new age was dawning in which old religions would undergo radical reinterpretations and new cults would emerge which, in the crucible of Alexandria, would bring the ancient world to an end and set history on a new path.

CHAPTER THIRTEEN

URBI ET ORBI

Behold now this vast city; a city of refuge, the
mansion-house of liberty, encompassed and
surrounded with his protection

John Milton, *Areopagitica*

While Alexandria may have looked little different, perhaps even improved, by Roman rule, the change in her fortunes had not left the minds of her inhabitants unaffected. As part of the Roman imperial project, Alexandrians were no longer their own masters, and what was decided in far-off Rome could have a direct effect on life in the city. A new era was dawning, an era of radical thought and new religions, many of which would take root in the city. In time the change would affect all parts of the population, but in the first years of the first century AD no one would be affected more than the Jews.

By the first century AD the population of Alexandria had risen to about 1 million people, and many, perhaps a fifth of this number, were Jewish. Since the days of Persian and then Macedonian rule this group had grown both in numbers and importance until the quarter of the city they mainly gathered in, known as Delta, was the largest Jewish community in the world outside Palestine. A cornerstone of the growth of the city, they had become Hellenized, writing and speaking and, since the writing of the Septuagint, even reading their holy books in Greek. They were, however, a population apart, without the automatic right of citizenship enjoyed by their Greek neighbors and so always vulnerable in times of crisis.

In Hero's days, the single most powerful Jew in Alexandria was Alexander Lysimachus—his names, both Greek, a testament to Hellenization. He was in charge of collecting all customs dues on goods imported from the East, and became one of the richest men in the ancient world. So powerful had he become that he could marry one of his sons to the great-granddaughter of Herod the Great. The other son, Tiberius Julius Alexander, had risen to extreme prominence in Rome. Renouncing Judaism, he became the first procurator of the province of Judea, and later prefect of all Egypt. But Alexander senior also had a brother, a man little interested in money, power, and worldly affairs. His name was Philo, and he would go down in history simply as Philo of Alexandria.

Philo is important to our story because he spent his whole life writing in Alexandria. Not many of his extensive works deal specifically with town life, but because he drew on his own experiences, he cannot help but give us a glimpse of the people of the city. In doing so he introduces us to an Alexandria missing from the records of geographers and philosophers and looks beyond the marble walls and ornamental gardens into the minds of its inhabitants.

Philo was born around 20 BC into one of the wealthiest and most privileged Jewish families in the city. As such, he was able to enjoy many of the liberties of citizenship, and at fourteen years of age he would have been taken to the Serapeum, where a priest would have shorn his long childhood hair and enrolled him as an *ephebos*—a young man suitable to receive the most select education available. He would then have set out on the *encyclia*, the secondary education program that included grammar, rhetoric, music, dialectics, geometry, and astronomy. As a physical counterpart to these mental exertions he would have been required to walk across from the lecture halls to the great gymnasium, where he would learn boxing and wrestling, the main sports of the day. In the extensive grounds here he would also have practiced the javelin and the discus, built his strength with the punching bag, and mixed with the other gilded youths who cooled their tired muscles in the fountains of the gymnasium's grounds. Outside his studies, he would also have become acquainted with some of the delights of his city, such as the theater, reached, according to Polybius, by a covered gallery that wound from the water gardens known as

Meander (after the winding river in Asia Minor), past the wrestling arena. Here he would have seen the classical plays he quotes in his own books and watched the politicians working the crowds. He and his friends would have bet on the outcome of the races in the hippodrome before retiring to their own clubs for an evening of banqueting.

This youthful regime was an entrée into a life of great privilege, and Philo, a believer in the Great Chain of Being that linked everyone and everything in order from the lowliest animals (and humans) up to God, knew he stood near the top, looking down over all but the mightiest leaders. His time as an ephebos probably also granted him full citizenship, marking him out from the ordinary Jews of the city. This gave him further rights—the right to marry as he chose and, most important, an exemption from the Roman poll tax. One of the most noticeable effects of Roman rule was an increase in taxation, particularly in Egypt, and a parallel increase in the brutality with which taxes were collected. Tax collectors were required to remit a certain figure to Rome, and Rome had no interest in how the collector went about gathering it, or what he did with any surplus. This made the tax collector a powerful and terrifying figure, as we see from the horror that Jesus' decision to dine with one provokes in the New Testament. Tax collectors were not suited bureaucrats; they were thugs, sadists, and bullies. Philo records one case he witnessed in the marketplace in Alexandria. A man owing tax had fled to avoid paying, and in response the collector seized his closest family members—the elderly, women, and children. These he then set about publicly torturing:

> He filled a large basket with sand and having hung this enormous weight by ropes round their necks set them in the middle of the marketplace in the open air. . . . They sank under the cruel stress of the accumulated punishments, the wind, the sun, the shame of being seen by passers-by and the weights suspended on them.

Philo of Alexandria, *De Specialibus Legibus,* book 3, chapter 160

The family would remain in the marketplace until the money was found, the tax evader returned, or they died. Either way the Alexandrians would know better next time than to run from him. We do not know what happened to the family Philo saw. He tells us that many cast pitying glances at them but, tellingly, fails to mention anyone coming to their aid. Such horrors were just a normal part of life under Roman rule.

Not being liable for the poll tax put Philo apart. He would never know the terror of the tax collector's call, never be humiliated in the marketplace—he was a man of position. But in the leisure hours that such privilege brought him, Philo was not wasting his time. At some point as a young man, it seems, he turned back to his Jewish roots, and he began applying the skills he had learned in the encyclia to analyzing his own religion.

Above all Philo was devoted to the Hebrew stories of his ancestors, in particular the revelatory teachings of the prophet Moses. He believed passionately that Moses was the original perceiver of divine wisdom and that his doctrine formed the basis of Greek classical philosophy, actually referring to him as "the summit of philosophy." When Philo compares Greek and Jewish scholarship he cannot help but give precedence to Moses over all others, and even when he is quoting Plato he has to add the caveat "but Moses said the same thing as Plato, only earlier and better" (Philo of Alexandria, *De Specialibus Legibus*, book 4, chapter 110).

This was not an entirely original position—something similar had been attempted in the first century BC by an unknown author in a work known as *The Wisdom of Solomon*. But ever since the Septuagint had been translated and Hebrew mythical thought came face-to-face with Greek philosophy, it had seemed inevitable that a figure would emerge who would try to develop a philosophical justification for Judaism in Greek terms. Philo was the man for the job, and set about it in great earnest. It would prove to be the happiest time of his life:

> *There was once a time when, by devoting myself to philosophy and to contemplation of the world and its parts, I achieved the enjoyment of that Mind which was truly beautiful, desirable, and blessed; for I lived in constant communion with sacred utterances and teachings, in which I greedily and insatiably rejoiced.*

> Philo, *On the Unchangeableness of God*,
> Loeb Classical Library, volume 3, pp. 1–6

Philo's works are generally divided into three groups. In the first he concentrates on a detailed analysis and paraphrasing of the biblical texts, with titles like *On Joseph, The Life of Moses, On the Creation of the World,* and *On the Migration of Abraham.* In much of this writing, Philo employs allegorical techniques to interpret the biblical stories, some of them very profound. For example, in his great *Commentary on Genesis* he argues that the whole of Genesis is a metaphor for the history of the soul, from its formation at the dawn of the perceivable world to its fall, followed by its mature development as wisdom after its restoration through repentance.

Interspersed among these biblical exegeses are more abstract pieces, where Philo the classically trained philosopher comes to the fore, with titles like *On the Virtues, On Drunkenness, On Flight and Finding, On the Unchangeableness of God,* and *On Dreams.* In these works it is almost as if Philo is saturating himself with Jewish mythology, wanting to ingest and absorb every tiny nuance of the text. It has even been claimed that he sometimes spent hours contemplating a single word from the Bible. And all the time with one foot in the traditions of the great synagogue and the other in those of the museum, Philo was comparing and contrasting Moses with Plato, the Septuagint with the works of Socrates and Aristotle, the classical world with the Jewish.

This process becomes much more transparent with the second series of his works, his philosophical treatises, such as *On the Liberty of the Wise, On the Incorruptibility of the World, On Providence,* and *On Animals,* where he discusses man's relations to the natural world. Here he is deliberately abstracting the messages he has found in the Bible and codifying them in moral, ethical, and spiritual terms; that is, he is subjecting them to the same sort of rational treatment and thought processes which we find in the classical Greek philosophers. It is as though Philo has made a magnifying lens from Alexandrian philosophy and through it is now minutely inspecting the Jewish books of law. The result was a modernizing of Jewish law which, quite by accident, also laid out the philosophical foundations for a new religion, one Philo himself would undoubtedly have had little time for, and one which was still barely struggling into existence: Christianity. And he did this in an extraordinarily thorough and creative way.

Philo, a firm believer in the Great Chain of Being, began by placing God at the apex of his philosophical landscape. But his God is so totally infinite and all-pervasive that no individual creations can be attributed to him. Instead, Philo states that God is creativity itself. God is in a permanent state of creation; his executor is a separate entity. In *The Wisdom of Solomon* the unknown author had called this entity Sophia, or "Wisdom." Philo decided this entity was Logos, the "Word" of God.

> *God is continuously ordering matter by his thought. His thinking was not anterior to his creating and there never was a time when he did not create, the "Words" themselves having been with him from the beginning. For God's will is not posterior to him, but is always with him, for natural motions never give out. Thus ever thinking he creates, and furnishes to sensible things the principle of their existence, so that both should exist together: the ever-creating Divine Mind and the sense-perceptible things to which beginning of being is given.*

> Philo, *De Presidentia*, 1.7

This whole idea is a modification, albeit a major one, of the Platonic doctrine, with God constantly generating the forms or ideas which then compose individual entities in the world, and actually brings the cosmic structure closer into line with the Jewish notion of angels and archangels as God's messengers, beings which Socrates calls "Daemons," a word later corrupted into "demons" by the Christians. In another passage Philo provides a splendidly Alexandrian analogy for this process when he compares it to planning a city in the mind of the builder:

> *Now we must form a somewhat similar opinion of God, who, having determined to found a mighty state, first of all conceived its form in his mind, according to which form he made a world perceptible only by the intellect, and then completed one visible to the external senses, using the first one as a model.*

> Philo, *De Opificio Mundi*, 19

It is hard to believe that, coming from such an erudite man who was brought up in and felt such passionate affection for Alexandria, there is not the smallest hint of Alexander and his lines of barley flour in this analogy. But from the theoretical perspective what Philo did was introduce the Greek concept of the Logos—the Word—into Jewish religious thought, and thus provide the foundation of Christianity in which Christ himself could be seen as a manifestation of the divine Word.

Philo had created the philosophical space in which the early church fathers would grow Christianity, apparently almost by accident, yet there is a possibility that Philo had closer links with this developing sect than first appears. We should bear in mind that Philo was alive at the same time as Christ, and that the New Testament documents were written in Greek by Jewish intellectuals who were part of the Hellenistic culture of the Greco-Roman world (even though they had, of course, converted to Christianity). Unlike Judaism, Christianity is a proselytizing religion, and the desire of the apostles to at least approach one of the most important figures in Hellenized Judaism seems highly plausible. Scholars have in fact argued that there are echoes of Philo, echoes of Alexandria, to be found in the writings of Saint Paul; in the Gospels, especially the book of John; and in the Epistle to the Hebrews.

There are also hints of early Christian practice in another of Philo's fascinations, with the contemplative, communal life. Philo, though believing that a family life was best for most people, was intrigued by religious groups that lived communally. He wrote about the Jewish Essenes of Palestine, now known to have been the guardians of the Dead Sea scrolls. But it was a community closer to home that most interested him. One of Philo's most popular works was a book called *Contemplative Life*. In it he describes a community of hermits, the Therapeutae, who lived on a low hill just outside Alexandria, on the banks of Lake Mareotis. This group held everything in common and spent their lives in rigorous religious study. Each member had a cabin in which was a room set aside for the study of sacred texts. Here they would study from dawn to dusk, six days a week, without food or drink, until they reached a state of religious ecstasy. On the seventh day they would gather together for holy service in their great hall before returning to their books.

The community Philo describes is clearly a Jewish one, but he hints that other such communities also existed, and these would seem to provide the model for the early Christian monastic groups, particularly the Nitrian monks of the Egyptian desert who would one day play such an important role in the life of Alexandria itself. It was the view of the Greek Christian historian Eusebius that the Therapeutae were in fact a community of early Christians, and he speculated that Philo himself may have been a Christian. This was certainly not the case, but what Philo did, in his rigorous synthesis of Greek and Jewish philosophy, was to delineate the landscape in which Christianity could develop. As such, Eusebius's claim that so great a philosopher must be a Christian is perhaps understandable, and we should at least be grateful to Eusebius for helping to preserve Philo's philosophy, whatever his reasons. By contrast, the Jewish and Greek establishments seem to have been less impressed with Philo's work, either ignoring or dismissing it. He describes their depressing reaction when he explained his revelations to them, "the sophists of literalness," as sneering and staring at him superciliously.

Philo was not to spend his whole life in simple contemplation, however. As one of the most influential Jews in the city, he had, whether he liked it or not, to take a part in civic affairs. For all its intellectual tolerance, Alexandria was still extremely volatile politically, even under the Romans. The populace was acutely divided by class, race, and creed, and anarchy was never more than a stone's throw away for the Alexandrian mob. It must have been a harsh comedown for Philo—from the ecstasies of contemplation to the real, dirty, racist, violent, and fearful world of street life. This would be the dangerous stage on which the battle for the hearts and minds of Alexandrians would be fought, and it was here that Philo would feel the grip of Roman rule.

The early days of Roman rule had promised much to the Jews. Augustus had favored them, as had his successor, Tiberius; but on Tiberius's death the appalling potential of imperial power became all too evident with the accession of the emperor Gaius, known today by his childhood nickname, Caligula, or "Little Boots." If we take the Roman historian Suetonius at his word, Caligula's rule was marked by arbitrary executions, forced suicides, and increasing megalomania. If his prefects and governors wished to keep their jobs (and their lives) they had to go to any length to please him. In Alexandria the man with that unenviable job was Avillius Flaccus, prefect of Egypt. In an attempt to ingratiate himself with the emperor he turned to three notorious marketplace rabble-rousers, Lampo, Dionysius, and Isodorus, who suggested that persecution of the

Jews, who had refused to worship Caligula as a god, would increase his popularity with the city mob and hence secure his position.

As the flames of anti-Semitic feeling were fanned, the Jewish community asked Herod Agrippa, a Jewish king in Palestine and a family friend of Philo's, to intercede on their behalf. It was his arrival in the city that sparked the first outrages. Gathering in the gymnasium, the mob began ridiculing the king. They had found a man in the marketplace whom Philo describes:

> There was a certain lunatic named Carabas, whose madness was not of the fierce and savage kind . . . but of the easier going, gentler style. He spent day and night in the streets naked, shunning neither heat nor cold, made game of by the children and the lads who were idling about.

> Philo of Alexandria, *The Embassy to Gaius*, 36

This poor creature, dressed by the mob as Herod, was paraded through the streets. When the mob reached the theater, it demanded that a statue of Caligula be placed in the synagogue, claiming that the Jews had failed to honor the divine emperor as they should. Not having a statue of Caligula at hand, they dragged an old, corroded statue of a charioteer from the gymnasium.

The prefect did nothing to stop this desecration; indeed, he issued a statement denouncing Alexandria's ancient Jewish population as foreigners with no legal rights. An orgy of looting ensued while the Jews were rounded up and forced into a small part of the Delta district. Philo explains their plan: "After driving these many myriads of men, women and children like herds of cattle out of the whole city into a very small portion as into a pen, they expected in a few days to find heaps of dead massed together" (Philo of Alexandria, *The Embassy to Gaius*, 124).

Those Jews who were caught searching for food outside this ghetto were beaten and stoned. Even Philo's own privileged class did not escape: Members of the Jewish governing body were rounded up and scourged like common criminals in the theater, and some were even crucified.

Eventually the situation calmed, and Flaccus found to his dismay that the pogrom had not had the desired effect. The extremely irrational (or perhaps calculating) Caligula had decided, for the moment, that this was not what he wanted, and when two of the governor's henchmen, Lampo and Isodorus, saw this change of heart, they were quick to condemn Flaccus to their paranoid emperor. Orders were soon sent for his arrest, and after exiling him on a barren Aegean island, Caligula eventually tired of him altogether and soldiers were sent to murder him.

Alexandria had shown itself to be a tinderbox; at one level the most cosmopolitan city on earth, it was always teetering on the brink of a dramatic descent into racial violence. Even with Flaccus gone the peace in the city remained fragile. Caligula had once more turned against the Jews, threatening to destroy the temple in Jerusalem if they persisted in refusing to worship him. If he did, all Jews in the empire would overnight become fair game for their persecutors. Alexandria was on tenterhooks, and in the following year both Jewish and anti-Jewish delegations headed for Rome to plead their case directly before the emperor; the Jewish group was headed by Philo himself. After months of prevarications the highly unstable Caligula agreed to meet Philo, but ominously began the interview with: "Are you the god-haters who do not believe me to be a god, a god acknowledged among all other nations but not to be named by you?" (Philo of Alexandria, *The Embassy to Gaius*, 353).

Fortunately for the Jews of Alexandria, Caligula seemed indifferent to the situation in the city and offered the anti-Jewish faction no more than he had offered Philo. In AD 41, on January 24, Caligula's assassination finally brought the sorry episode to an end. His successor, Claudius, ordered that the Greeks of the city show toleration to the Jews and that the violence stop forthwith. He did not want to be considered a god in his lifetime and he did not want his statue erected in the synagogue. Peace had been restored. But Roman Alexandria had shown another, ugly face which would change the whole complexion of the city.

Philo died peacefully in AD 50 or 55. He had witnessed a haunting warning of what was to come in the city, but he had also experienced the heights of philosophical ecstasy still accessible in the gardens and porticoes of the museum. And it was in those still-quiet groves that another great Alexandrian would soon rise to prominence, a man who would show that if the city's body was beginning to look diseased, its mind was still as healthy as ever.

Claudius Ptolemy looked beyond the confines of his turbulent city to the world outside, the whole world, and the heavens beyond that. His works would become the cornerstone of science until the Renaissance, and their influence is still seen today.

As with his illustrious antecedent Euclid, we know almost nothing of the life of Claudius Ptolemy. His name suggests that he was a Roman citizen of Greek extraction, as citizens usually took Roman first names. Though some have argued that he was born in the Egyptian town of Ptolemais (hence his surname), there is no solid evidence to support this claim. Nor is there any evidence that he was connected to the royal Ptolemies, though this mistake was made repeatedly in subsequent centuries and he is often portrayed with a crown and scepter. It is pretty certain, from the caliber of his work and the detail of the material he makes reference to, that he was educated and spent his working life in Alexandria, where a few years before his birth the Roman emperor Claudius, having brought peace to the streets, considerably expanded the museum. It is possible that while there he was either tutored by or received patronage from a man by the name of Syrus, to whom all his major works are dedicated, but this man has yet to be identified.

In the true Alexandrian tradition, Claudius Ptolemy was an extraordinary polymath, writing about mathematics, music, astronomy, astrology, optics, philosophy, geography, and cartography. But also in his work is a hint as to how the museum was changing. His books, magnificent as they are, are mainly syntheses. Where Ptolemy does venture into unexplored realms he is often wrong in his interpretation; indeed, there is even the suggestion that he made up data to match his hypotheses. However, there is no questioning the lucidity of his style and the clarity of presentation, and it is these which would carry his work and his name down the centuries. At the beginning of his mammoth work on astronomy, he tells us:

We shall try to note down everything which we think we have discovered up to the present time; we shall do this as concisely as possible and in a manner which can be followed by those who have already made some progress in the field. For the sake of completeness in our

treatment we shall set out everything useful for the theory of the heav-
ens in proper order, but to avoid undue length we shall merely recount
what has been adequately established by the ancients. However, those
topics which have not been dealt with by our predecessors at all, or not
as usefully as they might have been, will be discussed at length to the
best of our ability.

Claudius Ptolemy, *Almagest,* 1.i

Ptolemy was nothing if not comprehensive. In this massive work he suggests a complex mathematical model for the workings of the universe. And he produces a star catalog listing 1,022 stars in forty-three constellations, which is, incidentally, 22 more stars than Tycho Brahe could manage at the end of the sixteenth century. Ptolemy clearly considered his book to be a practical manual, not merely a reference work, and he wanted it used by and distributed to as wide a portion of the population as possible, and in doing this he became one of the world's first popular publishers. Having finished the main work, he collected together the tables of practical use to astronomers which are scattered throughout it and published them in a slim volume known as the *Handy Tables.* He then decided to write a popular account for lay readers, a sort of paperback version, called *Planetary Hypothesis.*

The *Almagest* is the second-most important and longest-lasting scientific textbook of all time, after Euclid's *Elements;* it held sway in the classical, then Arabic, and finally Western European world until Kepler unraveled the true movements of the "wandering" planets in 1618. But there is a problem. Whereas Euclid's work is substantially correct, Ptolemy's is not. In his researches in the library Ptolemy overlooked or ignored the observation by Aristarchus that the sun lies at the center of the solar system, and chose instead a geocentric model. Perhaps to be fair to him, Aristarchus's work may not have been there, destroyed in the fire started by Julius Caesar. Even if it had survived, other great men like Archimedes had dismissed the idea, so Ptolemy can perhaps be forgiven for doing likewise. Instead, using Aristotle's vision, along with data collected by the Babylonians and his illustrious Greek predecessor Hipparchus, as well as with some basic trigonometry, Claudius Ptolemy concocted what was by then a conventional view of the universe, with the earth static at its center and the sun, moon, planets, and fixed stars revolving steadily around it.

Observing that the planets do not move smoothly across the sky in one direction but sometimes appear to backtrack, Ptolemy ironed out these eccentricities by introducing the notion of "epicycles," little pirouettes the planets performed when they appeared to retreat along their paths. With this system, even previously unobserved erratic planetary behavior could be explained with the addition of a new epicycle or two. The addition of this catchy little device meant that cosmology became stuck in the rut of an earth-centered universe, a view which became so ingrained that it became pure dogma, to the point where, according to Arthur Koestler, on February 23, 1616, the church's qualifiers (theological experts) in Rome gave their decision concerning two propositions put to them:

1. *The sun is the centre of the world and wholly immovable of local motion.*
2. *The earth is not the centre of the world nor immovable, but moves as a whole, also with a diurnal motion.*

The Qualifiers unanimously declared the first proposition to be "foolish and absurd, philosophically and formally heretical in as much as it expressly contradicts the doctrine of Holy Scripture in many passages, both in their literal meaning and according to the general interpretation of the Fathers and Doctors."

The second proposition was declared "to deserve the like censure in philosophy, and as regards theological truth, to be at least erroneous in faith."

Arthur Koestler, *The Sleepwalkers*, part 5,
chapter 1, section 7, p. 455

Such was the gag order pinned on Galileo for daring to suggest that Aristarchus (plagiarized by Copernicus) was right and Claudius Ptolemy, after Aristotle, was wrong.

Claudius Ptolemy should not be criticized out of his time, however. The *Almagest*—a working, functioning model of the universe, creating mathematically based explanations for all the celestial movements as well as updating and expanding Hipparchus's star catalog into four figures— was still a stupendous achievement. It may not have been a correct model, but it fitted the observations of the day and provided a usable, working cosmological background to the whole of the Middle Ages.

Nor was Ptolemy about to leave the cosmos at that. His follow-up work, the *Tetrabiblos* ("The Four Books"), is concerned with the impact which the heavens have upon individual personalities and worldly affairs— that is, astrology. The very mention of the word incites passionate controversy. It did so then, too. But whether we believe in it or not, Ptolemy's *Tetrabiblos,* containing as it does a great deal of data drawn from Babylonian, ancient Egyptian, and earlier Greek sources, is *the* seminal work on the subject. The *Tetrabiblos* has had the longest life of all his works, being studied and employed by contemporary astrologers more than 1,800 years after he set down his basic principles.

As astrology, long dismissed as a pseudoscience by many, raises such passionate hackles, it is perhaps worth making some general observations on the subject before going into the details of Ptolemy's formulations. Astrology as we know it probably originated largely in Babylonia, where priestly watchmen studied the movements of the heavenly bodies in great detail and over very long periods of time. Their reputations as magi were widespread and attracted the attention of classical thinkers like Pythagoras.

This was of course an age of omens, when kings and slaves alike attempted to deal with the often cruel vagaries of life by looking for clues as to what the future might hold. The magi believed that in their observations of the movements of the stars they had found a unique method to do just that   to assess the personalities and fates of individuals by considering the positions of the heavenly bodies at the moment of birth or what is called today "natal astrology." Whether or not this connection is true or false, the least we can say about astrology is that it is humanity's first enormous attempt at human psychology. From their observatories every possible form of human personality trait was projected onto the cosmos, though of course the astrologers argued the other way around. So Mars projected warlike characteristics onto people born under its influence, love emanated from Venus, and so forth. And here of course lies the problem: The scientific skeptic simply has to ask the question, how do the planets and other celestial bodies transmit these qualities to individuals on earth? Over the millennia this matter of transmission has essentially been an article of faith, a mystery whose veracity is borne out only by the accuracy of its predictions.

Ptolemy's approach to astrology was that it was a conjectural rather than a precise science. So many variable factors had to be taken into account, such as race, country, and local culture, that absolute precision was difficult to achieve. And Ptolemy was also very aware that the subject was plagued by charlatans:

> As for the nonsense on which many waste their labour and of which not even a plausible account can be given, this we shall dismiss in favour of the primary natural causes. What, however, admits of prediction we shall investigate, not by means of lots and numbers of which no reasonable explanation can be given, but merely through the science of the aspects of the stars to the places with which they have familiarity.
> . . . It is the same with philosophy—we need not abolish it because there are evident rascals among those that pretend to it.

Claudius Ptolemy, Tetrabiblos, 3.iii

While Ptolemy displays no interest in the magical or mystical, or even the symbolic, aspects of astrology, he does draw on contemporary scientific thinking, which maintained that planetary characteristics were drawn from this relationship to the sun, where they received heat and light, and the earth, which was the source of moisture. Thus the moon was moist and dark, while Saturn, at the outermost position of all the known planets, was both cold and dark, and therefore thoroughly malevolent, the purveyor of death and destruction. His view was that the constantly changing positions of the celestial bodies created a continually fluctuating atmosphere to which all living creatures must respond.

Whether Claudius Ptolemy was right or not concerning astrology— and we should bear in mind that millions of people worldwide consult astrologers every day, as do countless millions of Western newspaper readers—it is his incredibly convincing presentation of the subject which gave his work its longevity. This is how he opens the Tetrabiblos:

Of the means of prediction through astronomy, O Syrus, two are the most important and valid. One, which is first both in order and in effectiveness, is that whereby we apprehend the aspects of the movements of sun, moon and stars in relation to each other and to Earth, as they occur from time to time; second is that in which by means of the natural character of these aspects themselves we investigate the changes which they bring about in that which they surround.

Claudius Ptolemy, *Tetrabiblos*, 1.i

With the thirteen books of the *Almagest* and the four books of the *Tetrabiblos* Ptolemy effectively created a model of the universe and its workings which would dominate the world for more than a thousand years. Even though we may now consider his work flawed, the fact remains that by all the standards of the time, Ptolemy's universe worked. And though for the most part his language remains couched in the scientific terminology of his day, he is not above occasionally letting us know his inner, spiritual attitude. For while his work was the first attempt to gather and systematize the mechanism by which the universe operates, his universe is not simply mechanical. Occasionally in his writing we can feel the inspiration behind his work, the sense of wonder that every astronomer knows and which must first have overwhelmed him when, as a child, he looked up through the clear Alexandrian night sky at the great vault of the heavens above him: "I know that I am mortal and ephemeral, but when I scan the multitudinous circling spirals of the stars, no longer do I touch earth with my feet, but sit with Zeus himself, and take my fill of the ambrosial food of the gods" (Claudius Ptolemy, quoted in W. Gunnyon, *A Century of Translations from the Greek Anthology*, epigram 33).

When Ptolemy looked back down to earth, however, he saw another challenge. Having completed his mammoth task on the heavens, he felt, like Socrates before him, it was time to bring his philosophy from the heavens down to earth.

That earth began for Ptolemy with Alexandria itself. Here in the markets were people from all over the earth, and piled in the warehouses along the waterfront were exotic goods gathered from as far as any traveler had ever reached. It was in part as a response to this cosmopolitanism that Ptolemy decided that the traders and explorers venturing out from this crossroads of the civilized world, which the Greek orator Dio Chrysostom called "the conjunction of the whole world," needed a new guidebook: a book that would take them to the very edges of the known world, and perhaps beyond.

Ptolemy's *Geography* is composed of eight books. Its intention was simple: to make and draw an account—an atlas—of the entire known world, and to construct maps which accurately reflected the texts. But as always, before proceeding to the work in hand it was necessary to review all the existing sources on the subject, evaluate their relative accuracy, and to devise and develop the necessary mathematical techniques for both the written geography and the accompanying cartography.

The idea of measuring the world (agreed by then to be spherical in shape) by dividing it into vertical and horizontal lines had been used by Eratosthenes when he made his astonishingly accurate measurement of the earth's circumference, but it was Ptolemy who developed this idea into the notions of longitude and latitude, divided into degrees and minutes. With this framework established, the next question was how to make the most accurate assessment of the positions of the major cities, rivers, lakes, and mountains of the known world. Ptolemy realized that as winds vary, so the speeds of ships fluctuate; further variations are caused by the effects of tides and currents, so simply logging times traveled at estimated speeds would not necessarily produce accurate positioning. Similarly, travelers proceeding on foot or horseback rarely traveled in a straight line or at a constant speed. He preferred Eratosthenes' method, measuring the angle of the sun's shadow at midday to estimate where a traveler might be longitudinally. This data he chose to combine with all the known reports from mariners, traders, travelers, and explorers, to come up with a list of more than eight thousand localities, each uniquely pinpointed by its own longitude and latitude.

His next problem was that of projecting the spherical world (of which he knew that only about half was known) onto a two-dimensional piece of paper, to produce a map. In book 1 of the *Geography* he shows us precisely how he planned to do it, dividing the hemisphere of the known world into eighteen "meridians" of 10 degrees each, the longitudinal lines converging on the North Pole, and at their widest at the equator. The remaining task was therefore to transfer the eight thousand plotted locations onto the grid-planned page and fill in the details of the map.

Ptolemy's *Geography* was lost from the fall of Alexandria until about AD 1300. When a copy of the great work was found it was in Arabic, and the world map, the twenty-six regional maps, and the sixty-seven maps of smaller areas were all missing. But the text was so detailed and comprehensive in explaining how to make the projections onto paper that enthusiastic cartographers found the maps relatively easy to reproduce. What then did they see as they put his world atlas together?

The first thing they must have noted was its sheer extent. Stretching from Iceland to China, it really did cover all of the Old World. Admittedly there were several oddities—much of India was not there, replaced by an enormous version of Sri Lanka named "Taprobana," and Africa below "Ethiopa" appeared to go on indefinitely, as did China as the easternmost point on the map. But most of Europe, North Africa, and the Near and Middle East were much as we see them today. Egypt and the Nile; the details of the Red Sea and Arabia; the Aegean Islands; Cyprus; the leg, high-heeled boot, and football of Italy and Sicily; the square box of the Iberian Peninsula; and France, Germany, and Denmark were easily identified. The British Isles grew an interesting extension jutting out from eastern Scotland, but the southwestern limb of the Cornish Peninsula was there, as were Wales, the Isle of Man, and a plausible outline of Ireland. Considering that Ptolemy constructed this map in the late second century AD and Britain was much more than a thousand miles away by sea, the accuracy of his work is truly astonishing.

Little wonder then that Claudius Ptolemy has come to be known not just as the last, and perhaps the greatest, of the classical astronomers, but as the father of geography too.

Claudius Ptolemy's achievement was to lay out a whole system by which the world, the universe, and indeed the fates of men might be known. In it he hoped to live up to the ideals of Alexandrian philosophy, ideals which had been known to Eratosthenes, Callimachus, and Aristarchus before him. In this, for all its failings, Ptolemy's work was a spectacular success. What he could never have known as he wrote, however, was that his system would provide the framework for a new age, the Christian age, which was already sparking to life in the streets around him.

CHAPTER FOURTEEN

DAWN OF THE ICONOCLASTS

Now, says Solomon, defend wisdom, and it will exalt thee, and it will shield thee with a crown of pleasure.

Clement of Alexandria, *Stromata*

For Ptolemy, Philo, and the Alexandrian philosophers in whose footsteps they trod, spiritual enlightenment came from two interconnected sources. It was in the unending search for wisdom which might allow them to see beyond the sordid, material world to Plato's. Coupled with this was a personal code by which their bodies and minds might be in a suitable condition to search out such truths. This path was by no means easy, requiring moderation and temperance, a willingness to shun the obvious temptations of the physical world and to strive to find divinity in ideas alone. As such it was a path suitable only for the chosen few. Neither Philo nor Ptolemy believed that just anyone could enjoy the insights they had received. They were the highest link in the human portion of the Great Chain of Being, with the privilege, and perhaps the duty, of understanding the world on behalf of lesser humans—the uneducated, the women, and the children.

In second-century Alexandria, however, a new force was stirring which took a radically different view of man's (and woman's) destiny. During Ptolemy's lifetime access to this protoreligion had been largely by word of mouth, with just a few accounts of the life and works of the new man-god in circulation. However, those stories had not died out as so many other religious tales had, and now, just a century after his crucifixion at the hands of the Roman authorities, tales were rife that the Messiah had emerged among the Jews. His appeal lay partly in the fact that he had renounced the Great Chain of Being: He hadn't said that the poor and downtrodden must accept their place in society, however meek. In fact he had said the reverse, something radical and dangerous—he had said that the meek were going to inherit the earth.

Christianity, as preached by Jesus and passed on by his disciples, was a truly revolutionary doctrine, which, for all its overt pacifism—"turn the other cheek, love thine enemies"—clearly challenged directly the established social order. In a world dominated by the brute force of the Roman Empire, powered by slavery, awarding most of its inhabitants, particularly women, second-class status at best, the evangelizing zeal of Christianity, preaching damnation for the rich and powerful and salvation for the meek and oppressed, was almost certain to catch on. The highly publicized persecutions and martyrdoms of its early adherents only added fuel to the fires of this passionate new faith.

Alexandria, with its free and tolerant attitude to intellectual debate, as well as its burgeoning population of the downtrodden—slaves, Egyptians, and women from across the known world—was perfectly positioned to become the first great center for Christian study. It would be here that the new teachings would be refined, formalized, and shaped into the first proselytizing religion the world had ever known. This would also be the stage on which Christianity's main opponents voiced their opinions. In the streets these academic disputes between rich and poor, Jews, Christians, and pagans, would increasingly be fought out not only with words but with lives.

The most penetrating and comprehensive assault on Christianity came from a man named Celsus, who wrote a book titled *The True Word* or *The True Discourse* around the time of Claudius Ptolemy's death in the mid-170s. It gives us a unique insight into what some of the wealthy and educated ruling classes in Alexandria really thought about this new religion; but also, in the extraordinary story of its survival, the book demonstrates the passions such arguments would arouse and the lengths to which people would go to suppress views that differed from their own.

Not a single copy of Celsus's book survives, as every one was ordered destroyed by the Christian emperor Valentinian III and Archbishop Theodosius in 448. Early Christianity took great pleasure not just in the annihilation of anyone or anything deemed to be pagan, but in wiping out any trace of dissent from its own historical records. Paradoxically, this zeal could sometimes protect the very material that the church wished destroyed. About seventy years after he wrote it, a copy of Celsus's book was sent to the preeminent Christian theologian of the time, a man named Origen of Alexandria, with a request that he refute it. After some hesitation, Origen consented, and wrote his famous treatise *Contra Celsus*— "Against Celsus." This work immediately entered the Christian canon as a revered early defense of the faith, and it has been carefully conserved ever since. But Origen did such a thorough job (he was an Alexandrian scholar, after all) that he quoted almost all of Celsus's book verbatim— how else could he refute him point by point? Indeed, so much did he quote that in the nineteenth century scholars were able to reconstruct 90 percent of the original just from Origen's rebuttal. In this deliciously ironic way, the greatest early onslaught on Christianity was conserved almost word for word in the church's own sacred annals.

We know next to nothing about Celsus as a person, and, just as his book itself is a reconstruction, what little we do know of the man himself has had to be reconstructed from that book. For many years it was thought that Celsus must have been a Roman, living in Rome and hence displaying all the contempt for a foreign peasant religion that we might expect from the then masters of the world. But in his work there are clues to his real origins. His writing clearly shows a deep knowledge of Egyptian customs, something people in Rome had little interest in. His description of Judaism is also unusual for a Roman, not dealing with the Western tradition but instead speaking of the idea of Logos, the Word. This is a unique aspect of Oriental Judaism and one we have heard expressed before by Philo. So all indications are that if we had gone looking for Celsus in the second century we would have found him not in Rome but at the museum in Alexandria.

His *True Word* consists of a preface followed by an attack on Christianity, first from a religious, Jewish point of view, then from a philosophical standpoint. This is followed by a detailed refutation of Christian teaching and an appeal to Christians to renounce their faith and return to the pagan fold of the True Word (Logos). Celsus opens his attack by accusing both Christianity and Judaism of arrogant "separatism" in that both claim a special relationship with God as chosen races that casts them as superior to the rest of society. This, Celsus claims, is false. In reality all peoples share the same relationship with divinity. In fact, he suggests that the evidence of how Christian and Jewish peoples have fared in the world might be taken to imply that God actually was prejudiced against them. The Christians were, after all, a persecuted people, and the Jews still had no homeland. These seemed to Celsus odd rewards for "chosen" peoples.

Turning then to Christ and his teachings, Celsus begins by attempting to set the record straight with regard to the virgin birth. Pointing out that there are many examples of divine inseminations of mortals in Greek mythology which the Christians have crudely copied, he gives his own stark version of what he imagines were the real events. Jesus was

> born in a certain Jewish village, of a poor woman of the country, who gained her substance by spinning, and who was turned out of doors by her husband, a carpenter by trade, because she was convicted of adultery; . . . after being driven away by her husband, and wandering about for a time, she disgracefully gave birth to Jesus, an illegitimate child.

> Origen, *Against Celsus*, 1.28

He then moves on to provide his explanation of how Jesus, from this unpromising beginning, went on, thanks to the superstitious Egyptians, to return to Palestine with a religious mission. Celsus claims he became a servant in Egypt in order to raise money and there learned some "miraculous powers"—the sorts of tricks that Egyptians loved and were famous for. He was so pleased with these that when he returned home he declared himself a god.

Celsus maintains that on his return, however, Jesus was not able to persuade his fellow countrymen of his divinity, merely attracting a following of ten or twelve infamous publicans and fishermen—hardly company fitting for a god. Celsus goes on to claim that Jesus failed to keep his promises to the Jews, and even failed to sustain the loyalty of his followers. Of his claims to have predicted his own death, Celsus asserts that this was merely fabricated by his followers, like the story of the resurrection, another trope which appears so often in Greek mythology. If Christ rose from the dead, he asks, why did he show himself only to his disciples and not to his persecutors?

It becomes clear that Jesus does not measure up to Celsus the Platonist's notion of divinity. Using Philo's term "Logos" to mean the executor of God's will, he piles on the sarcasm:

> The Christians put forth this Jesus not only as the son of God but as
> the very Logos—not the pure and holy Logos known to the philoso-
> phers, mind you, but a new kind of Logos: A man who managed to get
> himself arrested and executed in the most humiliating circumstances.

Celsus, On the True Doctrine, 64

Celsus goes on to attack both Christians and Jews even for claiming that theirs are separate religions when in fact Christianity derives directly from Judaism. His view is that because the Jews revolted against the Egyptians, and the Christians against the Jews, sedition lies at the root of both traditions. He complains too of the lack of any cohesion or agreement among the many fledgling Christian cults which were flourishing at the time, claiming that they have almost nothing in common except the name.

But it is the way that he has seen Christianity spreading through Alexandria and the empire that most baffles Celsus. Alexandria is a city of wisdom, where men dedicate their lives to study so that they might understand the true nature of divinity. Study draws men further up the Great Chain of Being, yet Christian evangelists seem to ignore this, shunning the well educated and concentrating their efforts on the lowliest and most ignorant parts of society. Why is it, Celsus asks, that it is

> only foolish and low individuals, and persons devoid of perception, and
> slaves, and women and children of whom teachers of the divine word
> wish to make converts. . . . For why is it an evil to be educated and
> to have studied the best opinions, and to have both the reality and the
> appearance of wisdom? Why should it not rather be an assistance, and
> a means by which one might be better able to arrive at the truth?

Origen, Against Celsus, 3.64

His view is that the Christians have added nothing to the wisdom of the ancients and in fact have often distorted and perverted the tenets of the great classical thinkers. Philosophy, he maintains, clearly distinguishes between true wisdom and mere appearance, whereas the Christians demand that adherents believe what they don't understand and evoke the authority of their discredited leader as endorsement. Even Christ's apparently new doctrine of the resurrection he dismisses as a mere corruption of the ancient doctrine of the transmigration of the soul. This lies at the very heart of Celsus's concern. In his view, rationality—the logic of the museum scholars—is the path to understanding the divine. But Christianity does not require his sort of wisdom; it does not demand that its adherents spend their days in the philosophy lecture halls. Instead, it requires only one thing from them, one thing that anyone of any social standing can give and the one thing that can really threaten his world order: faith.

In this Celsus sees a terrifying future, where the knowledge that he stands for counts for nothing and the dangerous masses might threaten the established social order. Under Christian rule, he believes, the lower classes would rise up, fired not by a new love or understanding of philosophy, but inspired by a blind and unquestioning faith that actually revels in the ignorance of its adherents. With this antiacademic group in control there would then be no rule of law, and the classical world would be reduced to barbarism. What would follow would be chaos and the end of the world as Celsus knew it.

Prophetic words these, as we shall see as Alexandria's fate unfolds.

But Celsus believes he has a cure. Having identified the rotten worm within the apple, he appeals to the Christians to forsake their errant ways and return to the fold of true Platonic paganism. Some commentators consider that this was his intention all along, that his aim was a reconciliation and return to the true path, as is acknowledged in some passages of Origen's rebuttal. Celsus declares that his desire is to help all men, and bring them all to the ideal of a single religion.

Celsus has done, certainly in his own view, a classic Alexandrian analysis of Christianity, and found it wanting. Like so many scholars before him, he gathered the information, and sifted and ordered it, before applying the test of his own logic to it. In studying Christianity, which yet had a shortage of texts, Celsus must have spent long hours not in the library but in the market, talking to the evangelizing Christians as they sought converts. It must have made for some nervous and heated exchanges, but at the end of the day Celsus still hoped that they would return to the old order. In his mind this new religion was subversive but not yet truly dangerous. In the end the Great Chain of Being would reestablish itself, so he could afford to treat the Christians he met not as enemies but more as errant children. They should turn away from thoughts of liberation and return to their established place in society. But Celsus had overlooked one key issue, the issue of faith.

At its most fundamental, the debate Celsus raised with the Christians was about the nature of God. In the Platonic world God was an ultimate form, like Philo's God a constant creator, but one utterly divorced from the world of people, animals, cities, and wars. To remain in his pure form God must not have contact with our fallen, human world. So by definition a God on earth is a debased God:

> God is good, and beautiful, and blessed, and that in the best and
> most beautiful degree. But if he comes down among men he must
> undergo a change, a change from good to evil, from virtue to vice, from
> happiness to misery, and from best to worst. Who, then, would make
> such a choice?

>   Origen, *Against Celsus*, 4.14

But Celsus reached this appreciation of God's nature via the classical Platonic route. His ideas of divinity were to be found through *philosophia*, the love of wisdom, in which the philosopher refined himself in an attempt to reach closer to God through the purity of his spirit. What Jesus and his followers preached was not philosophia but credo: belief. Their God was to be found through faith, and faith alone, and no amount of intellectual and spiritual refinement would help the individual on that quest. Both parties agreed that there was a God, but only one party, the Christians, believed that access to the almighty was open to all and sundry through faith. Even though they may not have felt the benefit until they had shuffled off this mortal coil, Christian converts lived their lives in faith and in hope of a better life thereafter. This appealed to those who could never afford to enroll their children in the encyclia—to people for whom the next life could, in truth, only be better than this one. These ideas—faith and hope—the cornerstones of Christianity, were barely to be glimpsed in the canon of Hellenistic philosophy.

Celsus was also making a mistake if he thought that Christianity was something new in Alexandria, or just another passing craze. Eusebius, the Greek bishop and ecclesiastical historian, claims that the religion's roots in Alexandria go right back to the apostles. According to him, Saint Mark came to Egypt preaching the gospel around 41–44 and created a center for discipleship and education in the city, becoming the city's first patriarch. In truth, reconstructing the life of Mark is fraught with difficulty, and the fact that writers like Origen make no mention of him in connection with the city might suggest that placing him there is a later tradition. Even the nature of his death is uncertain. The Acts of Mark claims that the saint was gloriously martyred at Easter in 68 by an angry Alexandrian mob that dragged him to death through the city streets in reprisal for his attempts to turn them away from paganism. This story does not emerge before the fourth century, however, and may simply serve to provide the city with a major martyr. Though these stories may not be contemporary with Mark, they do demonstrate how quickly Christianity gained a foothold in the city and how even early on its church fathers could associate themselves with a character as powerful as one of the apostles. They also contain a veiled warning of events to come.

Whether Christianity was established in Alexandria by Saint Mark or by a later disciple, it was certainly firmly rooted by the time of Celsus's denunciation; indeed, it was about to move out of the marketplace and into its own educational establishment. The dean of this institution, Pantaenus, was a brilliant Christian scholar, and the establishment he would preside over, the Didascalia, would go down in history as the first school of Christian religion in the world and the home of the first translation of the New Testament from Aramaic and Greek into Coptic, the language of the Christian Egyptians. Founded around 180, this school was intended to take on the Platonists at their own game. According to one ancient source, Pantaenus was originally a Stoic philosopher himself, and therefore well used to the classical form of education available in the city. This he now applied to the teaching of Christianity, forming a "catechetical" school, where his faith and other subjects were taught orally by repetition or by question and answer.

Pantaenus was a Sicilian, and his greatest pupil, and later friend and successor, was Clement of Alexandria. Clement was probably born and educated in Athens—his Greek is very proper—and so received a full classical education before he converted. After his conversion he set about finding the greatest Christian teacher in the world, someone who could not just inspire the people of the marketplace, but defend his religion against the relentless logic of the professional philosophers. Eventually, he found Pantaenus, in perhaps the only city that could have produced such a man—a classically educated convert who could bring Christianity into the same regard as the museum at which he himself had trained. Clement immediately knew his search was over: "Having tracked him out concealed in Egypt, I found rest. He, the true, the Sicilian bee, gathering the spoil of the flowers of the prophetic and apostolic meadow, engendered in the souls of his hearers a deathless element of knowledge" (Clement of Alexandria, *Stromata,* 1.1).

Clement stayed with Pantaenus until 189, when the dean was selected to go on a mission to India (in fact probably southern Arabia), and Clement took his place in the Didascalia. According to Clement, Pantaenus eventually returned from "India" bearing the copy of the Gospel of Matthew, in Hebrew, which had originally been carried there by Saint Bartholomew and which was now the treasured possession of the Alexandrian church. Pantaenus was not well rewarded for his trouble, however, and was apparently martyred in 216 in one of the anti-Christian pogroms which would become a feature of the pagan Roman Empire in that period.

The Didascalia had originally been conceived as a specifically Christian school, designed to educate converts to a point where they were ready for baptism, but it was set up in typical Alexandrian style. The school was open to anyone who wanted to learn, not just Christians. Subjects taught there included all the classical greats, not scripture alone, but science, mathematics, physics, chemistry, astronomy, medicine, and music. Classes were open to all comers, and non-Christians were encouraged to attend the introductory classes in Christianity. Catechumens (converts who had not yet been baptized) studied alongside students of Greek philosophy as well as ordained priests. Many of the students came from abroad, especially from Rome, and graduates from the school held prominent positions throughout the empire. Classes were held in Greek and the more everyday language of Coptic, and by the fourth century even blind students could study there using a system of raised writing on wooden boards, which predated Braille by fifteen centuries.

So education at the Didascalia under Clement's tutelage was truly eclectic, which fitted precisely with his own highly educated and open-minded personality and philosophy. The philosophy he taught was not to be "the Stoic, nor the Platonic, nor the Epicurean, nor that of Aristotle; but whatever any of these sects had said that was fit and just, that taught righteousness with a divine and religious knowledge, this I call mixed philosophy" (Clement of Alexandria, *Stromata*, 1.7).

Like Celsus, Clement was a universalist: He believed that all humanity could be united under one religion and thus all would be saved from damnation. But unlike Celsus, for Clement that universal religion would be Christianity, not Platonism. Under his guidance Alexandrian Christians brought intellectual rigor to its doctrines and adapted it to all classes of people, and in so doing they attempted to proclaim a world philosophy capable of being understood by all and sundry, from the highest to the lowest, from kings and emperors to slaves, women, and children. It was Clement's great genius, and a mark of his devout Christian faith, that in the face of Celsus's withering attack he "turned the other cheek" and sought to incorporate all that seemed good and of value in Celsus's Hellenistic philosophy into his own Christian doctrine.

The key to Clement's plans for the Didascalia was the same as the key to the Platonists' museum: writing. As Clement himself noted, he became a Christian at a time when most Christian teaching and thought was oral, handed down from the apostles to their followers and their followers' children. Yet Clement was a highly literate scholar in the true Alexandrian tradition, and felt it was his duty to attempt to make a written record of the original, oral tradition. By this time most of the New Testament had been written down, but nobody had employed the Alexandrian approach to Christianity: that is, to collect everything ever written on the relevant subject, refine it, subject it to "scientific" analysis, and finally incorporate it into a way of living and being—a Christian form of

Celsus's "right living." This is what Clement determined to do to: beat the Alexandrian philosophers at their own game, as it were.

Clement divided his great work into three parts. Some scholars equate this with the three degrees of the Neoplatonic mysteries: purification, initiation, and vision. Others see it more directly as a graduated initiation into Christian life as belief, discipline, and knowledge, or perhaps even more sublimely as reflecting the Holy Trinity of Son, Father, and Holy Ghost. More overtly, the first set of books, titled *The Exhortation to the Heathen* or more briefly the *Protrepticus* or *Exhortation,* aims to win pagans to the Christian faith; the second set, the *Paedagogus* or *Instructor,* sets out to teach the convert how to live a proper Christian life; the third part's full title is *Titus Flavius Clement's Miscellaneous Collection of Speculative (Gnostic) Notes Bearing Upon the True Philosophy.* It has come to be known as the *Stromata,* or *Tapestries,* and aims to provide the raw materials from a huge range of sources from which the trained disciple can gain a higher knowledge of the Christian mystery. It is perhaps the boldest literary undertaking in the history of the church and certainly the largest and most valuable record of early Christian thought to have come down to us. Together then, these form their own curriculum—a Christian version of Philo's encyclia.

So what would the young catechumen, or pagan philosopher, have heard in the halls of the Didascalia? In the first book, the *Exhortation,* Clement invites the reader to listen, not to the pagan legends of the gods, but to the "new song" of the Logos, the Word of God, the creator of the world. He points to the folly of idolatry and pagan mysticism and the horrors of pagan sacrifice. He also identifies what he sees as the weakness of pagan philosophy, which has only guessed at the real truth, while the divine Logos, as personified by Christ, has revealed the nature of truth, the living Word of God, in person, requiring only that his teaching be followed in order to awaken all that is good in the human soul and lead it toward immortality.

In the second book, the *Instructor,* Clement establishes Christ as the Divine Instructor and sets out in painstaking detail exactly how a Christian, one who has been rescued from the darkness and pollutions of heathenism, should live a good and virtuous life. In this book, divided into twelve chapters, he addresses the minutiae of conduct under the following headings: "On Eating," "On Drinking," "On Costly Vessels," "How to Conduct Ourselves at Feasts," "On Laughter," "On Filthy Speaking," "Directions for Those Who Live Together," "On the Use of Ointments and Crowns," "On Sleep," "On Clothes," "On Shoes," "Against Excessive Fondness for Jewels and Gold Ornaments." Each one of these chapters runs to several pages, giving a complete history of the usage of the subject under discussion as well as the views expressed both in the scriptures and in secular and philosophical writing, as well as Clement's own advice on how a good Christian should treat the subject. On drinking, for example, such as he would have witnessed in the festivals of Dionysus and the private banqueting clubs once frequented by Philo, he sounds a note of caution:

> *"Use a little wine," says the apostle to Timothy, who drank water, "for thy stomach's sake," most properly applying its aid as a strengthening tonic suitable to a sickly body enfeebled with watery humours; and specifying "a little," lest the remedy should, on account of its quantity, unobserved create the necessity of other treatment.*

> Clement of Alexandria, *Instructor*, 2.2

He does not condemn drinking alcohol outright, however. He takes the opportunity to explain the Holy Communion, in which Christians drank wine mixed with water in imitation of the Last Supper, when Christ told the apostles that it was his "blood" and they should drink in remembrance of him:

> *For the blood of the grape—that is, the Word—desired to be mixed with water, as His blood is mixed with salvation. . . .*
> *   Accordingly, as wine is blended with water, so is the Spirit with man. And the one, the mixture of wine and water, nourishes to faith; while the other, the Spirit, conducts to immortality. And the mixture of both—of the water and of the Word—is called Eucharist.*

> Clement of Alexandria, *Instructor*, 2.2

This is followed by a long discussion of the merits of wine as well as the demerits of excess. "Moderation in all things" is a major part of Clement's message. Typically of Clement, however, much of his message would have appealed just as much to Celsus as it did to his Christian converts. For him there was a place for the educated Alexandrian philosopher in Christianity, just as there was for the street peddler, and he appealed to their Platonic belief in "right living" to attract them. On the subject of choosing a bed, for instance, he uses language that could have come from any of those pagan or Jewish intellectuals trained in the encyclia:

> The bed which we use must be simple and frugal, and so constructed that, by avoiding the extremes (of too much indulgence and too much endurance), it may be comfortable. . . . But let not the couch be elaborate, and let it have smooth feet, for elaborate turnings form occasionally paths for creeping things which twine themselves about the incisions of the work, and do not slip off.

Clement of Alexandria, *Instructor*, 2.9

Of course Clement was considerably more ambitious than proponents of the Great Chain of Being in believing that there was a place for everyone in his philosophy. While Philo considered that a woman's place was in the home, and even secluded within that, Clement suggested that women too could be a part of his great project, provided that they also turned away from the more material aspects of Alexandrian life and adorned themselves not with gold but with the Word of God.

Having exhorted the heathen to turn to Christ and set out how they should live, Clement then moved on to his third work. The *Stromata*, or *Tapestries*, is aimed at the mature Christian believer, who by studying the work will be able to perfect his or her Christian life by initiation into complete knowledge of both man and God. It means to give an account of the Christian faith which will answer the questions of all men, even the pagan cynics who inhabit the museum in Alexandria, not through logical arguments but rather by building up a "tapestry" of spiritually nourishing thoughts of his own, drawn from the scriptures and, indeed, even from the pagan world around him. He had no intention of sticking to an ordered plan for the work, declaring that his intention was to create a work like a meadow where all varieties of flowers grow at random, or like a hillside planted with every possible variety of tree. In this way Clement aimed to reveal the innermost realities of his beliefs. His original intention was to do this in one book, but it steadily mushroomed into seven, or possibly eight, books, though if the eighth book ever existed it is now lost. Eusebius's speculation that the final book was composed solely of extracts taken from pagan philosophers might explain why it has not survived.

While the cornerstone of this work, like all the others, is the revelation and promotion of faith, and the assertion that such revelation is superior to philosophy, he does still have an eye toward the scholars of the museum. He insists that God's truth is to be found both in revelation and in philosophy. He opens the fifth chapter of the work with a section entitled "Philosophy—the Handmaiden of Theology":

> Accordingly, before the advent of the Lord, philosophy was necessary to the Greeks for righteousness. And now it becomes conducive to piety; being a kind of preparatory training to those who attain faith through demonstration. . . . Philosophy, therefore, was a preparation, paving the way for him who is perfected in Christ.

> Clement of Alexandria, Stromata, 1.5

Clement taught in Alexandria from 190 until 202, numbering among his pupils the same Origen who would later be called upon to write the rebuttal to Celsus's pagan broadside and who would succeed him as dean of the Didascalia.

But if Christianity was finding a place in Alexandria, it could still be considered a dangerous and seditious sect in Rome. It challenged Roman authority; it refused to acknowledge the divinity of the emperor and preached that the meek and not the imperial family were the inheritors of the earth. Anti-Christian purges, just like the frequent anti-Jewish pogroms, remained common, and the Alexandrian mob which had been so easily roused against Philo's friends was just as adeptly turned against Clement's.

In 202 the emperor Septimius Severus, a North African himself, ordered a purge of the Alexandrian Christians. In the ensuing persecution the seventeen-year-old Origen saw his father martyred, engendering in him a lifelong hatred for the Romans. Clement fled the city and took shelter in Palestine. From there he traveled to Antioch to stay with his star pupil, Alexander, by then archbishop of the city, who reported his master's death in a letter to Origen in 215.

Clement's flight proved to be a decisive moment in the history of early Christianity and the history of his home city of Alexandria. As a scholar of the city, he had attempted to bridge the gap between Christian, Jew, and pagan with a hopefulness and generosity which might eventually have drawn these disparate groups together. As the church historian F. W. Farrar once said, Alexandria was in its time "the cradle of Christian theology" (*Lives of the Fathers*, book 1, pp. 262–63), but the early life of the child born in that cradle would prove violent and bloody enough to turn many church fathers away from Clement's liberal views. A church born into purges and persecutions found his message too Hellenistic, too open to other philosophies, to the point where, some 1,500 years after his death, Pope Benedict XIV would have his name removed entirely from the church calendar.

A unique moment, when the old pagan and Jewish city and the new Christian one might have come together to set a new path, a new interpretation of the work the museum had striven for so many centuries to achieve, had been wasted. Instead, the seeds of a bitter and ultimately deadly struggle that would tear up the very roads and colonnades of the city itself were sown in their place. Imperial Rome and Christianity were on a collision course. If the infant religion was to survive, it would have to learn to fight even before it had learned to walk. Words were all well and good, but they had not safeguarded Clement in his city. His pupil Origen and the young catechumens had seen just how little the masters of the world cared for philosophy. If Rome wanted a fight, they could have it.

CHAPTER FIFTEEN

INTO THE SOFT MACHINE

Our body is a machine for living. It is organised for that, it is its nature.

Leo Tolstoy, *War and Peace*

While the talk in the markets and shops of Alexandria was now more often than not centered on the subject of religion, that was not yet the overriding consideration for either the provincial government or the museum. Rome had more serious worries than the growth of Christianity that were even now pressing on her borders.

The second half of the second century saw the emergence of a new threat to the Roman world order, not from within but from without. The barbarian German tribes, along with their Sarmatian allies, were massing along the northeastern frontiers of the empire, along the east banks of the Danube and Rhine, and threatening to flood into the empire itself.

It is an irony of history that the first emperor who tried to contain the threat was also one of its most sophisticated intellectuals, a man better suited to the museum and library in Alexandria than to the wilds of his empire's frontiers. Marcus Aurelius (ruled 161–80) was also known as Marcus Aurelius Antoninus the Philosopher, and the collection of imperial biographies known as the *Historia Augusta* says that "Plato's judgement was always on his lips, that states flourished if philosophers ruled or rulers were philosophers" (Anonymous, *Historia Augusta*, 27.7).

Sadly for this frail and thoughtful emperor, his rule would seem to prove otherwise. On his accession Marcus Aurelius had immediately taken his adoptive brother Lucius Verus into the emperorship with him, for the first time splitting the primary role in the empire between two people. It was a move born out of pity more than practicality, granting the man who had always been in his shadow an equal position that, unfortunately, he was unequal to. The timing also could not have been worse. At the very moment the two men were taking the imperial throne, hostilities were already breaking out on the British frontier along Hadrian's Wall and along the Danube, while in the east the Parthians had seized the province of Armenia, destroying two whole Roman legions in the process. For the first time the empire appeared vulnerable, and Alexandrians, despite their chafing against Roman rule, must have prayed that their occupiers would prove up to the task of keeping the barbarians outside their protected and, as they saw it, civilized world.

Marcus Aurelius, for all his love of philosophy, could still prove a man of action. While choosing to tackle the Danube problem himself, he sent the dithering and indulgent Verus to deal with Parthia, along with his best general, Avidius Cassius. Avidius was also from an academic family, his father having been a rhetorician in Syria, but under Verus's nominal command he fortunately showed himself also to be a great soldier, restoring peace in the East. For this he was rewarded with supreme command over the entire region, including Egypt, the same post Mark Antony had held before him. And it was perhaps this unfortunate precedent that then began to work on his mind.

Verus, for his part, returned west with a less welcome trophy—soldiers infected by a plague which then swept the ancient world. At the same moment the barbarians beyond the Danube finally broke out and swarmed into the empire, reaching Italy itself. In a mad scramble Marcus Aurelius recruited two new legions and saved the situation, eventually agreeing to peace terms and managing to take back Italy. On his triumphant return to Rome, his co-emperor Verus died of apoplexy in 169, removing at least one threat to Marcus Aurelius's rule.

But the impenetrable facade of imperial might had been breached, and Egypt itself was encouraged to revolt. When Avidius Cassius quickly suppressed the rebellion, Marcus Aurelius must have believed he had finally found an ally he could trust. He was very wrong.

Avidius Cassius's experience of imperial rule in the form of an ineffectual co-emperor had given him unusual ambition. Now as virtual ruler of the East, the inheritor of Mark Antony's mantle and perhaps seduced by his dream, he struck. Hearing that Marcus Aurelius had been killed on the northern frontier (or at least claiming that to be the case), he proclaimed himself emperor, possibly encouraged in this by Marcus Aurelius's own wife, Faustina. Faustina had long despaired of her husband's frequent bouts of ill health, something which in these turbulent times she knew could have direct effects on her and her children. If her husband suddenly died there was no one to guarantee her safety, and any new imperial candidate would almost certainly begin his campaign to gain legitimacy by killing the true heirs—her children. Perhaps in Avidius she found a guarantor for her children, or at least saw the opportunity to force the hand of history. Whether Avidius knew he was bluffing when he announced the emperor's death is uncertain, although the *Historia Augusta* is suspicious.

Nevertheless, Avidius evidently persuaded several senior officials to back his claim to the laurels, and among these was the governor of Alexandria, Lucius Maecianus, who had once been Marcus Aurelius's tutor and who may have had ambitions of joint sovereignty with Avidius. Egypt and Alexandria stood once again on the brink of king making, but once again it would prove a false dawn.

Marcus Aurelius was not dead; indeed, he was marching back toward Rome, and from there he would perhaps sail across the Mediterranean to Egypt. Certainly the specter of this was enough to unnerve Avidius's soldiers, and his three-month-old "empire" dissolved as quickly as it had appeared. Fearing the emperor's retribution, one of Avidius's own centurions turned on him and stabbed him to death. The assassination of the governor of Alexandria was not far behind.

It was with some trepidation then that the people of Alexandria turned out to greet their emperor when he arrived in their city in the winter of 176. No place had been more closely connected with the usurper, and the emperor could hardly be expected to leave the city unscathed. Julius Caesar had burnt the city and very possibly the precious library when he had arrived to remove the upstart Mark Antony, and many must have feared a reprise.

But Marcus Aurelius did nothing. Certainly he shed some crocodile tears for the dead Avidius, just as Caesar had "wept" for the murdered

Pompey, protesting that he would have spared his life if only he had reached Egypt in time. The *Historia Augusta* says that on receiving Avidius's head the emperor

> *did not rejoice or exult, but rather was grieved that he had lost an opportunity for showing mercy; for he said that he had wished to take him alive, so that he might reproach him with the kindness he had shown him in the past, and then spare his life.*

Anonymous, *Historia Augusta,* chapter 8

It was, of course, a story Alexandrians had heard before, but provided he chose to play the victorious Octavian rather than the vengeful Caesar, they were happy to go along. And Marcus Aurelius had no desire to harm such a spiritual homeland. So instead of a bloodbath, the citizens of Alexandria enjoyed the company of their philosopher-emperor, and he in turn took delight in the open and vibrant civic life of the city as well as the intellectual life of the museum and library.

If the emperor needed a reason to preserve Alexandria he had only to walk through the gardens and lecture halls in the museum to find it, for this institution was still the training ground for some of the greatest minds in antiquity. One of those who had benefited from an education here was his personal physician and the greatest doctor in the Roman world, Galen.

Galen was born in Alexandria's great rival city of Pergamum around 129, about a century and a half after Mark Antony had bequeathed the city's two-hundred-thousand-volume library to his lover Cleopatra. Despite this loss, the city had thrived and become particularly famous for its temple and sanctuary of Asclepius, the Greek god of healing, where people from across the empire came to seek cures both through prayer and through the ministrations of the doctors who gathered there. Galen's father, Nicon, had been a successful and affluent architect, and he had given his son a broad classical education in mathematics, logic, grammar, and philosophy, embracing all four major schools—those of Plato and Aristotle as well as Stoicism and Epicureanism.

But it was to medicine that young Galen turned when he was just sixteen—according to legend, after his father had a dream revealing the youth's destiny in the subject. In years to come, as Galen went on to become the greatest doctor in the Roman world, many of his patients must have thought that the dream had been sent by Asclepius himself. Galen began his studies at the Asclepian shrine in Pergamum before traveling on to study under other masters in Smyrna (now Izmir in Turkey), then in Corinth, before finally reaching the great medical school at Alexandria in 152. Alexandria was still the obvious place to finish an education in medicine in the second century, not simply because of its great heritage of physicians and anatomists but because in Alexandria, thanks to its Egyptian heritage, it was still possible to do there what could not be done elsewhere: dissect the human body. Such procedures were still taboo across most of the empire, and without a chance to look inside the body, most doctors were forced to rely on outward symptoms both to identify and to cure an ill. But here, Galen tells us, you could "look at the human skeleton with your own eyes. This is very easy in Alexandria, so that the physicians of that area instruct their pupils with the aid of autopsy" (Galen, quoted in translation by Kühn, vol. 2, p. 220).

These experiences gave Galen a passion for dissection, which would both make and, many centuries later, break his reputation. By opening human bodies, both living and dead, he was able to view the body as a machine, like one of Hero's automatons, and brilliantly deduce its functions. In his later career he would repeat his investigations on animals in front of astounded crowds, while he challenged the other doctors of the empire to disagree with his findings. A particularly famous experiment involved a rather gruesome operation on a live pig. Cutting an incision down its back, he would slowly sever groups of spinal nerves to show their function. Of course all the while the pig would squeal, until he tied off the laryngeal nerve and the pig suddenly stopped. And so he proceeded, removing or tying off various vital pathways and identifying their purpose from the effect. He tied off animals' ureters to demonstrate kidney and bladder function, and closed off veins and arteries to prove that, contrary to the popular theory of the day, they carried blood and not air.

On the basis of remarks made in Plato's *Laws*, it seems that prior to Galen the medical system in the Hellenistic world was two tiered. Physicians for the wealthy treated their patients in accordance with theoretical principles (they were known as Dogmatists). Physicians for slaves relied upon trial and error, and were known as Empiricists. Detractors claimed that the Dogmatists honored theory above observation and experience. Between these two extremes were the Methodists, whose sole concern was the disease itself, ignoring the patient, his or her medical history, and so on. Galen claimed to belong to none of these schools, though we know that he was certainly educated in the Dogmatic school and practiced both Empirically and Methodically. He recognized that it was necessary both to develop theories from practical observation and experience, and to test existing theory against observations, modifying or abandoning it if it seemed not to work.

Much of Galen's theory was based on the teachings of Hippocrates, the Greek "Father of Medicine." Hippocrates held that the human body was controlled by four humors: phlegm, blood, black bile, and yellow bile. Each humor was also related to parts of the body: head (phlegm), heart (blood), liver (black bile), and gallbladder (yellow bile). Imbalance in these four basic humors caused illness, and it was the job of the physician to right this balance. From Plato, Galen also employed the four-element theory (earth, air, water, fire) and the theory of contraries (hot/cold, wet/dry). Like the four elements, humors were characterized by two qualities. The earth was considered the heaviest of elements, and black bile, with its coldness and dryness, was seen as the heaviest of the humors, an excess of which caused melancholy. Blood (like air) had the qualities of heat and moisture, phlegm (like water) had coldness and moisture, and yellow bile (like fire) had heat and dryness. He then formulated an almost quantitative scale of admixture of such things, which he wrote up in a book called *On Mixtures*. So if a person was suffering from a cold, wet condition, such as a chest infection, he should be treated with a hot and dry drug, such as certain molds and fungi (penicillin, perhaps?). While Western medicine may have moved away from such elemental concepts (we should note that much Indian and Chinese medicine has not), what Galen was doing was making the task of diagnosis and treatment multidimensional, looking at both the illness and the cure from multiple perspectives. He himself acknowledged his eclectic, pluralist approach, and this is perhaps Galen's most enduring contribution to the history of medicine.

Inspired by this theoretical grounding and the anatomical mysteries he witnessed in Alexandria, Galen returned to his native Pergamum to begin his medical practice. Pergamum would prove a difficult place for him to work, however, as it did not allow its doctors to dissect human bodies. Fortunately, an official appointment came up that suited him perfectly—as physician to the gladiators.

Gladiatorial combat was a standard entertainment in the Roman world and was not always the deadly spectacle it is imagined to be. Gladiators were the football superstars of their day, the subject of adulatory graffiti in public baths and the pinups of young girls everywhere. A good gladiator, although a slave, was worth a fortune to his owner and hoped to win one day the "wooden sword" that would mark his retirement and freedom. So he would be attended on by the best physicians his master could afford—the sports physiotherapists of their day, whose job it was to keep the gladiator healthy and fighting.

Although Galen could not dissect criminals or corpses, he could use the skills he had learned in the Alexandrian anatomy theaters to cure the gladiators' often horrific wounds. Provided it was a gladiator who made the incision in the arena and not a doctor on the operating table, no one complained if he then used these wounds—or "windows onto anatomy" as he called them—to explore the inner workings of the body. At the same time he also pioneered the treatment of the more usual sports injuries—sprains, breaks, dislocations, and concussions. From these he developed 130 of the 150 basic surgical techniques that are still in use today—everything from brain surgery to repairing compressed fractures to the use of traction beds to straighten broken limbs. Even at the end of a gladiator's career there was one last procedure that Galen developed that would assist his patient in his new life as a free man: the removal of the tattoo that marked him as a slave.

It was not long before it became clear that Pergamum was too small a world for such a great doctor, and five years after his return there from Alexandria, he moved to Rome. Here he found medicine in a similarly primitive state, held back by its taboos against Alexandrian anatomy. The Roman poet Martial noted ironically: "Until recently, Diaulus was a doctor; now he is an undertaker. He is still doing as an undertaker, what he used to do as a doctor" (Martial, *Epigrams,* book 1.47).

Not surprisingly then this new doctor from the East dazzled the court, and as a superb self-publicist, Galen took every opportunity to put his rivals in the shade. One such occasion was provided by the arrival of a Persian merchant complaining of a loss of feeling in the ring and little fingers and half the middle finger of one hand. For some time Roman doctors had been applying unguents and creams to the fingers in the hope of stimulating them, but to no effect. Galen asked him an unusual question: Had he hurt his arm recently?

The question must have been quite surprising. The man's problem was clearly in his fingers. What did that have to do with his arm? But Galen was right. The man said he had taken a bad fall and hurt his back. Galen diagnosed a spinal lesion and recommended bed rest and soothing compresses for the injury site. It worked, and the man's fingers recovered. It may sound like a small thing, numb fingers, but in curing them Galen was laying the foundations of modern neurology.

Such demonstrations made Galen famous, while his arrogance, his outspoken attacks on his detractors, and his withering humiliation of less successful doctors made him many enemies. Galen was not a modest man, and in later life he would happily compare himself to a Roman emperor: "I have done as much for medicine as the Emperor Trajan did for the Roman Empire when he built bridges and roads through Italy. It is I, and I alone who have revealed the true path of medicine" (Galen, quoted in F. Marti-Ibanez, *The Epic of Medicine*, p. 93).

In 166, sensing a plot by his powerful enemies, Galen slipped secretly out of the city in the nick of time. Though he claimed the plot as the reason for his abrupt exit, an impending outbreak of the plague, which he had successfully identified, may have been the more compelling motive.

However, after a couple of years in obscurity he was recalled to Rome by none other than the emperors Marcus Aurelius and Lucius Verus, who asked him to accompany them on a military expedition against the invading barbarians. Galen was to be their personal physician. Some scholars claim that he turned down the offer to be imperial physician on the campaign, but either way a year or so later he was made personal physician to Marcus Aurelius, and this brought him back to the city of his training with his grateful rather than vengeful master.

During Marcus Aurelius's reign there were huge improvements in medical care in the army, and Galen must have had a hand in many of these. To keep their troops fit they built military hospitals. Tucked away in the corner of the fort, away from the noise and bustle of the army, such a hospital was a very modern-looking institution. Passing through the wide gatehouse, a patient would enter the first wing of a square building constructed around a wide courtyard. Ahead was a light, spacious ward where new arrivals waited. Beyond was the operating theater, projecting out into the courtyard to allow the maximum amount of light for the surgeons. At the hospital in Neuss, in modern Germany, raised hearths were even found in the operating theater. These were probably where the surgical tools were sterilized in the fire before use—just as Galen had suggested.

In one corner stood a complex of baths with a block of flushing toilets attached—hygiene was very important to doctors like Galen. In another stood the kitchens where the healthy balanced diets required by convalescing patients were prepared. In other wings lay a series of small wards designed to reduce the risk of cross-infection, consulting rooms, a dispensary, and—for the unfortunates that even a man as great as Galen couldn't save—a mortuary.

We know so much of Galen's work because, like the true Alexandrian scholar he was, he wrote prolifically. Although much has been lost, the definitive modern edition of his work, edited by K. G. Kühn, still runs to over twenty thousand pages. In these volumes he describes not only surgical procedures such as the removal of cataracts and the making of false teeth but the correct tools with which to perform operations. Galen was very particular that his instruments should be made with iron from Noricum, which could be made into what was basically surgical steel, and his bag contained the catheters, hooks, probes, needles, bone chisels, dilators, and forceps familiar to any modern surgeon. He also hypothesized about the cause of illnesses, particularly those contagious diseases such as the plague he witnessed tearing through the troops on Verus's return from Parthia. Though as late as the eighteenth century many thought the cause was "polluted air" or some evil miasma, Galen reasoned that there were tiny particles, or "bad seeds" as he called them, so small they could not be seen, which carried infection. He could not have seen them—

there were no microscopes in the ancient world—but using logic he inferred their existence. And he was absolutely right.

Galen lived to serve another two emperors after Marcus Aurelius, dying at the great age of eighty-seven. He was clearly a doctor who took his own medical advice. Because of his insufferable arrogance he was not popular, and few mourned his passing—indeed, not a single statue was ever known to have been erected to him. His works, however, achieved wide circulation and were still being taught in Alexandria in 500, although they largely disappeared with the demise of the classical world. But they were rediscovered by the Arab Renaissance in the ninth century. From the late eleventh century the Arabic versions of his works were then translated into Latin and rapidly became the core teaching materials in the medical schools of medieval universities all over Europe.

Galen's undoing came in 1543, at the hands of the Flemish anatomist Andreas Vesalius. As much of Galen's later work had been carried out in Rome, a city where human dissection was forbidden, he had been forced to use animals to study anatomy. When Vesalius, who had free access to human cadavers, compared what he saw in the anatomy theater with what was written in Galen, he realized that much of Galen's work was simply wrong. The inside of a dog, or even the inside of his preferred Barbary apes, was not the same as the inside of a human. So Galen was abandoned, and even his most insightful works forgotten. What Alexandrian inquiry had made, Roman taboos had broken. Suddenly his own boast seemed rather hollow: "Whoever seeks fame need only become familiar with all that I have achieved" (Galen, quoted in F. Marti-Ibanez, *The Epic of Medicine*, p. 92).

Galen and Claudius Ptolemy were the two great scientific comets blazing their way across the star-studded cosmos of second-century Alexandria, but there was a third figure, altogether darker and more mysterious but no less influential on the modern world.

Alchemy was a subject largely scorned and dismissed by modern scientists until the great economist John Maynard Keynes bought a box full of papers in 1936 at an auction at Sotheby's in London. The papers dismissed as of "no scientific value" when offered to Cambridge University fifty years earlier had been written by none other than Sir Isaac Newton. They were almost all concerned with his lifetime passion for alchemy, and they so amazed Keynes that he felt it necessary to entirely redraw the established view of who Newton was and how his mind worked. In 1942 Keynes addressed a distinguished group of members of the Royal Society:

> *Newton was not the first of the age of reason. He was the last of the magicians, the last of the Babylonians and Sumerians, the last great mind which looked out on the visible and intellectual world with the same eyes as those who began to build our intellectual inheritance rather less than 10,000 years ago. Isaac Newton, a posthumous child born with no father on Christmas Day, 1642, was the last wonder-child to whom the Magi could do sincere and appropriate homage.*

> John Maynard Keynes, "Newton the Man"

And where did Newton get his alchemy from? Why, Alexandria of course.

The roots of alchemy lie in the origins of metallurgy, in the discovery that by applying intense heat to specific rocks they can be purified and transformed into metal. From the very start this process acquired occult or secret status, and the objects produced by this sacred craft—ornaments, jewelry, and currency from gold and silver; weapons and tools from copper, its alloys, and iron—were always given high prestige and value. It's clear from ancient texts that iron especially had divine qualities: The Egyptians called it the "metal from heaven"; the Babylonians, "celestial fire." These and other sources make it seem likely that people first encountered iron as meteorites which had fallen from heaven to earth. When they later discovered the same metal underground, inside the womb of Mother Earth, it must have seemed like confirmation of the metal's divine status.

This notion of "Mother Earth" was the starting point for the alchemists. The first smiths and metallurgists were either farmers or pastoralists, both depending for their sustenance on the fecundity of the surface of the earth. When people began to extract both metals and precious stones from within the earth, from the womb of Mother Earth, they attributed life, or at least evolution, to the materials they extracted, albeit at a very different pace from the beings living on the surface. If left to gestate slowly in the womb of Mother Earth, rocks would gradually evolve into precious stones (for example, quartz was considered to be a juvenile, "soft" form of diamond). Likewise lead, if left in Mother Earth's womb, would eventually transform itself into gold, and copper would develop into iron. It was therefore the task of the early smiths and forgers to accelerate this natural process of gestation by purifying metal ores through the application of heat. The alchemist's task, however, was to transform, by secret occult means, the base materials from one form to the next on the scale of metallic evolution.

There are close parallels between Egyptian beliefs and practices concerning death and the afterlife and the theory and practice of alchemy that developed in the medieval world. More specifically, the Egyptian Book of the Dead offers precise prescriptions for the transfer of the human soul from life to death and then to rebirth in immortal form which are extremely close to the prescriptions adopted by alchemists. No great surprise, then, that all this occult knowledge and wisdom should come to Alexandria, where it would be systematically codified into a set of mystical beliefs and procedures recognizable by the likes of Isaac Newton some 1,500 years later.

The person (or persons) responsible for the Alexandrian alchemical canon is, without doubt, the most mysterious figure we shall encounter in the whole of the history of Alexandria. The canon itself is a collection of works purporting to contain secret wisdom and known collectively as the *Hermetica* (though the collecting was performed by a group of Italian scholars during the Renaissance). The majority of the works are concerned with alchemy and magic, and are written in Greek, though there are also extant Hermetic works in Syriac, Arabic, Armenian, Coptic, and other languages. From the language of the Greek versions it seems likely that they were written in the second to third century AD, though some scholars place them as early as the first century AD. The author names himself (or herself) as Hermes Trismegistus, that is, "Hermes, the thrice great." Hermes is the Greek name for the god of wisdom, Thoth in Egyptian.

Not just the god of wisdom and alchemy, Thoth also invented writing, mathematics, music, sculpture, and astrology, so he was a crucial deity in the Egyptian pantheon, and there is some evidence that these works attributed to his earthly incarnation may be expressions of the Egyptian population of Alexandria. Though mostly written in Greek, some of their contents are clearly anti-Greek and anti-Roman, and, curiously, the texts are almost never mentioned by the Alexandrian philosophers, even though they are frequently quoted by almost every other available doctrinal source. They frequently assert the superiority of the Egyptian language, and one work, the *Asclepius,* prophesies that there will be a bloody expulsion of "foreigners" from Egypt. Overall, then, it seems that these alchemical outpourings may well be the authentic voice of the ancient Egyptians, beset as they were at the time by the baying of the Romans and Greeks, the Christians and Gnostics, and all the other new cults which were thriving in Alexandria at the time.

Though we tend to think of alchemy as a quick, base-metal-to-gold, rags-to-riches fix, its practice, at least as expounded in Alexandria by Hermes Trismegistus, was far deeper and more complex than that. It involved in essence the transformation of the body into spirit in the quest for immortality. To acquire the ability to transform base metal into gold, the initiates would have to transform not just metals but themselves as well. They had to undergo an inner death and resurrection, a "baptism of fire," holding out the prospect of rebirth into immortality. Alchemical initiation was a reduction of the self to *Materia Prima,* the fluid, shapeless fundamental state of chaos, a time of darkness and night, symbolically corresponding to the meltdown of metals from solid to liquid form. Rebirth meant entering the cosmic creation, being admitted, as it were, to the "high church" of the scholar/philosopher/mystic as the *Filius Philosophorum,* son of the lovers of wisdom. These profound transformational processes guided the techniques and symbolism of the alchemist.

Thus the first stage of the alchemical process was colored black, for the descent into darkness and primordial chaos of the underworld. The second stage produced its opposite, the color white, symbolizing purity, the quality metal attains at white-hot temperatures. The third stage was golden, an enrichment and ascent to the sun. The final stage was the blood-red of vitality after rebirth here on this earth. In this way the alchemist was taken into the cosmos. This is Hermes Trismegistus's "fourfold way," best articulated in the *Emerald Tablet,* an obscure text first recorded around 800, which claimed to reveal the secrets of primordial substance and its transmutations. From this first version the short work appears to have been added to the twelfth-century *Secret of Secrets* by John of Seville, eventually finding its way into Renaissance texts and hence to Isaac Newton's laboratory, where he penned his own translation. In this he summed up the value of the occult way as he saw it: "By this means you shall have ye glory of ye whole world & thereby all obscurity shall fly from you" (Hermes Trismegistus, *Emerald Tablet,* trans. Isaac Newton).

This was the promise that so attracted Isaac Newton. He knew perfectly well that all this talk of transforming metals was just a facade, even a cover, for a far more profound spiritual awakening: "For alchemy does not trade with metals as ignorant vulgars think, which error has made them distress that noble science, but she has also material veins of whose nature God created handmaidens to conceive and bring forth its creatures" (Isaac Newton, *Alchemical Notes,* in KCL Keynes MS 33, fol. 5v). A more perfectly Alexandrian set of precepts is hard to imagine.

Newton was one of the first great men of science, but few realize that his occult work, his alchemical studies, gave him the keys to the biggest breakthrough in his life. Alchemy insists that there are unseen, invisible forces at work in the universe, capable of acting on objects at a distance. An apple may (or may not) have dropped on Newton's head, but beyond a shadow of a doubt, it was alchemy which prompted Newton to formulate the notion of gravity—alchemy which had been rendered into a coherent and communicable, if secret, code in Alexandria.

Alchemical writings continued to emerge from Alexandria and elsewhere in Egypt, in various scripts, long after the departure of the Romans and the fall of the Greek-dominated city, suggesting that as a cult it was indeed native to the peoples of Egypt.

Trismegistus not only foresaw the expulsion of the "foreigner" but also the demise of Egypt and the fall of the "temple of the world." He foresaw the faith of the worshippers failing and the gods leaving the earth and retreating to heaven. But he tells us the situation is never hopeless, and, as everything changes and reforms, so this great deterioration will be followed by a sudden resurgence, a rebirth that "will bring back the

238 THE RISE AND FALL OF ALEXANDRIA

world to its first beauty, so that this world may again be worthy of reverence and admiration, and so that God also, creator and restorer of so great a work, may be glorified by the people of that time in continual hymns of praise and blessing" (Hermes Trismegistus, *Hermetica*, 16).

At the beginning of the third century, it must have seemed to many Alexandrians that the apocalyptic moment of destruction which Hermes Trismegistus had prophesied had arrived, though the purveyor of the calamity was not a god but a vicious Roman emperor.

CHAPTER SIXTEEN

THE ASCENDANCY OF FAITH

All good moral philosophy is but a handmaid to religion.

Francis Bacon, *The Advancement of Learning*

After Marcus Aurelius's successful visit to Alexandria there were many in the city who believed that relations with their Roman masters were restored, and this view was endorsed when all Egyptian cities were granted a municipal council by Emperor Septimius Severus in 200. But if the people of the city believed they had woken from the rebellion of Avidius Cassius into a new Roman dawn, it was to prove a false one. Alexandria was used to speaking its mind, and Rome did not always like what it heard.

Septimius Severus had two sons, and it was his wish that both should succeed him on the imperial throne. Though the two boys, Aurelius Antoninus and Geta, were only eleven months different in age, they loathed each other from early childhood. To try to generate some rapprochement between the two, the aging Septimius took them off to Britain, where he placed his younger son, Geta, in charge of civil affairs while Aurelius Antoninus commanded the army in their campaigns against the northern barbarians. It was here that Antoninus got the nickname by which he would be remembered from thenceforth—Caracalla, from the hooded Gallic tunic, or *caracallus,* that he always wore.

After two years in Britain, on February 4, 211, Septimius died at York, and the two boys were declared joint emperors. They determined to return immediately to Rome to arrange their father's funeral, but such was their mutual antagonism that during the entire journey back they never traveled or ate together, and they slept every night in separate houses.

Back in Rome the imperial palace was split in half, doors were sealed, and guards were mounted at every entrance, as if each half of the building was under siege. The only hope of resolving the latent civil war lay with the two boys' mother, Julia Domna, a formidable woman who was renowned for her coteries of learned men, including Galen. Edward Gibbon, the famed eighteenth-century classicist, is full of praise:

> She possessed, even in old age, the attractions of beauty, and united to a lively imagination a firmness and strength of judgement seldom bestowed on her sex. . . . In her son's reign she administered the principal affairs of state of the empire with a prudence that supported his authority and with a moderation which sometimes corrected his wild extravagances. Julia applied herself to letters and philosophy, with some success and with the most splendid reputation. She was the patroness of every art and the friend of every man of genius.
>
> Edward Gibbon, The Decline and Fall of the
> Roman Empire, volume 1, chapter 6

That is not to say, however, that the somewhat prudish Gibbon found her character to be faultless. The more salacious ancient sources also suggest that Julia enjoyed more than just mental stimulation from the men around her, and Gibbon was forced to rather elliptically point out that if those sources were true, then chastity was "very far from being the most conspicuous virtue of the empress Julia" (Edward Gibbon, The Decline and Fall of the Roman Empire, volume 1, chapter 6).

Naturally it fell upon Julia to attempt to resolve her sons' differences. She convinced Caracalla to meet with his brother in her apartments to attempt a reconciliation. But the minute Geta entered the room he was set upon by a troop of Caracalla's men. According to the contemporary chronicler Cassius Dio, Geta died in his mother's arms while his faithless brother ran, blood-soaked, to the camp of the Praetorian Guard, pretending he had escaped an ambush aimed at assassinating both of them.

Now absolute ruler of the Roman Empire, Caracalla soon showed his true colors. There followed an appalling bloodletting in Rome in which all of Geta's supporters and their families—men, women, and children— were slaughtered, one contemporary observer putting the figure at twenty thousand dead. It was also rapidly becoming clear that the emperor's megalomania would allow for no criticism. Anyone who dared to offer a different opinion, from senators down to the charioteer Euprepes, who "showed enthusiasm for a cause that the Emperor opposed" (Cassius Dio, *Roman History,* book 77, chapter 1), was summarily executed.

This alone should have been warning enough to the outspoken Alexandrians, but already growing in the emperor's mind was an idea that would have far worse consequences for them. Caracalla was rapidly coming to the belief that he was the new Alexander, destined to recapture the Macedonian's empire in the East. According to Cassius Dio, he carried with him items that were said to have belonged to Alexander, including his personal weapons and the cups he was supposed to have drunk from. He created a new army unit, a traditional phalanx made up of sixteen thousand Macedonian soldiers, which he armed with period weapons already half a millennium out of date. From his reading of the histories of Alexander he had also come to believe that Aristotle had taken a part in his hero's murder, so Caracalla persecuted Aristotelian philosophers, arguing that their books should be burned and ordering the abolition of their communal dining room in the museum in Alexandria.

But it was when the emperor arrived in Alexandria in person that its citizens realized just what they had to fear from a man who considered himself the heir of their founder's destiny. At the time, certain Alexandrian satires appear to have been in circulation that criticized the murder of Geta and lambasted the emperor's claims to be another Alexander. In response he decided to visit the city in the winter of 215–16. His mission was ostensibly intellectual and religious, as Caracalla had a passion for religious institutions, having already stayed at the famous temple of Asclepius in Pergamum, where Galen trained, and received all the holy rites there. According to Cassius Dio, however, this was just a subterfuge. When Caracalla reached the suburbs he stopped and waited for the leading citizens of the city to come to meet him, as was customary. This they did, bringing with them the sacred symbols of the city and their offices. The emperor, in apparently jovial spirits, met them and led them to believe that they would enjoy a banquet and entertainments with the royal retinue before proceeding into the city. When they were thus put off their guard, he had them all slaughtered.

The emperor then marched into the city, taking up residence in the Serapeum and attending the temple's sacrifices and other rites. As he considered himself both a deeply religious man and a scholar, he doubtless also took advantage of the extensive library housed in this temple, although we cannot imagine that any Aristotelian texts housed there fared well. But if Caracalla hoped the chastised inhabitants of the city would now take him as their new Alexander, he was badly mistaken. Sporadic rioting seems to have erupted in the city, and rumors flew around town that the emperor intended to marry his mother, Julia—an idea Caracalla perhaps thought Egyptians would appreciate. Instead, it was whispered that he was Oedipus and his mother, Jocasta. Incestuous marriage might have been allowable among divine pharaohs, but in Roman emperors it was laughable.

Revenge was swift. Caracalla ordered all the young men of the city arrested, regardless of their race or creed. He then unleashed upon the city his army, which set to looting and pillaging. Next he had the city cordoned off into zones to prevent freedom of movement, and suspended the local games, abolished all the communal messes of the museum, and revoked all Roman privileges. Finally he gave the order which would scar the city's life for generations to come so that no one would forget what they called "the fury of Caracalla." The young men seized during the looting were taken to the city walls and systematically slaughtered. Within a few hours the flower of Alexandria's youth, some twenty-five thousand young men, lay dead. And then as a last tilt at his tormentors Caracalla had the governor of the city publicly executed.

Fortunately, Caracalla's reign of terror was not to last, and ironically, this ruthless emperor would meet his end pursuing yet another act of religious devotion. According to the colorful but not overly reliable *Historia Augusta,* in the spring of 217 he set off to make a visit to the temple of the moon god at Carrhae accompanied only by a select corps of bodyguards. On his way back he stopped to defecate, and at that moment a bodyguard named Martialis struck him down, only to be killed moments later by a loyal Scythian archer. The emperor died quickly. The scars he inflicted on Alexandria would take longer to heal.

Caracalla had certainly taught the Alexandrians a lesson they would never forget, but if he thought he had cowed them into silent submission in the process he was very wrong. From then on the city would be a focus of discontent and rebellion, and thus an almost irresistible magnet for rebellious generals and would-be emperors, who would be welcomed into the city with open arms.

It is uncertain just what effect the "fury of Caracalla" had on the museum and library beyond the statement in Cassius Dio that the emperor abolished the "communal messes" of the Alexandrians (Cassius Dio, *Roman History,* book 77, chapter 23). This may refer simply to the dining clubs in the city, but may also refer to the communal dining halls of the museum where the scholars, who held everything in common, ate together. Considering his loathing of the Aristotelians, this is not unlikely.

Academic life in the city was clearly not extinguished, however, as the few details we have of one of the great mathematicians of this era confirm. Diophantus of Alexandria, a Hellenized Babylonian, was probably just a child at the time of the fury, but he survived it, and went on to master enough of the knowledge left in the museum for him to become one of the greatest mathematicians of his or any age. By adapting Babylonian techniques and concentrating on arithmetic rather than geometry he invented a whole new area of mathematics, where numbers were replaced with symbols, allowing problems to be solved for any number, not just specific instances. As such he has become known as the "Father of Algebra," the originator of the hugely complex collections of Greek letters and symbols which fill the blackboards of modern mathematicians and the exercise books of their often baffled students. Indeed, it was his book the *Arithmetica,* a collection of 130 problems and their various solutions, that inspired one of the most complicated pieces of mathematical research of all time. When the great seventeenth-century mathematician Pierre de Fermat wrote in the margins of his copy of the *Arithmetica* that he had discovered a remarkable proof of a theorem suggested by Diophantus, he also noted that he hadn't the space to prove it there. Sadly, he never found time to write it out anywhere else either, setting off a 357-year mathematical search for the proof to what became known as "Fermat's Last Theorem." The problem, originated in the second century and formulated in the seventeenth, was not finally published until

1995, in a paper so complex that most modern mathematicians still don't fully understand it.

Nor was this the only riddle Diophantus left behind. As with so many Alexandrians, it can be painfully difficult to extract personal details from his work, but the Father of Algebra did leave us his own mathematical clues. His epitaph, describing his life, is itself an algebraic problem:

> *This tomb holds Diophantus. Ah, what a marvel! And the tomb tells scientifically the measure of his life. God vouchsafed that he should be a boy for the sixth part of his life; when a twelfth was added, his cheeks acquired a beard; He kindled for him the light of marriage after a seventh, and in the fifth year after his marriage He granted him a son. Alas! Late-begotten and miserable child, when he had reached the measure of half his father's life, the chill grave took him. After consoling his grief by this science of numbers four years, he reached the end of his life.*

Epitaph recorded in W. Gunnyon, *A Century of Translations from the Greek Anthology,* chapter 14, no. 126

Those with mathematical talents can rewrite the above as two equations which can be solved simultaneously to discover something of Diophantus's life. From this we learn that his boyhood lasted fourteen years, he entered his majority at twenty-one, was married at thirty-three, and had a son at thirty-eight. His son died aged forty-two while Diophantus lived on into great old age, dying four years later aged eighty-four.

Diophantus's biographical riddles may have illuminated the twilight of Alexandrian mathematics, but it was the spiritual investigations of the Alexandrians of this turbulent age that were now having the most profound effect not just on their city, but on the world as a whole. Uncertain times drive many to question the nature of the world and the motives of the gods, or even their very existence. Any Alexandrian street philosopher could have told you that Caracalla wasn't divine, but the question as to what *was* divine increasingly vexed the inhabitants of the museum. Strangely, for both the main schools of thought that would fight for supremacy in the city's final days, the answer came not from the porticoes of the library, but from the waterfront.

The somewhat unlikely father of this process was a man named Ammonius Saccas. Born into a very poor family, he may initially have had a Christian upbringing in the institution which preceded Pantaenus's catechetical school. After school Ammonius went to work on the Alexandrian harbor front as a porter or sack bearer, hence his second name—Saccas. There he enjoyed a second education, talking to the traders and captains with their travelers' tales of distant lands, surprising customs, and alien religions. For anyone who wanted to learn of the world, these wharves and quays were a university in themselves, a gathering together of people and goods from the whole known world, the most cosmopolitan place on earth. It was a setting to get anyone thinking, and that's exactly what Ammonius Saccas did, both on the dockside and in the public lectures in the pagan philosophy schools which he attended after work.

Ammonius was not content to follow any one school of thought, however, but was all the time developing his own theories. Indeed, so deeply did he think about what he heard during the days that, it was said, these ideas followed him into his dreams at night, and during these dreams he found his insights. That was how he came to be known as *theodidactos*, or "God-taught," though he referred to himself as merely a *philolethian*, a "lover of the truth."

At some point in the early third century, perhaps even during the upheavals of the fury, Ammonius set up his own school of philosophy. He taught only orally, and like Pythagoras, he bound his advanced students with a vow of secrecy, so it is difficult to discover what his actual philosophy was. There is a further complication in understanding Ammonius, in that he was formally adopted as the founder of Theosophy by the spiritualist medium H. P. Blavatsky when she founded the Theosophical Society in 1875. This led to an enormous amount of speculation about Ammonius's life and thoughts and a considerable attribution of eccentric Victorian quasi-religious ideas about universal brotherhoods and the like to Ammonius, with virtually no evidence to support it.

However, the pupils that Ammonius attracted do throw some light on the man and his ideas. Two of these pupils would go on to become the most influential thinkers and authors of the third century. From them we learn that Ammonius was very selective in allowing pupils to attend his school, taking on only a few pupils every year. His pupils were initially divided into three groups—novices, initiates, and masters—and he divided his teachings into two sections, the exoteric and the esoteric. This division was very widespread at the time and can be traced to many early philosophers, including Pythagoras. The exoteric teachings were openly available to all and were characteristically ethical, like the ones Ammonius himself attended as a young man. These were the lectures that the public could attend. The esoteric or "greater" mysteries were different. These were taught in private and were reserved for the fully trained and dedicated few.

Here Ammonius's pupils learned of his notion of absolute deity, utterly transcendent and indescribable, something that both Christ and Plato could agree upon. He believed that the human soul was an immortal radiation from the universal soul or ether, and that gave every individual the possibility of experiencing divinity. But he also considered that there was a universal ethical basis within all metaphysical systems, and that in essence *all* philosophies and religions shared this universal ethical and spiritual foundation. In short, therefore, there was no underlying conflict between the philosophies of Plato and Aristotle, and even Christ's teaching could be seen as an authentic expression of the timeless wisdom. In this way his views came to be known as "eclectic," capable of embracing all religious and philosophical systems.

Ammonius also posited that the best way to understand all sacred myths, legends, and mysteries was to interpret them by analogy, seeking correspondences between them and thus revealing the universality of their content. In this he is, of course, methodologically aligned with his illustrious Jewish predecessor, Philo. As his most able students began to employ these ideas, they became known as "Analogeticists."

The broad base of Ammonius's philosophy attracted students from a wide range of philosophical backgrounds, and among the most able of those were two young men who between them would describe the shape of Alexandria's last years. The first of these was a Greek speaker with a Roman name who was probably born in Egypt in 205—Plotinus.

Because Ammonius himself left no written testimony, the title of "founder" of the pagan movement that became known as Neoplatonism is usually given to Plotinus, although his own ideas were certainly born out of what he heard from Ammonius in those secret lectures. Neoplatonism was not merely a revival of Plato's teaching, but a whole new interpretation and development of his philosophy, as closely related to the original as, say, Protestantism is to Catholicism. Plotinus's philosophical ideas began with his physical being, and they were none too flattering. Recalling that in Plato's cosmos the waking, conscious world of humans and nature was the most debased and corrupted level of existence, he took the idea much more personally. He could hardly bear the thought that his soul was trapped in so base a thing as his body, which he sometimes called a "detestable vessel," one which acted as an obstacle to spiritual development. He insisted that "to rise up to very truth is altogether to depart from bodies. Corporeality is contrary to soul and essentially opposed to soul" (Plotinus, *Enneads,* 3, 6.6).

In a similar ascetic vein he refused to reveal his birthday, as he did not wish his friends to celebrate it, avoided eating meat, and took a daily massage instead of indulging in the rather Roman luxury of bathing. When a pupil, friend, and physician suggested he sit for a portrait, he castigated the unfortunate doctor, roaring that surely it was bad enough to be entrapped in the form in which nature had cast him without making an image of that image, as if that would be something worth staring upon.

Much of this idea of self must have come from the diminutive Alexandrian porter whom Plotinus first met when, at twenty-seven, he came to Alexandria in search of a philosophy teacher. At first he was depressed and disappointed with the offerings in the public lecture halls, until a friend mentioned Ammonius. They went to one of his lectures, after which Plotinus exclaimed, "This was the man I was looking for" (Porphyry, *Introduction to Plotinus*).

He stayed with Ammonius for eleven years, then decided he would travel to the East in search of the philosophies of the Persians, Chaldeans, and Indians. To this end he got himself attached to the army of the Roman emperor Gordian III, which was intent on invading Persia. However, Gordian was assassinated before he reached his destination and Plotinus found himself abandoned in the wilderness. It took him the best part of two years to make his way back to Antioch, and from there he took a ship to Rome, where he lived the rest of his life. He never returned to the city that had nurtured his dream.

In Rome Plotinus quickly became something of a star, commanding the respect of the emperor and his wife, along with many prominent citizens, particularly some of the more important and influential women. So deeply was he revered that several families decided to endow him with property and income in exchange for educating their children, so his house became full of young boys and girls who mixed with senators and foreign students—even Alexandrians—who had become his pupils.

One of his most able students was Malchus of Tyros, who was known in Rome as Porphyry, a humorous allusion to the purple robes of the emperor. It was he who eventually persuaded his master that for posterity's sake he must break with Ammonius's injunction never to write down the secrets of his philosophy, and commit his teachings to paper. So from about the age of fifty Plotinus started to record his ideas, his dialogues with his students, and his lecture notes. But he was not a patient scribe. His handwriting was tiny and very untidy, and he cared not a jot for spelling. Fortunately for us, Porphyry was the soul of patience and tact, and he both copied and edited Plotinus's meanderings, later completing the work and considerably reordering it, as well as writing a biography of his master, before the work was finally published under the title of the *Enneads,* meaning "Groups of Nine"—each book consisting of nine discussions.

In the *Enneads* we can look into the mind of the last great pagan philosopher of antiquity. Plotinus's universe is, broadly speaking, of a similar structure to Plato's, graded in the Great Chain of Being from the divine to the mundane, from the eternal to the mortal, from God the One to nature, matter, and the observed world.

At the top of this hierarchy is the One, beyond all categories of being and nonbeing. It is totally indivisible and even unthinkable. It is both self-caused and the cause of everything else in the universe. Thought cannot be applied to the One, as that would imply a distinction between the thinker and the object being thought of. The One is both thinker and thought. The One is the source of the world, not through any act of creation, though, as activity cannot be ascribed to this unchangeable idea. From this One then come "emanations" which are, of necessity, less perfect than the One, and which make up our universe.

The first of these is Thought or Intellect (*Nous*). Intellect is the home of all of Plato's forms, the repository of the cognitive identity of all things and the way we recognize things to be as they are, by perceiving them in ideal type. Intellect thus provides the principle or essence of all things. And from Intellect emanates the Soul.

Soul is related by analogy to Intellect in the same way that Intellect is related to the One; that is, put crudely, Intellect is the sum of all the Souls in existence. Beneath Soul is mere matter, the stuff of the universe, including our own bodies, which Plotinus so despised.

With respect to Soul, Plotinus departs from Plato by splitting it in two. His view is that in all things, and especially people, there is an upper Soul, which remains pure, divine, and untarnished eternally; and there is a lower Soul, which, though it is actually divine, may become tarnished and forget its divine origin as it provides the motivation for material beings (in our own cases our bodies) to find their way through the trials of a conscious life. In Plotinus's view the way to discover our upper Soul and restore our tarnished lower Soul is through ethics. The keys to human salvation are thus the cultivation of Virtue, which refreshes the Soul with divine Beauty; the practice of "dialectics" (debate), which reveals the true nature of Souls; and finally through Contemplation, which is the proper occupation of the purified Soul.

> Let every soul recall, then, at the outset the truth that soul is the author of all living things, that it has breathed the life into them all, whatever is nourished by earth and sea, all the creatures of the air, the divine stars in the sky, it is the maker of the sun, itself formed and ordered this vast heaven and conducts all that rhythmic motion, and it is a principle distinct from all these to which it gives law and movement and life, and it must of necessity be more honorable than they, for they gather or dissolve as soul brings them life or abandons them, but soul, since it never can abandon itself, is of eternal being.

Plotinus, *Enneads*, 5, 2.1

The legacy of these ideas was enormous, not just in the last days of the pagan ancient world but throughout later history. In the later classical world the theological traditions of Christianity (most particularly in the work of Saint Augustine), Islam, and Judaism all looked to Platonic philosophy, as described by Plotinus, as a method for formulating and articulating their own theologies. After the obscurity of the medieval period, the *Enneads* reemerged in 1492 as one of the driving forces behind the writings of the Italian Renaissance philosophers and in the works of humanists like Erasmus and Thomas More.

Plotinus's influence further continued into the seventeenth century in the works of the Cambridge Platonists, and by the eighteenth century Plotinus was recognized as one of the formative influences on Western Christianity, as the classicist Lemprière noted:

> *He was the favourite of all the Romans, and while he charmed the populace by the force of his eloquence, and the Senate by his doctrines, the emperor Galienus courted him, and admired the extent of his learning. . . . He was a great mystic, and his Neoplatonism had a profound effect upon the theology and philosophy of the Christian Church.*

> Lemprière, *Classical Dictionary Writ Large*, pp. 500–501

The German idealists of the following century, especially Hegel, considered Plotinus's work the basis for their opposition to the growing schools of scientific philosophy, and his influence can even be traced in the twentieth-century Christian imaginative literature in England, spearheaded by C. S. Lewis. Few philosophies have lasted so long, appealing to so many peoples of different nations and from different times, all of whom have in their own ways tried to live up to Plotinus's last injunction, as recorded by his student and personal physician, Eustochius of Alexandria, as the master lay on his deathbed: "Strive to give back the Divine in yourselves to the Divine in the All" (Eustochius of Alexandria, *Letter to Porphyry*).

Only one other philosophy has lasted as many centuries as that of Plotinus, and it was championed by his own fellow student in the secret lectures of Ammonius Saccas. He was about twenty years older than Plotinus and of the other great emerging school of thought in Alexandria: Christianity.

Origen, or more properly Origenes Adamantius, was born and brought up in Alexandria as a Christian by his father, Leonides, a Greek teacher, and his mother, who was Jewish and taught him to sing the psalms in Hebrew. His father gave him an excellent education, and as an adolescent he attended the lectures of both Clement at the catechetical school and those of Ammonius in his school of philosophy. His precocious brilliance attracted such attention, it is said, that by the time he was seventeen his father was known as "Leonides, father of Origen."

But in that year (202) the emperor Septimius Severus ordered another of the periodic persecutions of Christians, and Leonides was dragged from his house by Roman soldiers. Origen, the oldest of seven children, insisted upon accompanying his father, but, according to the story, his mother hid his shoes or his clothes. Still, he followed his father to the Caesareum, where he saw him executed, his head thrown onto a pile of heads, his body cast aside.

As was the practice in those days, all of the Christian Leonides' property was confiscated by the state, and Origen, his mother, and his six brothers were left destitute. Origen was forced to provide for his family by teaching and copying manuscripts until a new opportunity was presented to him by the bishop of Alexandria. The pogrom which had taken his father's life was the one that led Bishop Clement of Alexandria to abandon the catechetical school and seek refuge in Palestine, so the next year Bishop Demetrius appointed Origen as the new dean of the school, at just eighteen years old.

Origen's reformed school was open to all and taught a wide range of subjects besides Christian doctrine. Prayer and fasting were practiced by teacher and pupil alike, and simplicity of lifestyle was encouraged. It was clearly an immensely stimulating environment, and one of Origen's pupils, Gregory, later known as Thaumaturgus ("Wonder-Worker"), recalled that they were given complete freedom to find their way around the entire world of knowledge, and to investigate anything which took their interest, enjoying any mode of teaching and savoring the sweet pleasures of the intellect:

> To be under the intellectual charge of Origen was like living in a garden where fruits of the mind sprang up without toil to be happy with gladness by the happy occupants. . . . He truly was a paradise to

us, after the likeness of the paradise of God . . . and to leave him was
to renascent the experience of Adam and the Fall.

Gregory Thaumaturgus, *Address to Origen,* 13

Origen himself is said to have taught all day and studied the Bible for
much of each night, leading a life of exemplary asceticism. Perhaps because many of his students were women, and also because at that time he
wished to follow the gospel to the letter, one report claims he decided to
obey the words of Matthew literally and mutilate himself. The passage
from Matthew 19:12 concerns the nature of eunuchs—both those who
are born that way and those who decide to take matters into their own
hands "for the kingdom of heaven's sake." Matthew ends the discussion
with the words "He that is able to receive it, let him receive it," and this
Origen took as a direct order.

There is some debate as to whether Origen did actually castrate himself, and it has been argued that he put the story about to mask his own
homosexuality, though there is no evidence to support what sounds like
a slur from his detractors. Later in life he admitted that it was an extreme
act and probably beyond the call of his faith.

For ten years Origen devoted himself to teaching, with only two short
breaks—a brief visit to Rome in 211–12 and a journey to Arabia at the
request of the prefect of the province in 213 or 214, during which he
visited the rose-red city of Petra. On his return he became friendly with
Ambrose of Alexandria, a wealthy man whom Origen converted from
Valentinian Gnosticism—a heretical Christian sect formed by the original
Saint Valentine—to orthodox Christianity. From then on he acted as
Origen's sponsor and promoter.

When the fury of Caracalla was unleashed on the city, Origen and
Ambrose fled to Caesarea together. Around 218 Ambrose of Alexandria
made a formal agreement with Origen to promote his writings, and thereafter all his published works were dedicated to Ambrose. With the help
of seven stenographers to take dictation in relays, another seven scribes to
prepare longhand copies, and a team of girls to make copies of the copies,
Origen's output was phenomenal. He set to work on a huge commentary
on the Bible, two books on the Resurrection, and one of the most im-

portant works in early Christian literature, *On First Principles,* in which he began to lay out a systematic analysis of his vision of the Christian faith.

Over the following twenty years Origen set about teaching and writing, organizing his textual criticism of the Bible by the Alexandrian method. To do this, he took the unusual and hugely significant step of mastering Hebrew—the language in which the Bible had first arrived in Alexandria. Having mastered the language, he then gathered together all the known versions of the Old Testament in Hebrew and Greek and systematically compared them all.

Origen accepted the notion of the Holy Trinity, but he gave it a hierarchy. As in Plato, God the Father is the One, the omnipotent, all-encompassing, purely spiritual being. God the Son, however, is a product of the One, equivalent to Logos or Wisdom (Sophia) in Neoplatonism, the first emanation. The Holy Spirit, third element of the Trinity, emanates from the Son and is related to the Son as the Son is to the Father. A passage of Origen's writing, preserved in the original Greek, explains his position:

> The God and Father, who holds the universe together, is superior to every being that exists, for he imports to each one from his existence that which each one is; the Son, being less than the Father, is superior to rational creatures alone (for he is second to the Father). The Holy Spirit is still less, and dwells within the saints alone. So that in this way the power of the Father is greater than that of the Son and of the Holy Spirit, and in turn the power of the Holy Spirit exceeds that of every other holy being.
>
> Origen, *De Principiis* [*On First Principles*], book 1, section 8

This is a masterful synthesis of classical Platonic and mystical Christian perspectives, but it was this application of Neoplatonic cosmology to the Holy Trinity which would eventually lead to Origen's expulsion from the Roman Catholic Church several centuries later.

Origen is quite close to Plotinus in his view of the human soul. Though he doesn't differentiate the soul into upper and lower parts, he does state that in the first creation human souls were close to and "warmed" by

God. He sees Jesus as a perfect product of this first creation, his soul still warm and intimately close to God, his father. But "the Fall" led the rest of humanity's souls to fall away from God and become cool. The job of the faith is to return us to God's warmth and love.

An absolutely central tenet of Origen's theology is the resurrection of all beings, even ultimately the devil, his argument being that God would not create anything, even Satan, if he did not want all of creation to be saved at the end of time.

The devil, however, did seem to be snapping at Origen's heels. His work was repeatedly interrupted by persecutions. In 235, it is said, he was forced to hide in a house in Caesarea, where he stayed in hiding for two years. During this period he wrote a book appropriately entitled *On Martyrdom* which is preserved in a later text, the *Exhortation to Martyrdom*.

Origen is best remembered today for a work that we have already met. In 248 his old friend Ambrose, aware of the growing sophistication of anti-Christian literature, particularly among the Neoplatonists, prevailed upon him to write eight books refuting the damning critique of their religion composed by Celsus. This collection, *Against Celsus*, became the most celebrated defense of the faith produced by the early church, partly because it inadvertently preserved Celsus's own work. It also opens a window onto the dangerous religious politics of the day and shows the real fear and danger that lay behind the ethereal arguments of the philosophers. Here we see Origen not as simply the defender of the faith but as a man who knew that Celsus's clever words were often backed up by the tip of a sword, and that where persuasion failed, the empire was quite happy to force conformity. In dealing with Celsus's complaint that Christians were secretive whereas other great iconclasts, like Socrates, had been prepared to speak openly, regardless of the risk, when they knew themselves to be right, Origen answered that the situation was now different. Socrates had died for his philosophy and in the process proven the Athenians wrong—this they had quickly realized. Rome, however, had not learned from the deaths of many Christians: "But in the case of the Christians, the Roman Senate, and the princes of the time, and the soldiery, and the people, and the relatives of those who had become converts to the faith, made war upon their doctrine" (Origen, *Against Celsus*, book 1, chapter 3).

Prophetic words these turned out to be, as two years later what he termed the "whole world's conspiracy" against Christianity caught up with Origen himself. In 250 he was captured during yet another pogrom, this time ordered by the emperor Decius. Bound hand and foot for days on end, Origen was repeatedly tortured; but Decius died before him, and the old man was released. Crippled and broken, he died of his wounds shortly afterward.

By the time of his death Origen had done a thoroughly Alexandrian job on Christianity. In so doing he portrayed his religion for the Hellenistic world as a faith with a philosophy, not simply another localized cult. This was a religion that now offered a whole cosmology, not just the forlorn hope of a better life after death for those whose current life was almost unbearably hard. This was a religion that the scholars of the museum could understand. Origen's lifework was an act of integration, the conversion of a blind faith into a rationalized set of ideas, a plausible worldview and system of thought and action designed to elevate its practitioners, in this world and the next.

The two disciples of the Alexandrian porter Ammonius Saccas had accomplished extraordinary feats: the codification of the last great pagan philosophy of the ancient world and of the primary philosophy of the world that would follow. Yet these two ideas were not destined to grow happily side by side, and in Ammonius's secret lectures had been planted the seeds of Alexandria's destruction.

CHAPTER SEVENTEEN

THE END OF REASON

The dream of reason produces monsters.

Goya, *Los Caprichos*

I f Alexandria was the ideal crucible in which to forge new ideas about God and divinity, it was not prepared for the firestorm those new ideas would unleash. Alexandria was the city that questioned everything—from the shape of the earth to the divinity of the emperors—but not all of its subjects took this academic criticism well. The earth had not complained when Eratosthenes had measured it; triangles, circles, and cones had quietly surrendered their secrets to Euclid. But while a difference of opinion in geometry or astronomy was just that—a difference of opinion—a difference of opinion in religion was heresy. Opinions were met with counteropinions. Heresy was met with persecution and often death. So it was with explosive results that the greatest heresy of the early Christian church emerged in the one city with the pedigree to have created it.

Arius may not have been born in Alexandria, being of Libyan and Berber descent, but he arrived in the city in the later years of the third century and from that point on he would make it his only home. He had chosen a career in the fledgling church, but his questioning, some would say confrontational, perhaps even "Alexandrian," nature had made his rise uneven. In particular he had shown a dislike of the dogmatic authorities of the day, represented by Alexander, the patriarch of his home city. In an age when the church was obsessed with schism and heresy, arguing over the exact interpretation of the nature of God, Arius was almost deliberately provocative, backing schismatic causes and twice getting himself excommunicated while still just a presbyter. So it was that from what should have been a simple lecture by the patriarch to his young charges arose the greatest and most damaging heresy in the early church.

The church father Socrates Scholasticus tells us that Alexander had chosen to lecture his pupils, including Arius, on a particularly tricky subject. He had decided to speak in detail (too much detail, according to Socrates) about the greatest theological mystery of all: the unity of the Trinity, or how the Godhead was three parts, Father, Son, and Holy Spirit, yet also just one part and hence all equal.

Arius, ever quizzical and ready for an argument, took the bait, according to Socrates simply to annoy his master:

> *A certain one of the presbyters under his jurisdiction, whose name was Arius, possessed of no inconsiderable logical acumen . . . , from love of controversy took the opposite opinion . . . and as he thought vigorously responded to what was said by the bishop. "If," said he, "the Father begat the Son, he that was begotten had a beginning of existence: and from this it is evident, that there was a time when the Son was not. It therefore necessarily follows, that he had his substance from nothing."*
>
> Socrates Scholasticus, *Ecclesiastical History,* book 1, chapter 5

It was a perfectly logical piece of argument, and had this been a debate on logic in the porticoes of the museum, Arius might have expected some applause. But this was not a matter of logic, not a matter which Alexander wished to discuss. This was an article of faith, a matter of belief, and his presbyters were meant to accept it without question.

Arius would not and, receiving no conclusive answer to his point, began to elaborate his own idea further, acquiring his own adherents; and, as Socrates put it, "thus from a little spark a large fire was kindled" (Socrates Scholasticus, *Ecclesiastical History,* book 1, chapter 6).

Encouraged by the response from some Christians, Arius traveled to his friend Eusebius of Nicomedia, where he began codifying his ideas in a book that would turn that fire into an inferno. In this book, known as *The Banquet* or, in Greek, *Thalia,* Arius proposed that God the Father was the only God and that Christ was created by him, not an integral part of him. Today this may seem a rather dry and academic point, but in Alexandria it was dynamite. The idea created a sensation and the inns and churches of Alexandria were soon filled with arguments over the true nature of Christ. In the marble colonnades street philosophers argued for and against the idea, while the doctrine rapidly became the talk of Christian society. That Arius had written his work in an easily read, populist style made it even more fashionable.

But the arguments were not confined to the polite exchanges of the museum, or even the soapbox harangues of the street preachers. In an early church, battered and bruised from numerous bloody persecutions, desperately trying to assert its authority, arguments over Arius and his "Arianism" often ended in bloodshed. The doctrine in effect created a turf war between two opposing factions of the church, each of which of course claimed to hold the only true interpretation of the faith. As emperors came and went, so bishops and priests of each camp were excommunicated and exiled, reinstated and returned. The atmosphere was highly inflammatory, with both parties claiming their opponents were responsible for terrible atrocities, most of which probably never happened but all of which served to further enrage the street mobs and radical monks that both camps used to support their campaigns.

In the end the Christian emperor Constantine, who had himself converted to Christianity, at least nominally bringing the Roman Empire with him, decided to intervene. So he wrote to the head of each faction—the patriarch Alexander and Arius—in an attempt to ease passions, suggesting that they differed only on the interpretation of a small and obscure point of doctrine. Remembering the reputation of the city where the fight was raging, he patiently reminded them:

> You are well aware that even the philosophers themselves are united under one sect. Yet they often differ from each other on some parts of their theories: but although they may differ on the very highest branches of science, in order to maintain the unity of their body, they still agree to coalesce. Now, if this is done among them, how much more equitable will it be for you, who have been constituted ministers of the Most High God, to become unanimous with one another in such a religious profession.

> Letter of the Emperor Constantine, in Socrates Scholasticus, *Ecclesiastical History*, book 1, chapter 7

Despite this eminently sensible attempt to pour oil on troubled waters neither the Arians nor their opponents were prepared to listen, nor were they about to do as Constantine had suggested. The religious ideas now coming out of the city may have been created in an atmosphere of tolerance, but having defined their own positions, they would allow no further debate or diversion. This radicalism had been born in Alexandria and grown in Alexandrian soil, and it would poison and eventually kill the city that had nurtured it.

As Alexander would allow no differences in religion, so eventually the whole Christian church was forced to choose, and in 325 a weary Constantine ordered the bishops to gather in council at Nicaea to decide once and for all what the official church did and did not believe. The result was the Nicene Creed, still used in churches today. In it there was no place for Arianism. Patriarch Alexander seemed to have won and Arius was banished.

Some of the credit for Alexander's apparent triumph at Nicaea must go to his deacon Athanasius. He was a young and fervent Christian who had accompanied the patriarch to the council as his secretary, having already served at his side for several years. Athanasius was a unique product of his time and a man who could have been produced only by the city of his childhood—Alexandria. Here he had received the education still traditional among the wealthier elements of society, learning grammar and rhetoric before finishing his education in the lecture halls of the philosophers of the museum. He had then thrown himself into the life and controversies of the church, witnessing firsthand both the sophisticated academic arguments in the city for and against Arianism and the stark fundamentalist Christianity of the desert monks who from this date would play an increasing role in his city's fortunes.

Contemporaries describe him as relatively short and thin but full of energy, his "finely shaped" head crowned with sparse auburn hair. He was said to have a ready wit, be affable in company, pleasant in conversation, and quick to learn. But the passion of his religion betrayed itself in his unyielding and unsparing debating style. If there was an Alexandrian to answer Arius's criticism it was he, and his rise through the church hierarchy was rapid, until at just thirty-three, on the death of his mentor, he found himself the new patriarch of his home city.

Fourth-century Alexandria was as idiosyncratic and energetic as its new patriarch. The Ptolemaic temple of Serapis still functioned, and pagan philosophers still bowed to the great cult statue there, created centuries before by Bryaxis. Nearby the Jewish synagogues familiar to Philo and perhaps even the writers of the Septuagint still flourished, and in between them Christian churches had now sprung up. In the streets the pagan fortune-tellers still offered glimpses of the future to those with a few coins in their pockets, while populist Neoplatonist and evangelical monks vied for the ears and hearts of passersby. In this multicultural, multilingual milieu the new patriarch began his turbulent career, one that would change the face of his city and his religion forever.

Athanasius inherited one niggling problem from Alexander. Arianism, though condemned at Nicaea, was not dead, despite the death of Arius himself, who—one church father claimed—died when, seized with the realization of his own wickedness, he became so incontinent that he passed his own bowels. Under a series of weak emperors the fortunes of pro- and anti-Arian factions waxed and waned, during which time Athanasius was alternately feted and denounced, expelled and reconciled. During his episcopate he was variously charged with sorcery, corruption, and murder. Somewhere between five and seven times he was driven from his city and forced to take refuge with the desert monks, in western Europe, and once even in his own father's tomb. But for each reverse there was a restoration, and Athanasius himself recorded in ever more polemical detail his changes of fortune, stoking the political fires in Alexandria. On the occasion of one return the Arians claimed that people complained and even wept at the news of his return and refused to meet with him.

He responded furiously (referring to himself in the third person):

> *Now such was not the case, but, quite the contrary, joy and cheerfulness prevailed, and the people ran together, hastening to obtain the desired sight of him. The churches were full of rejoicings, and thanksgivings were offered up to the Lord everywhere; and all the Ministers*

and Clergy beheld him with such feelings, that their souls were possessed
with delight, and they esteemed that the happiest day of their lives.

Athanasius, *The Orations of St. Athanasius Against the Arians,* chapter 1

Every swing of the Arian pendulum brought a more emphatic, more violent, more fundamentalist response from the protagonists. Athanasius himself was now known as *"Athanasius contra mundum"*—"Athanasius against the world." Suspicions were stoked, factions formed, sects became mobs, and their cry in the streets was not "think" but simply "choose."

Perhaps fortunately, Athanasius would not live to see the end results of his church's radicalization. After an exhausting and turbulent career he died peacefully in his bed, having spent a lifetime fighting for the view of Christianity that he had heard agreed to at Nicaea—a fight which would gain him the titles "Doctor of the Church" and "the Father of Orthodoxy." On these foundations would be built the medieval Catholic Church, but they would be laid in the ruins of the city he had ruled.

With the Christian church apparently absorbed with its own internal battles, life for those outside its influence in Alexandria may have seemed little changed. Indeed, on the surface the city was still an eclectic center of learning. Christians found enlightenment at the catechetical schools; Jewish philosophy was taught at the rabbinical school; and the museum and library, whatever the predations of previous centuries, were still filled with scholars. Among this last group, around the middle of the century, lived a little-known member of the museum whose family was also about to have a profound effect on both the life of the city and the fortunes of the world beyond.

Theon first appears in the record as an astronomer and mathematician who in 364 was credited with correctly predicting eclipses of both the sun and the moon. He was in many ways the archetypal member of the museum of this era, a local scholar who never left his city and whose epithets, "Egyptos" and "Alexandreus," suggest that he traced his lineage back through both Greek and Egyptian roots. Because some of his writings survive we know something of his passions and can gain one of our last glimpses of the great library at work. Theon studied in the Alexandrian way, building his own work around the creation of new editions of the great books in the library and preparing his own commentaries on them. He produced editions of Euclid's *Elements, Data,* and *Optics,* and wrote commentaries on Claudius Ptolemy's *Almagest* and *Handy Tables.*

But Theon also had philosophical interests that were very much of his own time. Amid the bitter recriminations of the Arian heresy it might seem that Christianity was already the only religion in town and that faith had been reduced to a matter of which Christian interpretation one chose to follow. This was not the case, however, and the uncertainty of their modern world encouraged even some of the philosophers of the museum to seek answers beyond logic in the more mystical aspects of Neoplatonism.

In this religiously charged atmosphere Theon had taken an interest in divination. In this city of soothsayers and priests he looked for divine truths in the books of the library and the circling of the stars. The chronicler Malalas tells us that he wrote commentaries on the books of the legendary father of alchemy, Hermes Trismegistus, and the mystical Orphic oracles. He is also said to have written a work entitled *On Signs and the Examination of Birds and the Croaking of Ravens* as well as treatises on the function of the star Sirius and the influence of the planetary spheres on the Nile River.

These may seem like unusual departures for a man who spent his days studying the very down-to-earth geometry of Euclid. But although Theon was at one level a scientist by any modern definition, in his eyes the world was a magical place, filled with omens and hints of the Platonic forms that lay beneath the veneer of reality. For him, to study the heavens was to study the minds of the gods, from which might be deduced not only the physical operation of the world, but clues to the future of individuals and nations. These thoughts found expression in poems attributed to him on astrological themes, one of which survives in the *Corpus Hermeticum,* a collection of texts of "secret wisdom" compiled during the Renaissance from various classical materials. In this Theon speaks of the seven sparkling spheres of heaven and how their interaction determines the lives of everyone on earth. To him destiny lay in the stars, in the crystal spheres whose mathematical precision reflected universal laws laid down by the supreme God behind all things, the everlasting Aion.

Nor was Theon alone in these beliefs. In this uncertain age it was not only the Christians, Jews, and pagan cults that looked to the supernatural for answers. In the museum itself Theon could have met, and probably knew well, other occultists such as Paulus of Alexandria and the anonymous writer now known to us simply as "the Astrologer of the Year 379." It was against this background that the Christian patriarch Theophilus came to power in Alexandria in 385. In his eyes the paganism of Theon and the members of the museum was not simply harmless hocus-pocus but a threat, like any belief that deviated from the patriarch's orthodox views. The early, bloody history of the church and its hard-won agreement on what was orthodox and what was heresy had made it combative. The Christians of the empire had often been persecuted for their beliefs, but now their moment in the sun had come. The empire was Christian, and for Theophilus that could mean only the destruction of paganism altogether. In June 391 an opportunity came to do just that: The news reached Alexandria that the emperor Theodosius had banned all pagan practices.

The focus of Theophilus's attack would not be the museum itself but the Serapeum, home to the ancient Ptolemaic cult of Serapis and the location of the "daughter library." As news of the edict of suppression spread, fear gripped the city's pagans. The prophetic Antoninus, son of Sosipatra, had already foretold the fall of the temple, and a group of pagans now fearfully barricaded themselves inside, under the unlikely command of a cabal of philosophers.

These men were a cross section of an ancient world on the verge of disappearing. They included Olympius, a servant of Serapis, the seven-hundred-year-old god of the Ptolemies who had been forged by the Greeks to help them rule a foreign land; Ammonius, a priest of the Egyptian god Thoth, whom the Alexandrians associated with the Greek god Hermes but whose Egyptian roots lay in a religion older than the pyramids; Helladius, a priest of Ammon, the oracular god who had informed Alexander of his own divine origins at Siwa; the poet Palladas, known for his bitter epigrams written in the persona of a pagan schoolteacher forced to live in a Christian city; and finally Claudian, whose icy poetry would one day find him favor in Rome as court poet. But these eclectic representatives of Alexandria's old guard were not there simply to await martyrs' deaths; they intended to go out fighting.

From their stronghold they organized repeated sorties against the Christian mob, picking fights where they could and dragging away any Christian foolish enough to approach the compound unprotected. So bitter had the enmity between these groups become that reports speak of them crucifying those they caught. It must have made for an extraordinary and terrifying sight as Theophilus's Christians and Olympius's pagans became caught up in the white-hot zealotry of a religious war. It seems almost impossible today to imagine poets and philosophers battling in the streets with monks and Christian converts, but both were battling not for ideas but for beliefs—beliefs that both would die for.

In the end the pagans paid the highest price. The street battles dwindled into occasional skirmishes, and the pagans dug in inside the Serapeum had nowhere to go. When the running battle came to the attention of the Christian emperor he ordered his representatives in Egypt—the *praefectus augustalis* (prefect) and the *dux aegypti* (military commander)—to intervene. The pagans were ordered out of the Serapeum, and the Christian mob flooded in. Olympius and his compatriots had to watch as Bryaxis's 750-year-old statue of Serapis, a wonder of the world to many who had seen it, was dragged out into the street and smashed with a soldier's ax.

No reports survive of what happened when the mob reached the daughter library, which Bishop Epiphanius of Salamis, who died in 402, claims in his *Weights and Measures* was still stored in the Serapeum. In fact his is the only source which claims the library was still there; all other descriptions of the temple's sacking are silent on the issue, including even that of the vehemently anti-Christian Eunapius of Antioch, whom we might expect to put any thinkable atrocity at Theophilus's door. So in this moment the fate of one of Alexandria's great libraries again slips through our fingers. It may be that the collection had already been moved, althrough if so, we have no record of where it went. If it did remain in the Serapeum, then the centuries of writing kept in a pagan temple could only have raised suspicions. Whatever was contained in those scrolls belonged to the old world, the pagan world, and could have no place in the new Christian Alexandria. The early Christian writer Paulus Orosius in his *Seven Books of History Against the Pagans* does not mention specific temples but seems to think the destruction of books kept within them was commonplace: "Today there exist in temples book chests which we ourselves have seen, and, when these temples were plundered, these, we are told, were emptied by our own men in our time, which, indeed, is a true statement" (Paulus Orosius, *Seven Books of History Against the Pagans*, book 6, chapter 15).

So we must presume that the Serapeum library was destroyed. One thing alone is certain: If it was kept there or elsewhere, the daughter library was never heard of again.

Those philosophers who had actively fought to preserve the Serapeum now either fled, like Claudian, to Rome, or were deprived of their religious positions and state funding. Of the effect of the destruction on Alexandria and her pagan citizens we have only the cold verses of Claudian and the bitter and rueful lines of Palladas's epigrams, in one of which he can't help but compare the vicissitudes of his life with the fate of the seafarers whom he must have watched come and go through the Great Harbor of his city every day:

> *Life is a dangerous voyage; for tempest-tossed in it we often strike rocks more pitiably than shipwrecked men; and having Chance as pilot of life, we sail doubtfully as on the sea, some on a fair voyage, and others contrariwise; yet all alike we put into the one anchorage under earth.*

> Palladas, "The Voyage of Life," in J. W. MacKail, *Select Epigrams of the Greek Anthology,* chapter 12, epigram 22

But not everyone had fought for or against Theophilus; not every Neoplatonist had cast off his philosopher's robes to take up arms in the name of Serapis, Hermes, or paganism in general. Though Claudian had fled and Palladas had sunk into a sea of despair, their loss had not left the lecture halls of Alexandria empty quite yet.

CHAPTER EIGHTEEN

HYPATIA

Revered Hypatia, ornament of learning, stainless star of wise teaching, when I see thee and thy discourse I worship thee, looking on the starry house of Virgo; for thy business is in heaven.

Palladas, *Greek Anthology*, 11

The highly charged religious atmosphere in Alexandria was making it a dangerous place to have an opinion—any opinion—and rough seas now buffeted what had once been the intellectual safe haven of the museum. Indeed, Theon is the last name we can definitely associate with the institution that has been at the center of our story since the earliest days of the city. He is its last known member, the last in that roll call of the most brilliant names in antiquity. But it is his daughter who will always be associated with its fall.

In the early years of the fifth century Theon's daughter seemed to have emerged from the religious crisis of her father's era unscathed. From early childhood she had been her father's greatest collaborator, and we find her name first in his introduction to his commentary on the *Almagest*: "Commentary by Theon of Alexandria on Book III of Ptolemy's Almagest, edition revised by my daughter Hypatia the Philosopher" (Theon, recorded in A. Rome, *Commentaires de Pappus et de Théon*, volume 3, p. 807).

Hypatia was the inheritor of her father's mantle; indeed, many sources claim she was much more than that, and according to the philosopher Damascius "she was by nature more refined and talented than her father" (Damascius, *Life of Isidore*, excerpted in *The Suda*).

She was a mathematician of noted brilliance, writing commentaries on the works of Apollonius of Perge and the notoriously complicated

Arithmetica of the third-century inventor of algebra, Diophantus. Indeed, it has been doubted whether, without her clear, patient explanations of the works of this famously opaque mathematician, his work, crucial in the development of modern mathematics, would even have survived. The bitter irony is that today none of Hypatia's original works survive, and therein lies the key to one of Alexandria's most tragic episodes, the beginnings of its disappearance back into the Egyptian sands.

Hypatia was born around 355 into the academic elite of Alexandria. At her father's side she learned astronomy and mathematics as well as the practical skills first mastered by such luminaries of the museum as Eratosthenes and Archimedes, including the building of planispheres and astrolabes. But her interests went far beyond the stars into the realms of philosophy, a philosophy far removed from her father's mystical occultism.

There is no evidence that Hypatia was ever herself a member of the museum, let alone the "last librarian," as some have claimed. Indeed, after the death of her father we have no evidence for the museum or library, in the sense that Archimedes or Euclid might have understood them, existing at all. According to the church father Epiphanius of Salamis, whose life roughly coincided with Hypatia's (he died in 403), the Brucheum quarter of the city where this institution had once stood among gardens, royal palaces, and summerhouses now made for a rather startling sight. In describing the founding of the library he makes the casual aside that it was "in the [part] called the Brucheum; this is a quarter of the city today lying waste" (Epiphanius of Salamis, *Weights and Measures*, chapter 9).

We do not know which of the various Roman emperors left the most beautiful quarter of this city in ruins. It may be that this iconic part of the city had never recovered from the fury of Caracalla. But as Alexandria stands on a geological fault line that produced a major earthquake and subsequent tsunami in 365, we can't even be sure that it wasn't simply nature that tore down the marble halls.

If the buildings of the old museum were gone, however, the idea of it was not dead, and the philosophy schools, now perhaps housed in the homes of the teachers, survived. From the late 380s Hypatia had formed her own such school in the city, attracting the sons of some of the most influential and wealthy men in the empire. Among them she lectured in the subjects her father had taught her—ethics, ontology, astronomy, and mathematics—but to a smaller and more select group she also taught philosophy, including the ancient pagan ideas of Pythagoras, Plato, and Aristotle as well as the Neoplatonism of Ammonius Saccas and Plotinus.

This group of initiates became an intensely loyal family around Hypatia; they called each other "brother," maintained their contacts over a lifetime, and would only hint to the outside world at what secrets they had heard in Hypatia's house. But this was not a crypto-pagan cult, not simply another band of disinherited priests reminiscing over the old days like the embittered Palladas. Nor were they the augurs and fortune-tellers that Theon counted among his friends. They instead represented both the old and the new in the empire and the city—and as such represented perhaps a chance for Alexandria to reinvent itself, and so save itself, one last time.

The guarded nature of Hypatia's pupils and her own fate make it hard to unlock the secrets of her school, but thanks to the surviving letters of one of her closest followers we can reconstruct something of her life and times and gain a window into a very unexpected world.

Synesius of Cyrene was a young and wealthy landowner from Alexandria's sister city who came to Egypt's capital in the 390s to gain what even then must have been considered a classical education. In his 156 surviving letters we gain tantalizing glimpses of the life of a fourth-century aristocrat in the city and at home. In a letter to his best friend, Herculian, later prefect of Constantinople, he remembers their arrival in Alexandria and their time with Hypatia, the "lady who . . . presides over the mysteries of philosophy":

> If Homer had told us that it was an advantage to Odysseus in his wanderings that he saw the towns and became acquainted with the mind of many nations, and although the people whom he visited were not cultured, but merely Laestrygonians and Cyclopses, how wondrously then would poetry have sung of our voyage, a voyage in which it was granted to you and me to experience marvelous things, the bare recital of which had seemed to us incredible! We have seen with our eyes, we have heard with our ears the lady who legitimately presides over the mysteries of philosophy.

> Synesius, Letter 137 (to Herculian)

From his letters we also learn something of the other "disciples" in Hypatia's house, including Olympius, a hugely wealthy Syrian landowner with whom Synesius talked of hunting and horses; his little brother Euoptius; Ision, who told stories like no other; Syrus, "our friend"; his uncle Alexander; "father" Theotecnus, "the worthy and holy"; Theodosius, "a grammarian of the first order"; Auxentius, his childhood playmate; and Gaius, "the most sympathetic."

At one level these seem exactly what might be expected from an old aristocracy—young men looking to a heroic and already ancient past. Synesius talks about happy days on his estate outside Cyrene that reminded him of the "golden age," and in Alexandria, gazing across the heptastadion to the Pharos and walking down the marble colonnades of the Street of the Soma, he must have imagined he walked with the ghosts of Alexander, Callimachus, and Archimedes. But Hypatia's "family" were not all they appeared. These were not, as they have so often been characterized by later writers, the last of the old guard. She was a pagan— true—or at least she was a Neoplatonist, but astonishingly, perhaps half of her students were Christians.

Synesius himself married a Christian and went on to become bishop of Ptolemais in Cyrenaica, where he was succeeded in that position by his little brother, the fervent Euoptius. The mysterious "Petrus" mentioned in one letter has a name which suggests his Christian pedigree as well, while Synesius's friend Herculian became bishop of Cotyaeum in western Turkey. This perhaps explains how, when others were barricading themselves in the Serapeum or fleeing abroad, Hypatia continued teaching unhindered.

So just what was Hypatia teaching this eclectic inner circle who gathered at her house in the city in the last years of the fourth century and the first decade of the fifth? From Synesius we can discover that it must have been a form of Neoplatonic philosophy far removed from the radicalism of the defenders of the Serapeum—a gentler and older Hellenism that had bound all those who had worked in the library and museum regardless of politics or creed. In a letter to Herculian Synesius exhorts him to "go on digging up the eye that is buried within us" (Synesius, Letter 137 [to Herculian]).

And in that phrase we probably hear an echo of Hypatia's own words, as she taught her charges to release the "luminous child of reason" (Synesius, Letter 139 [to Herculian]). It seems that what Hypatia wanted most from her students was that they love and seek wisdom, but not simply knowledge divorced from the real world around them. The course that she advocated required physical purity and mental wisdom. Learning was not of itself enough, nor was "right living," as Synesius tells Herculian:

> The masses think that uprightness of life does not exist for the end of wisdom, but stands by itself, and is itself the perfection of man, and that the way is not a way merely, but the goal itself at which we must aim. In this view they are mistaken. An unreasoning self-control and an abstinence from eating of meat, have been given to many unreasoning creatures by nature. We do not commend a raven or any other creature that has discovered a natural virtue, because they are devoid of reasoning power. To live according to reason is the end of man.
>
> Synesius, Letter 137 (to Herculian)

Hypatia, at least in the minds of her followers, perfectly combined the two. She was a teacher who remained a virgin all her life, who always wore the simple white *tribon* robe of a philosopher, and who practiced moderation in everything. Those lucky enough to spend time with her referred to themselves as the "fortunate chorus that delights in her divinely sweet voice" and called her "divine spirit" and "blessed lady." Even in her ordinary lectures her disciples seem to have found divine truths, learning that mathematics is a stepping-stone to understanding and, as Synesius puts it, that "astronomy is itself a divine form of knowledge."

Her influence in Alexandria reached far beyond her private teaching circle. The chronicler Socrates Scholasticus tells us that she also gave public lectures where city officials and ordinary citizens might hear her, and says that she achieved such "heights of erudition" that she surpassed all the other philosophers of her day. He also claims that she "succeeded to" the Platonic school derived from Plotinus (although it is unclear if this means she was the official head of the Neoplatonic school) and "delivered all the philosophical lectures to those who wished to listen" (Socrates Scholasticus, *Ecclesiastical History*, book 7, chapter 15).

This public speaking spread her fame throughout the higher echelons of the government, and she seems to have been consulted at least informally by senior officials, including councillors, military commanders, and even the prefect. Socrates Scholasticus tells us, "On account of the majestic outspokenness at her command as the result of her education, she maintained a dignified intercourse with the chief people of her city, for all esteemed her highly and admired her" (Socrates Scholasticus, *Ecclesiastical History,* book 7, chapter 15).

Yet her teachings do not seem to have brought her into conflict with either the Christians among her group or the church authorities in the form of Alexandria's patriarch Theophilus. Indeed, Synesius writes to both Theophilus and the philosopher Hypatia asking for similar favors as though the two were on a comparable level. That she avoided such trouble during Theophilus's antipagan campaigns tells us that her Hellenism was cultural rather than religious, centered on the raison d'être of the museum, the pursuit of knowledge, and the self-knowledge that leads to understanding. The schools of Alexandria didn't yet separate pupils on religious grounds, so all religions could seek wisdom with Hypatia—a wisdom born not from dogma, magic, augury, or sacrifices, but from thought alone.

But this understanding was not for everyone. Her group considered themselves an elite (as indeed they were, both in education and fortune), and the squabbles of "believers"—those who considered belief enough in itself—were, in their eyes, beneath them. Synesius himself rails against both the "white mantles"—the street philosophers peddling quick-fix paganism to the masses—and the "black mantles"—zealous monks preaching Christian salvation. For him, and his teacher, divine knowledge was not for the masses but reserved for the favored few who could survive the arduous mental journey to enlightenment. For them the path to "truth," be it Neoplatonist truth or Christian truth, was an intellectual obstacle course whose end could be reached only by great mental effort, physical moderation, and ethical purity. Belief of itself would never be enough— the road still had to be traveled—and that journey was the subject of Hypatia's private classes and the reason for the great secrecy that surrounded the discussions of their inner circle. Pogroms, fighting, and desecrations were for believers who took on an idea without thinking, but had nothing to do with them. It was an extraordinary concept, and one which could hold both pagans and Christians together; but just as it formed, so its hour was already passing.

The patriarch Theophilus died on Tuesday, October 15, 412. He had spent his years in office antagonizing both pagans and Christian heretical sects but had never touched Hypatia's circle. He had been known to the people of Alexandria as the "church pharaoh," yet he had been careful not to overextend his power into the secular administration of the city—the preserve of the prefect and dux—nor had he sought to interfere in the philosophical education of men such as Synesius, who he knew would one day take high office in his church. It had been a delicate balancing act, and Theophilus's death left a dangerous power vacuum. And into that vacuum exploded his nephew Cyril.

Two candidates were nominated to succeed Theophilus, and the nature of the subsequent election campaign would give an unpleasant foretaste of what was to come. The stronger candidate was said to be Timothy, Theophilus's archdeacon, who had a lot of backing within the church hierarchy as well as the support of one of the military commanders in the city. The other was Cyril, Theophilus's nephew, an impetuous, self-promoting radical who believed in backing up the power of the Word with the power of the mob. This was not to be an election decided by debate or even a vote. Three days of street fighting ensued, after which, on October 17, a triumphant Cyril was installed as patriarch. This brutal election had been a testing ground for Cyril's influence, involving as it did secular imperial figures as well as church fathers, and from his victory Cyril drew some new and deadly lessons. Just as the state had become involved in an ecclesiastical struggle (although bearing in mind the violence of the struggle, it had actually had little choice), so now, as patriarch, Cyril believed he had a right to a say in the secular administration of the city. This belief in a new, wider mandate would have terrible consequences, as Socrates Scholasticus says:

> Cyril came into possession of the episcopate, with greater power than Theophilus had ever exercised. For from that time the bishopric of Alexandria went beyond the limits of its sacerdotal functions, and assumed the administration of secular matters.
>
> Socrates Scholasticus, *Ecclesiastical History*, book 7, chapter 7

Cyril wasted no time in suppressing any groups in the city that either disagreed with him or did not accept his absolute power over them. The first to suffer in his "purification" of the church was the entirely harmless Christian Novatian sect. The Novatians followed the teachings of the Roman priest Novatian, who had split from the official Catholic Church because he considered it too lax in readmitting former Christians who had, in the face of persecution, renounced their religion. His followers called themselves "the Pure" and required considerably greater self-discipline among themselves than Cyril's followers did. Indeed, perhaps that is why he set upon them. Socrates Scholasticus certainly had some sympathy for Novatians, and notes: "Cyril immediately therefore shut up the churches of the Novatians at Alexandria, and took possession of all their consecrated vessels and ornaments; and then stripped their bishop Theopemptus of all that he had" (Socrates Scholasticus, *Ecclesiastical History*, book 7, chapter 7).

It seems that in Alexandria, at least, Cyril would have no bishop but himself.

Next he turned from those he considered "too religious" to those he considered not religious enough—the Jewish community. It had come to his notice that some Jews in the city did not celebrate the Sabbath in a particularly "religious way," preferring instead to visit the theaters rather than staying at home in prayer. For Cyril this presented an opportunity not just to confront the Jews but to draw the state authorities into his arguments and make them decide whose side they were on as well.

Since his election campaign, Cyril had skillfully used the Christian mob in the city and groups of radical Nitrian monks from the desert to stir up trouble. He now stationed his people in the theaters to goad the Jewish population into taking violent action. On one of these occasions the prefect of Egypt, Orestes, happened to be in the theater giving a speech, when a brawl broke out. Some of the Jews in the audience shouted out to Orestes that Hierax, an agent of Cyril, was fomenting trouble and begged for his arrest. Orestes, already wary of Cyril's attempts to extend his influence into the government of the city, was only too happy to oblige, and Hierax was arrested and tortured.

But if he hoped to put Cyril in his place and remind him of the terrible powers of the prefect, he was very much mistaken. Cyril immediately summoned the Jewish leaders of the city as though he were governor himself and warned them in the most patronizing terms to behave and leave his agents alone. It was the last straw of antagonism for some Jews in the audience, first goaded and threatened by Cyril's thugs, then sternly told off like children by their leader when they tried to fight back. At that moment some decided to take physical action and in doing so played straight into Cyril's hands.

The event that gave Cyril the opportunity he had been looking for occurred late one night. Having set an ambush around the church of Saint Alexander, a group of radicalized Jews ran through the streets shouting that the church was on fire. Local Christians jumped from their beds and ran to the building to help, only to find they had run into a trap. A bloody fight ensued in which many of them were killed.

Cyril now had his martyrs, and he rushed to surround the main synagogues with large crowds of his supporters, whom he only too easily whipped into a frenzy of retribution. Authorizing the looting of Jewish sites, he then ordered the expulsion of the entire Jewish population, who, as Socrates Scholasticus notes, had been there since the days of Alexander. Stripped of all their property and possessions, they were then cast out and "dispersed some in one direction and some in another" (Socrates Scholasticus, *Ecclesiastical History,* book 7, chapter 13).

Cyril quickly wrote to the emperor to tell him of the outrageous behavior of the Jews and the necessity of the action he had taken, but it was a dangerously provocative move. As Socrates Scholasticus records, the Jewish population had been a vital part of the running of the city from its earliest days. This was the city of the Septuagint, the home of Philo, and the removal of this ancient population would have a profound economic as well as social impact on the functioning of the city. The prefect Orestes was, not surprisingly, incensed, and sent his own report to the emperor. If the emperor did respond, not one of the contemporary chroniclers records his judgment. In truth it was a subject low on his list of priorities— a spat between two local officials—with just the sort of dangerous religious edge he wished to steer clear of. So the chroniclers probably failed to record the imperial verdict for a simple reason—none came.

This was a problem Alexandrians would have to work out for themselves. In the face of the prefect's anger Cyril seems to have made at least a tentative attempt at reconciliation, although his reported waving of the gospels under Orestes' nose made it clear that any rapprochement would be on his terms and his terms alone. But Cyril's provocation had now brought Orestes to the breaking point. Seeing his power eroding before him, the prefect decided finally to try to face Cyril down and rebuffed his overtures of peace. So Cyril turned back on his other tried and tested method of getting his own way.

His call went out again to the radical Nitrian monks of the desert, and some five hundred quit their monasteries and headed for the streets of Alexandria. There they came across Orestes riding in his chariot and surrounded him. Socrates tells us that "they called him a pagan idolater, and applied to him many other abusive epithets. He supposing this to be a snare laid for him by Cyril, exclaimed that he was a Christian, and had been baptized by Atticus the bishop at Constantinople" (Socrates Scholasticus, *Ecclesiastical History*, book 7, chapter 14).

This was not enough for the monks, who were intent on action, not argument. One of their number, Ammonius, seized a rock and threw it at the prefect. It struck him on the head and blood immediately began to pour down his face. In the ensuing panic Orestes' own guards abandoned him, and it was only thanks to the intervention of other passersby, the ordinary people of Alexandria, that he got away.

The wounded prefect ordered the immediate arrest of Ammonius, who was caught and tortured to death. Two more letters were now dispatched to the emperor, one from Orestes decrying the patriarch's behavior, the other from Cyril, claiming Ammonius, or "Thaumasius" ("the Wonderful") as he now called him, as a martyr. The emperor's response, once again, was silence, and Cyril and Orestes were left to resolve the problem alone. The race was now on to decide who would rule Alexandria—the state or the church, logic or belief. Only one could survive.

First blood seemed to go to Orestes. Cyril had overstepped the mark and misread popular opinion. The response in Alexandria was not what he had hoped for, and the Christians did not take "Saint Wonderful" to their hearts.

But the more sober-minded, although Christians, did not accept Cyril's prejudiced estimate of him; for they well knew that he had suffered the punishment due to his rashness, and that he had not lost his life under

the torture because he would not deny Christ. And Cyril himself be-
ing conscious of this, suffered the recollection of the circumstance to be
gradually obliterated by silence.

Socrates Scholasticus, *Ecclesiastical History,* book 7, chapter 14

So Saint Wonderful slipped from sight, his elevation among the realms of the martyrs proving only temporary. Cyril would need another way of getting to the prefect if he wanted to exert his power over the city as a whole, and, fatally for her, he would find it in the quiet person of Hypatia.

Up to this point Hypatia had been invisible in the record. Philosophically she may well have felt that the squabbles of believers were unworthy of her consideration, but her regular contact with the authorities, and Orestes in particular, must have created within her a growing sense of dread. In this situation it was simply not enough to ignore Cyril and his attempts on power. With his brand of Christianity he intended to be the central core of the running of the city. His interpretation of religion was his politics, and by claiming to be executing the will of God he gave himself carte blanche to act in any way he saw fit. This was undoubtedly a threat to the freedoms of the city Hypatia loved, and she could do little but throw her considerable influence behind the moderate Orestes.

That Hypatia, who was now about sixty, had been distancing herself from her circle—perhaps to protect them as the situation deteriorated—is clear from one of Synesius's last letters to her. In it he says:

> *If I could only have had letters from you and learned how you were*
> *all faring—I am sure you are happy and enjoying good fortune—I*
> *should have been relieved, in that case, of half of my own trouble, in*
> *rejoicing at your happiness. But now your silence has been added to*
> *the sum of my sorrows. I have lost my children, my friends, and the*
> *goodwill of everyone. The greatest loss of all, however, is the absence*
> *of your divine spirit. I had hoped that this would always remain to*
> *me, to conquer both the caprices of fortune and the evil turns of fate.*

Synesius, Letter 10 (to "The Philosopher," Hypatia)

But there was little happiness or good fortune to be had in Alexandria. Hypatia's support for Orestes was a thorn in Cyril's side. One chronicler tells of how he stopped at her house one day and was overcome with jealousy when he saw the huge crowds clamoring to hear her speak. She was widely respected in the city, had close connections with the council and government, and counted among her friends and pupils some of the most important people in the empire, including men at the imperial court. But she did have a weakness. Orestes was a moderate Christian, as had been many of Hypatia's school, but Hypatia herself was apparently not a Christian at all. She was of the old Alexandria, the last of the Hellenes. This was the wedge that Cyril now drove between prefect and philosopher.

Cyril circulated a rumor that she was a practitioner of black magic—a sorceress who was "devoted at all times to magic, astrolabes and instruments of music" (R. H. Charles, *The Chronicle of John, Bishop of Nikiu*, 84.87–103). To the city mob who had little to do with the museum or library it must have had a certain ring of truth. What did go on in her secret meetings with her inner circle? Had her father not been an astrologer and alchemist? Even the tools of science she had learned to make at her father's knee could be turned against her. Astrolabes, hydroscopes, and the like were not simply scientific tools, they were also regularly used for divination among the superstitious Alexandrians. So Cyril ensured that the slander spread that it was Hypatia who stood between him and Orestes—two good Christians—and she who was trying to undermine the religion and well-being of the state.

It was of course a lie, but a powerful one, and one which took deep root among Cyril's most fervent supporters, the Parabolans. The job of the Parabolans was, in theory at least, to help ill and destitute Christians in the city to find a place in hospitals or almshouses, but under recent patriarchs they had become almost a private army. These poorly educated but fervently religious young men obeyed the patriarch without question and were only too happy to put their imposing presence (there were eight hundred of them) and any degree of force necessary behind his commands. It was this group, no doubt encouraged by Cyril, who now decided to take direct action against Hypatia.

Fired with hatred, this band was led by a man called Peter, a lector in the church whom the Christian chronicler John of Nikiu called a "perfect believer in all respects in Jesus Christ" (R. H. Charles, *The Chronicle of*

John, Bishop of Nikiu, 84.87–103), and under his command the Parabolans now began searching the city for Hypatia. She was not hard to find, regularly riding in her chariot through the streets, very much living her life in public. They came across her as she was heading home, outside the Caesareum, the temple built for Mark Antony by Cleopatra shortly before their deaths, and since converted into a Christian church. There, by the three obelisks known as "Cleopatra's Needles," they surrounded her and dragged her from her chariot. In the street this most modest of women had her tribon torn from her and was stripped naked, but even her Parabolan attackers did not have the nerve to execute the next part of their plan in full public view. Dragging her inside the church, they threw her on the floor of the nave and, in the sort of rage that only blind zealotry brings, set upon her with broken pieces of roof tile, flaying her alive. Her torn and mutilated body was then carried beyond the walls to a place called Kinaron, where her remains were burned on a bonfire—a witch's death. No one is recorded as having come to her aid. The last of the Alexandrian Hellenes was gone.

Cyril now had to work quickly to ensure that the blame for this horrific act did not fall directly on him, but he can only have been delighted at the outcome. Orestes now disappears from the historical record, either having been recalled by the emperor or simply having fled. Some Alexandrian councillors did attempt to intervene with the emperor, but Cyril's friends at court ensured that the affair was hushed up, and the only response was a mild attempt to reorganize and reduce the numbers of Parabolans, taking their recruitment away from Cyril and resting it with the prefect. Even that did not last long, and by 418 Cyril had that power back as well. Cyril carefully portrayed the death of Hypatia as a fight between Christians and pagans, distancing himself in the process from the real cause of the tension, his attempt to seize power from a Christian prefect. John of Nikiu sums up perfectly how Cyril wished the story to be told: "All the people surrendered to the Patriarch Cyril and named him 'the new Theophilus,' for he destroyed the last remains of idolatry in the city" (R. H. Charles, *The Chronicle of John, Bishop of Nikiu,* 84.87–103).

Socrates Scholasticus, himself a revered historian of the early church, took a more sober view: "This affair brought not the least opprobrium, not only upon Cyril, but also upon the whole Alexandrian church. And surely nothing can be farther from the spirit of Christianity than the allowance of massacres, fights, and transactions of that sort" (Socrates Scholasticus, *Ecclesiastical History*, book 7, chapter 15).

But Cyril had won and now settled down to live out his patriarchy more quietly. He died in June 444 after an episcopate of nearly thirty-two years. He would later be remembered as a doctor of the church and be raised to sainthood.

CHAPTER NINETEEN

THE SHIPWRECK OF TIME

Come and see my shining palace built upon the sand!
Edna St. Vincent Millay, "A Few Figs from Thistles"

With the death of Hypatia, her city also began to die. Philosophers were still to be found in the city's streets, and the "Alexandrian school" continued quietly—ever more quietly—to refine pagan Neoplatonism. Plato, Aristotle, and Plotinus were still read and talked of, but in truth the whole complexion of the city had changed.

In the streets violent religious extremism and an associated rise in ethnic tensions were fanning the flames of nationalism. Customs were changing, shunning the "foreign" Greek influence of Hypatia's Hellenism, despite the fact it had been the cornerstone, indeed the very raison d'être, of the city. Even the language was slowly transforming, still written in a Greek alphabet but with the addition of six hieroglyphic characters, its structure now more influenced by ancient Egyptian. This new, hybrid language would eventually emerge as Coptic, the language of the Christians of Egypt.

After Theon we no longer hear of the work of the museum, if indeed it survived the antipagan policies of the emperors and patriarchs. It was, after all, a temple to the Muses, and as such ripe for suppression. As mystical religion had taken hold in the city, as control of the government had slipped from Alexandrian to Roman hands, so the whole nature of academic life in the city had slowly been changing. Academics were now obsessed with compiling and editing older works, not creating new thoughts and new books. The creators had been replaced by the codifiers and critics, who, in the manner of their theological counterparts who pored over the holy books in which they said all answers lay, searched for truth in old ideas rather than seeking out new ones. The spirit of adventure had left the halls of the museum; the minds which once reached beyond its colonnades to the ends of the earth and beyond, far into space, were gone.

And what of the books? The fate of the libraries of Alexandria is one of the greatest mysteries of the ancient world. It would still be tragic, but at least convenient, if a single moment for their destruction could be found, a moment at which the curtain came down on the classical world and a new and darker age commenced. But it is not that simple. We know from the scholarly references which fill Synesius's letters that he gained access to a large number of classical texts during his time in Alexandria, although he probably did not get these from one great central library. That institution had died, not with a bang but a whimper. It may well be that the majority of the ancient collection of the Ptolemies was destroyed when Julius Caesar burned the Egyptian fleet in the Great Harbor and the flames carried over the roofs of the old city. Livy tells us there were four hundred thousand scrolls in the collection at that time, and their loss might have inspired Mark Antony to present the library of Pergamum to Cleopatra as a lover's gift.

Of course books were still created and collected after this date, although they may have been stored separately in either a library attached directly to the museum or in the daughter library in the Serapeum. It was perhaps from those shelves that Synesius took the works of Homer and Plato from which he so often quoted. But other books were probably even then missing, even then forgotten. Were Varro's forty-two lost books of *Antiquities* still there? Were the "lost decades" of Livy's Roman history still rolled up with the books that survive to this day? Very possibly not. The ravages of the fire of 48 BC, the literary pretensions and furious retributions of Roman emperors, and a simple dimming of the spark that had inspired the early Ptolemies to collect every book they could find had all taken their toll. There were already empty shelves in the libraries that Hypatia and her followers knew, and perhaps only a dim memory, preserved in Callimachus's lists, of what treasures they once held.

But it had been in Hypatia's own era that some of the final nails in

Alexandria's coffin were driven home. Emperor Theodosius's order to shut all pagan temples in 391 had a profound effect upon learning in the city, not because Christianity opposed learning—Hypatia's own circle proved the opposite—but because its more extreme proponents equated pre-Christian learning with paganism. The Serapeum had been created by the Ptolemies specifically to appeal to Egyptians and had been designed on an ancient Egyptian model, as not just a temple but a library and college. It was the logical home for the daughter library, but in finding a home in a pagan building the books themselves became tarred with the brush of paganism. Knowledge has always been the enemy of extremism, and for the most radical elements among Alexandria's Christians, the books in the Serapeum were a threat. So they simply destroyed them.

If any books survived by this date in any great library in the city, they too can only have come under suspicion. The museum, like all schools of the Greek model, like Plato's Academy and Aristotle's Lyceum, was at least nominally a religious institution. Only by centering his Academy on a temple had Plato gained for it the protection of the city of Athens—it was simply how these things had always been done. But the idea of a temple to the pagan Muses in Alexandria, in Christian Alexandria, could not have sat well with the Parabolans or the Nitrian monks who so readily chose to impose their will by force of arms rather than by force of argument. In the aftermath of Hypatia's death, much of whatever was left of the great bookstores of antiquity must have gone. From now on those who wished to read non-Christian texts probably did so in secret, collecting their own small libraries in the privacy of their houses. Cyril's Alexandria had no reason to spend civic or church funds on collecting old and idolatrous tomes.

So Alexandria stumbled on, now shorn of its unique attribute. Even Patriarch Cyril was aware that the city he had fought so hard to possess was now the sickly little brother to the "New Rome" of Constantinople, whose influence spread far beyond his city's limited sphere. Perhaps aware that the city he had cut loose from its classical past was not now free but simply adrift, he did make one final bid to achieve his dream and make Alexandria the center of the new world—the Christian world. Using his tried and tested technique of accusation and confrontation he charged Nestorius, the patriarch of Constantinople, with heresy and succeeded in having him expelled. But it was far too late for Cyril to take his place or for Alexandria to become a new Constantinople. Learning in the city was dying, the monuments of previous ages had been looted, and her books, her precious books, were gone—some up in flames, a few spirited away.

Yet, ironically, Cyril's last desperate move did save some small part of Alexandria. Of the few books that had survived from the great library, some had recently reappeared in Constantinople, and these were taken east by the banished Nestorius and his followers, out of the reach of the book burners and into the Syrian Desert, where they were once again lost to Western scholarship.

By the seventh century Alexandria had become an anomaly, a rebellious Christian outpost on the coast of North Africa. The Brucheum and Jewish quarters were long abandoned, and the museum and the tomb of Alexander lay in ruins. Christian communities clustered around the Caesareum and Serapeum, both of which had now become churches, and only the Heptastadion and the area around the Pharos remained densely populated. In 616 the city fell briefly to the Persian emperor Khosrau II, only to be regained a decade later by the Romans. But by this date a new force was already heading her way and was soon to overtake her.

The emperors had taken little notice of the unification of the peoples of the Arabian Peninsula under the prophet Muhammad; the *History of the Patriarchs of Alexandria* records an almost certainly apocryphal, but telling, story of how Emperor Heraclius failed to see the signs: "And in those days Heraclius saw a dream in which it was said to him: 'Verily there shall come against you a circumcised nation, and they shall vanquish you and take possession of the land'" (Severus of Al-Ashmunein, *History of the Patriarchs of the Coptic Church of Alexandria,* part 2, chapter 14).

Perhaps not surprisingly, Heraclius thought this must be a reference to the Jews and so ordered that all the long-suffering Jews and Samaritans in his empire were to be rounded up and compulsorily baptized. He soon realized, however, that he had made a mistake: "But after a few days there appeared a man of the Arabs, from the southern districts, that is to say, from Mecca or its neighbourhood, whose name was Muhammad" (Severus of Al-Ashmunein, *History of the Patriarchs of the Coptic Church of Alexandria,* part 2, chapter 14).

Under the prophet Muhammad the Arab world was uniting in a way it had never done before, and if the Roman world was unaware of it, it was not unaware of the Roman world. Under Muhammad's successors, the caliphs, this new nation was already vigorously expanding through a program of military conquests across the Near East. In 639 Omar I ordered his general, Amr ibn al-Asi (better known as simply Amr), west to conquer in the name of Islam. Damascus, Syria, and Jordan had already fallen, and Egypt would be next.

Amr conquered Egypt with just four thousand cavalry. The Byzantine viceroy Cyrus, who was also patriarch of Alexandria, was found hiding in the citadel of Babylon (a Roman fortress in Cairo) and rapidly offered his country's capitulation. John of Nikiu tells us that Amr congratulated him on coming forward. Cyrus replied, "God has delivered this land into your hands: let there be no enmity from henceforth between you and Rome: heretofore there has been no persistent strife with you" (R. H. Charles, *The Chronicle of John, Bishop of Nikiu*, 120.17–20).

Cyrus was putting a brave face on a rather unequal situation. Amr would certainly agree to peace, but it would be entirely on his terms. First a tribute in gold was to be paid, and then the Roman garrison in Alexandria was to be disbanded, although the troops were allowed to leave with their possessions and "treasure" intact. The Romans would promise no further military intervention in Egypt, and Amr would take 150 soldiers and 50 civilians as hostages to ensure they kept to the deal. The final part of the peace was more evenhanded and perhaps offered a last chance for peace in Alexandria. John of Nikiu summed up the deal succinctly: The Romans were to cease warring against the Muslims, and the Muslims were to stop seizing Christian churches and interfering in Christian religious practice.

Sadly, this was not a peace that would last. The caliph's forces did not immediately take Alexandria, partly because the Arabs chose to avoid the place. In their eyes it was dangerous and corrupt, an ancient town of evil fortune, filled with philosophers and monks—and the notoriously truculent city mob. By the time Amr did arrive in the city in September 642 the garrison was gone and there was little resistance as his cavalry rode in through the Gate of the Sun. The city he found still impressed him with its ancient temples converted into churches and the still-dazzling marble of the colonnades on the main streets, and he seems to have treated its people with the respect he had promised. Those who wished to leave were allowed to, while those who wished to remain were permitted to continue worshipping in their churches unmolested, provided of course that they paid the appropriate tribute.

Now as master of all Egypt Amr could write to the caliph telling him he had seized a city of 4,000 palaces, 4,000 baths, 12,000 dealers in fresh oil, 12,000 gardeners, 40,000 Jews who paid tribute, and 400 theaters or places of amusement. The caliph seemed unimpressed, perhaps wary of the somewhat inflated figures from his general. He reportedly just nodded nonchalantly at the messenger and rewarded him with a loaf of bread, a bottle of olive oil, and a handful of dates.

Perhaps Caliph Omar was right to be cautious, for the people of Alexandria did not keep to their side of the bargain. The Muslim writer Al-Baladhuri in his *Conquest of Alexandria* (*The Origins of the Islamic State*, volume 1, pp. 346–49) recorded that the Alexandrians wrote to Emperor Constantine (the son of Heraclius) explaining how his subjects were humiliated by the Muslims and forced to pay a poll tax—effectively making them second-class citizens. They then casually added that the Muslim garrison was rather understrength and hence vulnerable.

Constantine, roused to righteous indignation, immediately took advantage of the situation and sent an expeditionary force to recapture the city for the empire: "Constantine sent one of his men, called Manuwil, with three hundred ships full of fighters. Manuwil entered Alexandria and killed all the guard that was in it, with the exception of a few who by the use of subtle means took to flight and escaped" (Al-Baladhuri, *The Origins of the Islamic State*, volume 1, p. 346).

When Amr returned to this situation around 646 he was no longer in a mood to deal generously with the inhabitants, nor were they foolish enough to think he would. Ancient Alexandria was about to fight its final battle. Al-Baladhuri finishes the tale:

> *Amr made a heavy assault, set the ballistae, and destroyed the walls of the city. He pressed the fight so hard until he entered the city by assault, killed the fathers and carried away the children as captives. Some of its Greek inhabitants left to join the Greeks somewhere else; and Allah's enemy, Manuwil, was killed. Amr and the Moslems*

destroyed the wall of Alexandria in pursuance of a vow that Amr had made to that effect, in case he reduced the city. . . . Amr ibn-al-Asi conquered Alexandria.

Al-Baladhuri, *The Origins of the Islamic State,* volume 1, pp. 346–49

The city had become a minor irritant in the Muslims' conquest of Egypt, and its repeated calls on the Byzantine Empire for military help created unwanted friction. The solution of the Muslim general charged with bringing the city back to heel was simple: He tore it down. Flour once again flowed in the sands around the island of Pharos, as the city's famous granaries were demolished.

It is at this point, with Amr back in control of the city's remains, that the final legend associated with the great library is set. The story comes from a much later source, Bar-Hebraeus's *History of the Dynasties,* written in the thirteenth century, and is almost certainly fictional, but it does prove that the fame of the library and the need to explain its terrible loss was still felt centuries after it had vanished. Bar-Hebraeus tells the story that John the Grammarian, a Coptic priest present at the destruction of the city, was, due to his great learning, on good terms with Amr and eventually plucked up the courage to ask him about the fate of the library. "'You have examined the whole city, and have set your seal on every kind of valuable: I make no claim for aught that is useful to you, but things useless to you may be of service to us.' 'What are you thinking of?' said Amr. 'The books of wisdom,' said John, 'which are in the imperial treasuries'" (Bar-Hebraeus, quoted in E. A. Parsons, *The Alexandrian Library,* p. 416).

He then patiently described how the Ptolemies had collected books on all subjects from the four corners of the world, regardless of expense, and then rather extraordinarily claimed that they still existed in the warehouses of the city which Amr had sealed following his victory. While the city was now Amr's to do with as he pleased, would he not consider leaving intact this rare collection, as it could be of no use to either him or his soldiers?

Amr, renowned for his own scholarship, declared himself amazed at this news but warned that it was not in his power to hand such a library over to John. However, he would write to the caliph and seek his advice on the matter. In time the caliph wrote back with bad news: "Touching the books you mention, if what is written in them agrees with the Book of God, they are not required: if it disagrees, they are not desired. Destroy them therefore" (Bar-Hebraeus, quoted in E. A. Parsons, *The Alexandrian Library*, p. 416).

So Amr, faithful to his master's decision, ordered the books distributed among the bathhouses of the city, where they provided fuel for the boilers for six months. "Listen and wonder," concluded Bar-Hebraeus.

The origin of this story is uncertain, and it occurs in none of the earlier chronicles. By the thirteenth century, however, not long after the disastrous failure of the Third Crusade against Saladin, it suited a Christian writer like Bar-Hebraeus and his audience to characterize the Muslim world as barbaric and backward. And even if the enemy was wrong, there was a ring of truth to the idea that religious bigotry had after a thousand years of enlightenment finally dragged Alexandria into oblivion. Ironically, however, it was Muslim scholars who were even then preserving and translating the few great works from Alexandria's library shelves that had survived.

What the story does powerfully demonstrate is that any conqueror might consider the contents of a library as dangerous as the contents of an arsenal. Building that arsenal of ideas had been a driving force behind Ptolemy I's creation of Alexandria, and the insecurity of conquerors and the intolerance of extremists had been its downfall. Alexandria had been a city of ideas where the greatest freedom was the freedom to think, but Roman emperors, Christian patriarchs, and Muslim caliphs had all, in attempting to control those thoughts, whittled away at the library, the city, and the idea that lay behind them. A thousand years after the walls of Alexandria fell, the traveler George Sandys reached her sad remains and wrote her epitaph:

> *Queene of Cities and Metropolis of Africa: who now hath nothing left but her ruines; and those ill witnesses of her perished beauties: declaring that Townes as well as men, have their ages and destinies.*

> George Sandys, *The Relation of a*
> *Journey Begun An. Dom. 1610*, book 2

EPILOGUE
A Distant Shore

I picked up a bottle half buried in the wet sand, covered with barnacles, but stoppled tight, and half full of red ale, which still smacked of juniper,—all that remained I fancied from the wreck of a rowdy world,—that great salt sea on the one hand, and this little sea of ale on the other, preserving their separate characters. What if it could tell us its adventures over countless ocean waves! Man could not be man through such ordeals as it had passed. But as I poured it slowly out on to the sand, it seemed to me that man himself was like a half-emptied bottle of pale ale, which Time had drunk so far, yet stoppled tight for a while, and drifting about in the ocean of circumstances, but destined ere-long to mingle with the surrounding waves, or be spilled amid the sands of a distant shore.

Henry David Thoreau, *Cape Cod*

As the monk Maximos Planudes lifted the copy of Ptolemy's *Geographia* from the tomes piled around the book dealer's stall in Constantinople, that day back in 1294, one piece of the wreckage of Alexandria began a new journey.

Planudes had turned the ancient words into maps, which were added to and improved on by the Byzantine court. One of these had itself found its way from the edges of Asia to a wealthy Florentine with the time and money to translate its Greek text back into the Latin that the scholars of Europe still understood. From Florence that map found its way to Rome, to the Apostolic Library of the pope, then the most powerful man on earth. And from there copies made their way across Europe, to the palaces and castles of the princes of Christendom.

One of those would reach the Portuguese capital, Lisbon, where in 1484 a young explorer named Christopher Columbus was, like Ptolemy before him, beginning to think the unthinkable. What if the world was indeed a sphere? What if he could sail west to Cathay? What if the book he held in his hands that day was correct? A book called the *Geographia* by Claudius Ptolemy. A book from the library at Alexandria.

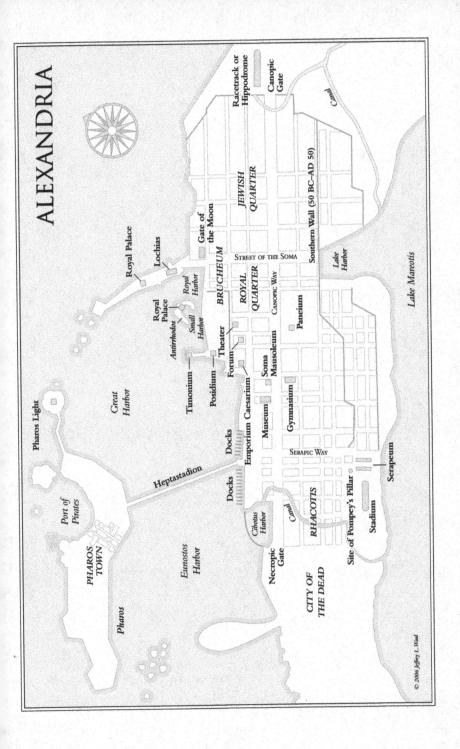

ALEXANDRIA

Pharos Light

Port of Pirates

PHAROS TOWN

Pharos

Great
Harbor

Eunostos
Harbor

Heptastadion

Docks

Docks

Emporium Caesarium

Cibotus
Harbor

Canal

Necropic
Gate

CITY OF
THE DEAD

RHACOTIS

Site of Pompey's Pillar

SERAPIC WAY

Stadium

Serapeum

Museum

Soma
Mausoleum

Gymnasium

Forum

Posidium

Timonium

Theater

Small
Harbor

Antirrhodos

Royal
Palace

Royal
Harbor

Lochias

Royal Palace

Gate of
the Moon

BRUCHEUM

ROYAL
QUARTER

Canopic Way

Street of the Soma

Pancium

JEWISH
QUARTER

Racetrack or
Hippodrome

Canopic
Gate

Canal

Southern Wall (50 BC–AD 50)

Lake
Harbor

Lake Mareotis

© 2006 Jeffrey L. Ward

CHRONOLOGY

336–323 BC	Reign of Alexander III the Great, king of Macedon.
Early in 331 BC	Alexandria founded by Alexander the Great.
	Later in year Alexander departs for Asia.
Late fourth century BC	Dinocrates of Rhodes designs the city. Intention is to give Alexander a secure naval base and to act as link between Macedonia and the Nile Valley.
332–331 BC	Cleomenes of Naucratis appointed financial manager of Egypt and administrative chief of Eastern Delta district. He makes himself satrap illegally but is then recognized.
	Continues to build Alexandria, but also squanders its wealth, becomes very unpopular.
323 BC	Alexander dies of fever in Babylon (June 10); conference held there to discuss the succession. Ptolemy is made satrap of Egypt but Cleomenes is made hyparchos.
323–306 BC	Ptolemy acquires (hijacks) Alexander's body (322). Wrapped in linen and bound in plates of gold, it is eventually placed in magnificent tomb of rare Greek and Egyptian marbles.
	Egypt ruled by Ptolemy, Macedonia and Greece by Antigonids, Persia by Seleucids. Alexander's half brother, infant son, and mother all murdered.
323–321 BC	Ptolemy brings charges against Cleomenes and executes him.
322–321 BC	Ptolemy conquers Cyrene.
307 BC	Demetrius Phalerus of Phaleron—tyrant of Athens 317–307—takes refuge in Alexandria from Demetrius Poliorcetes; persuades Ptolemy to found the library. Ptolemy writes (toward end of life) one of the best biographies of Alexander.

305 BC (or early 304)	Ptolemy assumes title of king (Ptolemy I). Known as Ptolemy Soter (Savior). Promotes new religious cult of Serapis bull hybrid with Greek gods.
300–294 BC	Strato of Lampsacus, "the Physicist," is tutor to Ptolemy II. Ptolemys adopt customs of pharaohs, including royal brother-sister marriage. Ptolemy II marries his sister, and takes the title Philadelphus (brother-loving).
c. 300 BC	Euclid teaches in Alexandria.
	Herophilus of Chalcedon founds a school of anatomy in Alexandria.
	Erasistratus of Ceos is active as a physician and anatomist.
First half of third century	Theocritus creates pastoral poetry as a form.
285 BC	Ptolemy I resigns in favor of son Ptolemy II.
285–246 BC	Ptolemy II is king of Egypt. Theocritus writes praises for Ptolemy I and II. Ptolemy II patronizes the Pleiad of seven tragic poets, of which the five most noted are Homerus, Lycophron, Philicus, Sositheus, and Alexander Aetolus.
c. 285–283 BC	Lycophron makes preliminary sorting of the comedies collected in the library.
	Ptolemy II greatly extends the library.
c. 284 BC	Zenodotus becomes first head of the library at Alexandria. He is the first person to piece together scientifically the *Iliad* and the *Odyssey* by comparing different manuscripts to reveal the original texts.
281 BC	Aristarchus of Samos observes the summer solstice at Alexandria. Aristarchus's conception of the universe includes an accurate understanding of the solar system and the comparative sizes of the heavenly bodies, in which the earth is much smaller than the massive sun, and both are tiny in the immensity of space.
c. 276 BC	Ptolemy II marries (second) his uterine sister Arsinoe II.
c. 270 BC	Architect Sostratus builds the Pharos (lighthouse).
	Death of Arsinoe II.
264–241 BC	First Punic War between Rome and Carthage.
c. 264 BC	Callimachus of Cyrene is active as poet and scholar.
c. 260 BC	Apollonius of Rhodes succeeds Zenodotus as librarian. Renowned poet. Writes the *Argonautica*, recounting Jason's quest for the Golden Fleece.
Mid–third century BC	Archimedes probably studies with successors of Euclid at Alexandria.

Third century BC	The first five books of the Bible are translated into Greek in Alexandria, possibly for the Hellenized Jewish colony there. In the following centuries the remaining books are also translated there.
Second half of third century BC	Apollonius of Perge, mathematician known for treatise on conic sections, flourishes, known as the "Great Geometer."
246–221 BC	Ptolemy III, son of Ptolemy II, king of Egypt. Third Syrian War begins. Ptolemy III the conqueror brings back the ancient statues of the Egyptian gods carried off to Persia by Cambyses III centuries before. The restoration of the statues earns him the title Euergetes ("Benefactor"). He is a great patron of literature and science. He enlarges the library and orders that all books coming into the country be sent to the library, where they are copied. (Contains 490,000 scrolls.)
c. 245 BC	Conon of Samos names the star cluster Coma Berenices after Ptolemy III's wife cut off her amber-colored tresses and placed them in the temple of Venus.
241 BC	End of Third Syrian War; Ptolemy III regains Syria, southern Asia Minor, and some Aegean ports.
c. 235 BC	Eratosthenes succeeds Apollonius as librarian. Not only does he write on geography, math, philosophy, grammar, and literary criticism, he goes on to calculate the obliquity of the ecliptic, the tilting of the earth's axis which causes the seasons. He made it 23'51". It is in fact 23'46". Not content to stop there, he goes on to discover the circumference of the earth by measuring the angle of the sun at midday on the summer solstice. He comes up with 24,650 miles as the girth of the earth; it is in fact 24,875.
194 BC	Eratosthenes, wearying of life, starves himself to death. He is in his early eighties.
230 BC	Aristarchus of Samos dies. Ptolemy IV (Philopator), son of Ptolemy III, is king of Egypt.
218 BC	Start of Second Punic War—Hannibal crosses the Alps.
217 BC	Philopator defeats Antiochus III, the Seleucid king at Raphia, with the help of 20,000 native Egyptian troops—thenceforth the latter increase their influence.
202 BC	Scipio Africanus defeats Hannibal at Zama.

201 BC	Peace between Rome and Carthage.
c. 194 BC	Aristophanes of Byzantium succeeds Eratosthenes as head of library. He and Aristarchus are the first grammarians. He makes first major improvement of the *Iliad* and the *Odyssey* since Zenodotus.
c. 153 BC	Aristarchus of Samothrace succeeds Aristophanes as head of library. Probably the greatest literary critic in antiquity. Makes careful studies of Homeric language and meter. The successive librarians collect, edit, and preserve the existing monuments of Greek literature.
c. 130 BC	Hipparchus discovers precession of the equinoxes.
80 BC	Ptolemy X, last of legitimate male line of Ptolemys, is killed by the enraged populace after killing his wife-stepmother, Cleopatra Berenice. Romans later claim Egypt is willed to them by Ptolemy XI.
48 BC	Gaius Julius Caesar defeats Pompey, who flees to Egypt, where he is assassinated. Caesar then sets fire to Egyptian fleet in the harbor of Alexandria. Supposed burning of the library by Caesar.
47 BC	Caesar departs Egypt.
41–40 BC	Mark Antony spends the winter in Egypt with Cleopatra.
40 BC	Mark Antony presents the library of Pergamum to Cleopatra.
31 BC	Octavian declares war on Cleopatran Egypt and defeats Antony and Cleopatra at Actium.
30 BC	Cleopatra kills herself, and the Ptolemaic dynasty ends. Alexandria becomes the capital of a Roman province. Alexandria is an important center for grain production, exporting 20 million bushels per year to Rome. Most exacted as tribute. Alexandria also continues to trade in spices and other luxury goods with Arabia and India.
AD 41–54	Emperor Claudius expands the museum.
Second half of first century AD	Hero of Alexandria writes numerous works on mathematics, physics, and mechanics, also inventing slot machines, a fire engine, a water organ, and many other devices worked by water or steam.
First century AD	A new school emerges in Alexandria, its character determined largely by Oriental mysticism and Jewish (and later Christian) elements. It results in the speculative philosophy of the Neoplatonists (early third century

AD) and the religious philosophy of the Gnostics and early church fathers.

AD 127–141   Claudius Ptolemy makes observations of the heavens. A polymath, Ptolemy produces two works that become standard texts for a thousand years after he wrote them. First is the *Almagest,* on astronomy, in 13 books; it contains the oldest surviving star catalog, listing 1,022 stars in 48 constellations. In his books, the movements of the planets are geocentric. His system is accepted for the next 1,400 years.

Geography, in eight books, covers the positions of all the known towns and geographical features at the time. He is probably the first to systematically use longitude and latitude. *Optics* (three books of five survive) includes discussion of refraction, and the elaboration of theory from experiment. The *Tetrabiblios,* in four books, is his summation of astrology, complementing the astronomy of the *Almagest.* Derived from Chaldean, Egyptian, and Greek folklore, it remains a standard work right up to modern times because it is so complete and well organized.

140s AD   In reign of Antoninus Pius there is a serious riot in Alexandria in which the prefect is killed.

AD 157   Galen starts practicing medicine in Pergamum. Born AD 129, he has a spectacular career rise from gladiators' physician to physician in the court of Marcus Aurelius in Rome. Researches and writes in Alexandria, and demonstrates that both the veins and the arteries carry blood; his research is unrivaled for fullness and accuracy. Died in AD 199, the outstanding scientist of the second century AD.

AD 172   Revolt of an Egyptian priest named Isodorus in the Nile Delta; defeats a Roman force and nearly captures Alexandria, which is saved by the army of Avidius Cassius.

AD 175   Revolt of Avidius Cassius; Alexandria declares for him. But Avidius is slain by a centurion and the revolt is over. Marcus Aurelius spends the winter (175–76) in Alexandria and treats it lightly.

AD 199 or 200   Septimius Severus seals the tomb of Alexander together with his texts, so that no one thereafter may see them or the body.

First half of third century AD	Ammonius Saccas, one of the founders of Neoplatonism, teaches at Alexandria.
AD 215	Alexandrian youths are murdered by order of Caracalla, who is visiting the city at the time and is incensed by the satire leveled at him by the Alexandrians. He first kills all the boys in the city, then systematically loots it: "the fury of Caracalla."
	At this time Alexandria is developing into a center for theology, both Christian and otherwise (e.g., Arianism).
AD 244	Plotinus, chief exponent of Neoplatonism, begins lectures on philosophy in Rome (born Egypt AD 205).
c. AD 250	Diophantus, reputed inventor of algebra, flourishes in Alexandria.
AD 273	Aurelian puts down a revolt in Alexandria led by a wealthy local merchant named Firmus.
AD 296	Diocletian subdues a fresh revolt in Egypt, after laying siege to Alexandria for eight months, killing many thousands of its citizens; much of the city set to the torch.
AD 323	Constantine I chooses Byzantium as new capital.
AD 325	Constantine calls the Council of Nicaea, at which the Nicene Creed is adopted.
AD 328–373	Athanasius is patriarch of Alexandria.
AD 330	Byzantium renamed Constantinople.
c. AD 365	Severe earthquake followed by tidal wave hits Alexandria; seaward part of Alexandria, including the palace complex, falls into the sea.
Second half of fourth century AD	Oribasius is personal physician of Emperor Julian and compiles a medical encyclopedia.
	Theon of Alexandria edits Euclid's *Elements* and writes a commentary on the *Almagest*. Theon is the father of Hypatia.
AD 385–412	Theophilus is bishop of Alexandria. The Christian Roman emperor Theodosius orders the destruction of the Serapeum, and Theophilus leads the crowd to destroy it. The library is also pillaged by the Christians.
AD 400	Hypatia becomes head of Neoplatonic school in Alexandria. During this period there is constant friction between Christian zealots, Jews, and pagans.
c. AD 415	Hypatia is murdered by a mob incited by Cyril, archbishop of Alexandria; she is stripped naked in the Caesareum, which has become a Christian church, and her

	flesh is torn off her bones with broken pieces of roof tile. Her body is burned.
AD 428	Nestorius is appointed patriarch of Constantinople. He preaches that there are two Christ natures, one human, one divine, and therefore two Christ persons.
AD 431	Nestorius is deposed for heresy and banished to the Syrian Desert. His followers are persecuted and flee eastward, to Mesopotamia and Baghdad. There they translate the works of some classical masters into Syriac. These are later translated into Arabic and will help to develop Arabic science. These books in turn are eventually translated into Latin, Hebrew, and modern Western languages, forming the basis of the Renaissance.
Fifth century AD	The Brucheum and Jewish quarters are abandoned.
AD 529	Justinian I forbids the study of all "heathen learning" in Athens; the school of Athens dies. Many Alexandrians migrate to Athens and later to Constantinople.
AD 616	Alexandria is taken by Khosrau II, king of Persia.
AD 640	Egypt is surrendered (640) to the Muslim general Amr (Amr ibn al-Asi) by Cyrus, patriarch of Alexandria and governor of Egypt.
AD 646	Amr conquers Alexandria (or the city is betrayed) and destroys it, tearing down the city walls.

APPENDIX

GENERAL PERIODS OF ALEXANDRIA

332–c. 215 BC	Hellenistic Period 1
c. 215–c. 145 BC	Hellenistic Period 2
c. 145–31 BC	Hellenistic Period 3
30 BC–AD 516	Roman Period
AD 516–AD 642	Byzantine Period
AD 642–present	Muslim Period

THE PTOLEMAIC LAGID DYNASTY, 305–30 BC

All dates are BC.

305–283 (or 282)	Ptolemy I Soter (satrap of Egypt from 323)
285–246	Ptolemy II Philadelphus (co-regent 285–283 or 282)
246–221	Ptolemy III Euergetes
221–204	Ptolemy IV Philopator
204–180	Ptolemy V Epiphanes
180–145	Ptolemy VI Philometor
145	Ptolemy VII Neos Philopator
145–116	Ptolemy VIII Euergetes II Physcon
116–80	Ptolemy IX Soter II (Lathyros)
107–88	Ptolemy X Alexander I
80	Ptolemy XI Alexander II and Berenice III
80–58	Ptolemy XII Auletes (first reign)
58–55	Berenice IV
55–51	Ptolemy XII Auletes (second reign)
51–47	Cleopatra VII and Ptolemy XIII
47–44	Cleopatra VII and Ptolemy XIV
44–30	Cleopatra VII and Ptolemy XV Caesarion

ROMAN EMPERORS

All dates are AD unless BC is stated.

Julio-Claudian Dynasty

January 16, 27 BC–August 19, AD 14	Augustus
August 19, 14–March 16, 37	Tiberius
March 18, 37–January 24, 41	Caligula
January 24, 41–October 13, 54	Claudius
October 54–June 11, 68	Nero

Year of the Four Emperors

June 8, 68–January 15, 69	Galba
January 15, 69–April 16, 69	Otho
January 2, 69–December 20, 69	Vitellius

Flavian Dynasty

July 69–June 24, 79	Vespasian
June 24, 79–September 13, 81	Titus
September 14, 81–September 18, 96	Domitian

The Five Good Emperors

September 18, 96–January 27, 98	Nerva
January 28, 98–August 7, 117	Trajan
August 11, 117–July 10, 138	Hadrian
July 10, 138–March 7, 161	Antoninus Pius
March 7, 161–March 17, 180	Marcus Aurelius
March 7, 161–March 169	Lucius Verus
177–December 31, 192	Commodus

Severan Dynasty

January 1, 193–March 28, 193	Pertinax
March 28, 193–June 1, 193	Didius Julianus
April 9, 193–February 4, 211	Septimius Severus
198–April 4, 217	Caracalla
209–February 4, 211	Geta
April 11, 217–June 218	Macrinus
May 217–June 218	Diadumenian
June 218–222	Elagabalus
March 13, 222–March 235	Alexander Severus

Crisis of the Third Century (Emperors During the Height of the Crisis)

February/March 235–March/April 238	Maximinus Thrax
Early January/March 238–late January/April 238	Gordian I
Early January/March 238–late January/April 238	Gordian II
Early February 238–early May 238	Pupienus Maximus
Early February 238–early May 238	Balbinus
May 238–February 244	Gordian III
February 244–September/October 249	Philip the Arab
249–June 251	Decius
Early 251–July 1, 251	Herennius Etruscus
251	Hostilian
June 251–August 253	Gallus
July 251–August 253	Volusianus
August 253–October 253	Aemilian
253–June 260	Valerian
253–September 268	Gallienus
260	Saloninus

Gallic Empire, 260–274

260–269	Postumus
269	Marius
269–271	Victorinus
271–274	Tetricus I

Illyrian Emperors

268–August 270	Claudius II Gothicus
August 270–September 270	Quintillus
August 270–275	Aurelian
November/December 275–July 276	Tacitus
July 276–September 276	Florianus
July 276–late September 282	Probus
September 282–July/August 283	Carus
Spring 283–summer 285	Carinus
July/August 283–November 284	Numerian

Tetrarchy and Constantinian Dynasty

November 20, 284–May 1, 305	Diocletian
April 1, 286–May 1, 305	Maximian
May 1, 305–July 25, 306	Constantius I Chlorus

May 1, 305–May 311	Galerius
August 306–September 16, 307	Severus II
October 28, 306–October 28, 312	Maxentius
307–308	Maximian
307–May 22, 337	Constantine I the Great
November 11, 308–September 18, 324	Licinius
May 1, 310–July/August 313	Maximinus Daia
December 316–March 1, 317	Valerius Valens
July–September 18, 324	Martinianus
337–340	Constantine II
337–361	Constantius II
337–350	Constans
November 361–June 363	Julian the Apostate
363–February 17, 364	Jovian

Britannic Empire, 286–297

286–293	Carausius
293–297	Allectus

Valentinian Dynasty

February 6, 364–November 17, 375	Valentinian I
March 28, 364–August 9, 378	Valens
August 24, 367–383	Gratian
375–392	Valentinian II
383–388	Magnus Maximus

Theodosian Dynasty

379–January 17, 395	Theodosius I the Great
383–January 395	Arcadius
January 23, 393–395	Honorius

Western Empire

395–August 15, 423	Honorius
421	Constantius III
425–March 16, 455	Valentinian III
March 17, 455–May 31, 455	Petronius Maximus
June 455–October 17, 456	Avitus
457–August 2, 461	Majorian
461–465	Libius Severus
April 12, 467–July 11, 472	Anthemius
July 472–November 2, 472	Olybrius

March 5, 473–June 474	Glycerius
June 474–April 25, 480	Julius Nepos
October 31, 475–September 4, 476	Romulus Augustulus

BYZANTINE EMPERORS

All dates are AD.

518–527	Justin I
527–565	Justinian I
565–578	Justin II
578–582	Tiberius II
582–602	Maurice Tiberius
602–610	Phocas
610–613	Heraclius
613–638	Heraclius, Heraclius Constantine
638–641	Heraclius, Heraclius Constantine, and Heraclonas

EARLY ISLAMIC CALIPHS

All dates are AD.

(570–632)	(The prophet Muhammad)
632–634	First caliph Abu Bakr
634–644	Second caliph Omar
644–656	Third caliph Uthman

LIBRARIANS OF ALEXANDRIA

All dates are BC and all are uncertain.

	SUCCESSION	NAME
c. 285	First	Zenodotus of Ephesus
c. 270	Second	Apollonius Rhodius (the Rhodian)
c. 245	Third	Eratosthenes of Cyrene
204/1	Fourth	Aristophanes of Byzantium
c. 189/6–175	Fifth	Apollonius of Alexandria the Eidograph
c. 175–145	Sixth	Aristarchus of Samothrace

Uncertain librarians following the persecution of scholars by Ptolemy VIII Euergetes II:

From c. 145	Cydas
120–80	Ammonios
	Zeno
	Diokles
	Apollodoros
In period 118–80	
(reign of Soter II)	Onasander, son of Nausicrates

ACKNOWLEDGMENTS

This book is a synthesis of many people's work, so our first debt is to all those scholars who, for so many generations, have striven to recover ancient Alexandria from the ashes. Though only fragmentary today, the great corpus of knowledge gathered and nurtured in the libraries of Alexandria, and the scholarly titans who both studied and contributed to it, are the source of our inspiration in this book. We still find it hard to conceive of the breathtaking scope and originality of minds like those of Callimachus and Claudius Ptolemy.

It is now more than six centuries since scholars began to rediscover Alexandria's unique heritage, and successive generations have labored to translate the originals and to take up the torch themselves in pushing forward the frontiers of learning. Our bibliography names those whose works we have relied upon, and we wish to thank all of them for providing us with the bread and butter of this work. On a rather narrower stage, several living scholars' works have been especially helpful in orienting us with regards specifically to Alexandria. The writings of Alan Bowman on Egypt after the pharaohs are seminal, as is the work of Gunther Holbl on the Ptolemaic Empire. Theodore Vettros's work on Alexandria itself, and in particular on Neoplatonism and early Christianity, opened our eyes to the crucial role Alexandria played in the formulation of theology in general, and Christianity in particular. We therefore acknowledge our debt to these scholars. We would also like to thank Dr. Christopher Kelly of Cambridge University for reading the manuscript and suggesting many changes that have not only greatly improved it but saved us from many an error. Away from the ivory tower, out there in the big wide world, the author Bill Bryson has recently shown the reading public that you don't have to be an academic to write about the history of knowledge and ideas. His work has encouraged us to think as widely and deeply as possible in this book, pursuing the notion that we too could write *A Short Classical History of Nearly Everything*.

At the conception of this book we received generous enthusiasm and support from John Lloyd of Quite Interesting Limited, for which we are extremely grateful. Our agents Mark Lucas and Julian Alexander of the LAW agency in London and George Lucas at Inkwell Management in New York have provided unstinting support and keen editorial insights throughout, and we'd like also to thank Hilary Redmon and Wendy

Wolf at Viking Penguin in New York for excellent editorial input throughout the project.

Finally, we want to thank our wives and families—for Howard, Val, Amie, Leila, and Maya; for Justin, Stephanie and Constance—for their patient support and tolerance as we waded our way through the huge amount of reading and writing this book has required. Last of all, we'd like to acknowledge each other, for getting through this considerable undertaking with ne'er a crossed word, all undertaken in a spirit of scholarly adventure which has been a great pleasure for us both!

SELECTED BIBLIOGRAPHY

Aelian. *Varia Historia.* Translated by D. O. Johnson. New York: Edwin Mellen Press, 1997.

Al-Baladhuri. *The Origins of the Islamic State.* Translated by P. K. Hitti. New York: Columbia University Press, 1916.

Anonymous. *Historia Augusta.* Translated by D. Magie. London: Heinemann, 1921–32.

Apollonius of Rhodes. *Jason and the Golden Fleece [The Argonautica].* Translated by R. L. Hunter. Oxford: Oxford University Press, 1993.

Appian. *The Civil Wars.* Translated by John Carter. London: Penguin, 1996.

———. *Roman History.* Translated by H. White. London: Bohn's Classical Library, 1899.

Aristotle. *Metaphysics.* Translated by H. Lawson-Tancred. London: Penguin, 1998.

———. *Politics.* Translated by H. Rackham. Cambridge, MA: Harvard University Press, 1932.

———. *Politics and Economics.* Edited by E. Walford. Honolulu: University Press of the Pacific, 2002.

Arrian. *Anabasis.* Translated by E. I. Robson. Cambridge, MA: Harvard University Press, 1929.

Athanasius. *The Orations of St. Athanasius Against the Arians.* London: Griffith, Farrah, 1889.

Austin, M. M. *The Hellenistic World from Alexander to the Roman Conquest.* Cambridge, UK: Cambridge University Press, 1981.

Bacon, F. *The Advancement of Learning.* Oxford: Oxford University Press, 1868.

Baines, J., and J. Malek. *Atlas of Ancient Egypt.* London: Phaidon, 1980.

Bell, H. I. *Cults and Creeds in Graeco-Roman Egypt.* Liverpool: Liverpool University Press, 1953.

———. *Egypt from Alexander the Great to the Arab Conquest.* London: Greenwood Press, 1977.

Bevan, E. R. *The House of Ptolemy.* Chicago: Ares, 1927.

Bigg, C. *The Christian Platonists of Alexandria.* Oxford: Oxford University Press, 1886.

Boardman, J., J. Griffin, and O. Murray. *The Oxford History of the Classical World.* Oxford: Oxford University Press, 1986.

Bottomley, G. *Poems of Thirty Years.* London: Constable, 1925.

Bowman, A. *Egypt After the Pharaohs, 332 BC–AD 642: From Alexander to the Arab Conquest.* London: Guild, 1986.

Bradford, E. *Cleopatra.* London: Hodder & Stoughton, 1971.

Braund, D., and S. Wilkins, eds. *Athenaeus and His World: Reading Greek Culture in the Roman Empire.* Exeter, UK: University of Exeter Press, 2000.

Caesar Caius Julius. *Commentary on the Gallic and Civil Wars.* Translated by W. A. Macdevitt. London: Bohn's Classical Library, 1851.

Callimachus. *Aetia, Iambi, Lyric Poems.* Translated by C. A. Tripanis. London: Heinemann, 1975.

Canfora, L. *The Vanished Library.* Translated by M. Ryle. London: Hutchinson Radius, 1989.

Cassius Dio. *The Roman History: The Reign of Augustus.* Translated by I. Scott-Kilvert. London: Penguin, 1987.

Celsus. *On the True Doctrine: A Discourse Against the Christians.* Translated by R. J. Hoffmann. Oxford: Oxford University Press, 1987.

Celsus, Cornelius A. *Of Medicine, in Eight Books.* Translated by J. Greive. London: T. Chidley, 1837.

Chadwick, H. *Early Christian Thought and the Classical Tradition.* Oxford: Oxford University Press, 1966.

Charles, R. H. *The Chronicle of John, Bishop of Nikiu.* London: Williams & Norgate, 1916.

Cicero. *On the Nature of the Gods.* Translated by Rev. Dr. Giles. London: Cornish & Sons, 1872.

———. *Tusculan Disputations.* Translated by C. D. Yonge. London: Bell & Daldy, 1865.

Claudian. *Epigrams.* In *The Works of Claudian.* Translated by A. Hawkins. London: Langdon & Son, 1817.

Clement. *Stromateis Books 1–3* [*Stromata*]. Washington, DC: Catholic University of America Press, 1991.

Dillon, J. *The Middle Platonists.* London: Duckworth, 1977.

Dio Chrysostom. *Dio Chrysostom.* Translated by J. W. Cohoon (and H. Lamar Crosby). 5 vols. London: Heinemann; New York: Putnam, 1932–51.

Diodorus Siculus. *Library of History.* Translated by C. H. Oldfather. Cambridge, MA: Harvard University Press, 1933.

Diogenes Laertius. *The Lives and Opinions of Eminent Philosophers.* Translated by C. D. Yonge. London: G. Bell and Sons, 1915.

Dionysius of Cyzicus. *Anthologiæ Græcæ Erotica.* In *Palatine Anthology.* Translated by W. R. Paton. London: D. Nutt, 1898.

Dzielska, M. *Hypatia of Alexandria*. Cambridge, MA: Harvard University Press, 1993.

Eliade, Mircea. *The Forge and the Crucible: The Origins and Structure of Alchemy*. Translated by S. Corrin. Chicago: University of Chicago Press, 1978.

Empson, W. *Complete Poems*. London: Allen Lane, 2000.

Eusebius. *Praeparatio Evangelica*. Translated by H. Street. London, 1842.

Farrar, F. W. *Lives of the Fathers*. Edinburgh: Adam & Charles Black, 1889.

Fildes, A., and J. Fletcher. *Alexander the Great: Son of the Gods*. London: Duncan Baird, 2001.

Forster, E. M. *Alexandria: A History and a Guide*. London: M. Hagg, 1938.

Fraser, P. M. *Ptolemaic Alexandria*. 3 vols. Oxford: Oxford University Press, 1972.

Gibbon, Edward. *The Decline and Fall of the Roman Empire*. Edited by Hans-Friedrich Mueller. New York: Modern Library, 2003.

Goya, F. *Los Caprichos*. Barcelona: Gustavo Gili, 1978.

Gunnyon, W., trans. and ed. *A Century of Translations from the Greek Anthology*. Kilmarnock, Scot.: Dunlop & Drennan, 1883.

Hardy, E. R. *Christian Egypt: Church and People*. Oxford: Oxford University Press, 1952.

Heath, T. L. *Aristarchus of Samos*. Oxford: Oxford University Press, 1913.

————. *A History of Greek Mathematics*. Oxford: Clarendon Press, 1921.

————. *Works of Archimedes*. Cambridge, UK: Cambridge University Press, 1897.

Heraclitus. *Herakleitos and Diogenes*. Translated by G. Davenport. Bolinas, CA: Grey Fox Press, 1981.

Hermes Trismegistus. *Hermetica*. Translated and edited by W. Scott. Oxford: Clarendon Press, 1924.

Hero of Alexandria. *The Pneumatics of Hero of Alexandria [Pneumatica]*. Translated by J. G. Greenwood. London, 1851.

Herodotus. *The Histories*. Translated by A. de Sélincourt. London: Penguin, 1972.

Heuer, K. *City of Stargazers*. New York: Scribner's, 1972.

Holbl, G. *A History of the Ptolemaic Empire*. Translated by T. Saavedra. London: Routledge, 2001.

Holden, J. H. *A History of Horoscopic Astrology*. Tempe, AZ: American Federation of Astrologers, 1996.

Homer. *The Iliad*. Translated by A. Lang. London: Macmillan, 1883.

————. *The Odyssey*. Translated by T. E. Shaw (Col. T. E. Lawrence). Oxford: Oxford University Press, 1935.

Hornung, E. *Conceptions of God in Ancient Egypt*. Translated by J. Baines. London: Routledge, 1983.

Iamblichus. *The Life of Pythagoras*. Translated by T. Taylor. London: J. M. Watkins, 1926.

Ibn Battuta. *Travels in Asia and Africa, 1325–1354*. Translated by H. A. R. Gibb. London: Routledge, 1929.

Jones, A. H. M. *Cities of the Eastern Roman Provinces*. Oxford: Oxford University Press, 1971.

Jones, C. P. *The Roman World of Dio Chrysostom*. Cambridge, MA: Harvard University Press, 1979.

Jung, C. *Psychology and Alchemy*. Translated by R. F. C. Hull. London: Routledge, 1953.

Keynes, John Maynard. "Newton the Man." In Royal Society, *Newton Tercentenary Celebrations*. Cambridge, UK: Cambridge University Press, 1947.

Kingsley, C. *Alexandria and Her Schools*. Edinburgh: McMillan, 1854.

Koch-Westenholz, U. *Mesopotamian Astrology: An Introduction to Babylonian and Assyrian Celestial Divination*. Copenhagen: Museum Tusculanum Press, 1995.

Koestler, A. *The Sleepwalkers: A History of Man's Changing Vision of the Universe*. London: Hutchinson, 1959.

Kühn, C. G. [K. G.], ed. *Claudii Galeni Opera Omnia*. 20 vols. Leipzig, 1821–23.

Lawrence, D. H. *Fantasia of the Unconscious*. London: Secker, 1923.

Lefkowitz, M. R., and M. B. Fant. *Women in Greece and Rome*. Toronto: Samal-Stevens, 1977.

Leick, G. *The Babylonians: An Introduction*. London: Routledge, 2003.

Lemprière, J. *Lemprière's Classical Dictionary of Proper Names Mentioned in Ancient Authors Writ Large*. 1788. London: Routledge, 1879.

Lewis, N. *Life in Egypt Under Roman Rule*. Oxford: Oxford University Press, 1983.

Lloyd-Jones, H. *Myths of the Zodiac*. London: Duckworth, 1978.

Loeffler, C. M. T. *Evocation: On Lines from the Select Epigrams of the Greek Anthology by J. W. MacKail for Women's Voices and Orchestra; Score*. Boston: C. C. Birchard, 1932.

Lucan. *Pharsalia*. Translated by J. D. Duff. London: Heinemann, 1928.

Lucian. *Dialogues of the Dead*. Translated by H. Williams. 1913. Whitefish, MT: Kessinger, 2004.

———. *How to Write History*. In M. D. MacLeod, ed., *Lucian: A Selection*. Oxford: Aris & Phillips, 1991.

MacLeod, R., ed. *The Library of Alexandria—Centre of Learning in the Ancient World*. London: I. B. Tauris, 2004.

Mariette, A. *Itineraire de la Haute-Egypte comprenant une description des monuments antiques des rives du Nil entre le Caire et la première cataracte*. Paris: Maisonneuve et Cie, 1880.

Marshall, P. *The Philosopher's Stone: A Quest for the Secrets of Alchemy*. London: Macmillan, 2001.

Martial, M. V. *Epigrams*. London: Bell & Daldy, 1871.

———. *A Roman Wit: Epigrams of Martial*. Translated by P. Noxon. Boston and New York: Houghton Mifflin, 1911.

Marti-Ibanez, F. *The Epic of Medicine: A Pictorial History of Medicine.* London: Spring, 1965.

Merton, T. *Clement of Alexandria.* New York: New Directions, 1962.

Millay, E. St. V. *A Few Figs from Thistles.* New York: Harper & Bros., 1928.

Milne, J. G. *A History of Egypt Under Roman Rule.* Chicago: Ares, 1997.

Milton, J. *Areopagitica.* London: Macmillan, 1904.

———. *Paradise Lost.* Edited by A. W. Verity. Cambridge, UK: Cambridge University Press, 1921.

Newton, Isaac. *Alchemical Notes.* In KCL Keynes MS 33, fol. 5v, King's College Library, London.

Nutton, V. *Karl Gottlob Kühn and His Edition of the Works of Galen.* Oxford: Oxford Microform Publications, 1976.

Origen. *Against Celsus.* Translated by J. Bellamy. London, 1680.

———. *On First Principles.* Koetschau's text translated by G. W. Butterworth. London: SPCK, 1936.

Orosius, P. *Seven Books of History Against the Pagans.* Translated by R. Woodworth. New York: Columbia University Press, 1936.

Pack, R. A. *The Greek and Latin Literary Texts for Graeco-Roman Egypt.* 2nd ed. Ann Arbor: University of Michigan Press, 1967.

Pagels, E. H. *The Gnostic Gospels.* London: Weidenfeld & Nicolson, 1980.

Pappus. *La collection mathématique: Oeuvre traduite pour la première fois du Grec en Français avec une introduction et des notes par Paul Ver Eecke.* Paris: Albert Blanchard, 1933.

Parsons, E. A. *The Alexandrian Library.* London: Cleaver Hume Press, 1952.

Pfeiffer, R. *History of Classical Scholarship.* Oxford: Oxford University Press, 1958.

Philo of Alexandria. *The Works of Philo.* Translated by C. D. Yonge. Peabody, MA: Hendrickson, 1993.

Plato. *Republic.* Translated by R. A. H. Waterfield. Oxford: Oxford University Press, 1994.

———. *Theaetetus.* Translated by J. McDowell. Oxford: Clarendon Press, 1973.

Plotinus. *The Enneads.* Translated by S. McKenna and B. S. Page. London: Library of Philosophical Translation, 1917–1930.

Plutarch. *Lives.* Translated by J. Dryden. 2 vols. New York: Random House, 2001.

———. *Moralia.* Translated by P. H. De Lacy. London: Heinemann, 1959.

———. *On the Face Which Appears on the Orb of the Moon.* Translated by A. O. Prickard. London: Simpkin, 1911.

———. *Parallel Lives.* Translated by B. Perrin. Cambridge, MA: Harvard University Press, 1914.

Polybius. *The Histories.* Translated by W. R. Paton. London: Heinemann, 1922.

Pomeroy, S. B. *Women in Hellenistic Egypt.* New York: Schocken Press, 1988.

Pope, A. *The Rape of the Lock*. Oxford: Clarendon Press, 1909.

Porphyry. *Introduction to Plotinus*. Translated by J. Barnes. New York: Oxford University Press, 2003.

Proclus. *A Commentary on the First Book of Euclid's "Elements."* Translated by G. R. Morrow. Princeton: Princeton University Press, 1970.

Ptolemy, Claudius. *The Almagest*. Translated by G. J. Toomer. London: Duckworth, 1984.

———. *The Geography*. Translated by E. L. Stevenson. New York: Dover, 1991.

———. *Tetrabiblos*. Translated by J. Wolson. London: William Hughes, 1820.

Rice, E. E. *The Grand Procession of Ptolemy Philadelphus*. Oxford: Oxford University Press, 1983.

Roberts, A. *My Heart My Mother: Death and Rebirth in Ancient Egypt*. Rottingdean, UK: Northgate, 2000.

Roberts, C. H. *Manuscript, Society, and Belief in Early Christian Egypt*. Oxford: Oxford University Press, 1979.

Rufus, Quintus Curtius. *Alexander the Great*. Edited by W. S. Hett. Wauconda, IL: Bolchazy-Carducci, 1987.

Sandys, G. *The Relation of a Journey Begun An. Dom. 1610*. London: printed for W. Barrett, 1615.

Severus of Al-Ashmunein. *History of the Patriarchs of the Coptic Church of Alexandria*. Translated by B. Evetts. Paris: Firmin-Didot, 1915.

Shakespeare, W. *Complete Works*. Oxford: Oxford University Press, 1919.

Shaw, I., ed. *The Oxford History of Ancient Egypt*. Oxford: Oxford University Press, 2000.

Singer, Charles, trans. *Galen on Anatomical Procedures*. Publications of Wellcome Historical Medical Museum. New series, no. 7. London: Oxford University Press, 1956.

Sly, D. I. *Philo's Alexandria*. London: Routledge, 1996.

Smith, H. S. *A Visit to Ancient Egypt: Life at Memphis and Saqqara*. London: Aris & Phillips, 1974.

Smith, T. *Euclid: His Life and System*. Edinburgh: T. Clarke, 1902.

Socrates Scholasticus. *Ecclesiastical History*. London: Bell, 1880.

Spencer, A. J. *Death in Ancient Egypt*. London: Penguin, 1982.

Stewart, Z., ed. *Essays on Religion and the Ancient World*. Cambridge, MA: Harvard University Press, 1972.

Stone, M. E. *The Armenian Texts of Epiphanius of Salamis De mesuris et ponderibus*. Leuven, Belgium: Peeters, 2000.

Strabo. *Geography*. Translated by H. L. Jones. Cambridge, MA: Harvard University Press, 1932.

Synesius of Cyrene. *Letters*. Translated by A. Fitzgerald. London: Humphrey Milford, 1926.

Tarn, W. W. *Alexander the Great*. Cambridge, UK: Cambridge University Press, 1948.

Tennyson, A. *The Holy Grail and Other Poems*. London: Strahan, 1870.

Thaumaturgus, G. *Address to Origen*. Series: Translations of Christian Literature, ser. 1; Society for Promoting Christian Knowledge. Translated by W. Metcalfe. London: SPCK, 1920.

Theocritus. *Idylls*. Translated by R. C. Trevelyan. Cambridge, UK: Cambridge University Press, 1947.

Tolstoy, L. *War and Peace*. Translated by R. Edmonds. London: Penguin, 1978.

Toynbee, J. *Death and Burial in the Roman World*. Baltimore: Johns Hopkins University Press, 1996.

Treweek, A. P. *A Critical Edition of the Text of the Collection of Pappus of Alexandria*. London: University of London, 1950.

Trigger, B. E., B. J. Kemp, D. O'Connor, and A. B. Lloyd. *Ancient Egypt: A Social History*. Cambridge, UK: Cambridge University Press, 1983.

Vaughan, H. *Silex Scintillans*. 1650 facsimile. Menston: Scolar Press, 1968.

Vernant, Jean-Pierre. *The Universe, the Gods, and Mortals: Ancient Greek Myths*. Translated by L. Asher. London: Profile, 2001.

Vitruvius Pollio, M. *Architecture*. Translated by J. Gwilt. London: Priestly & Weale, 1826.

Vrettos, T. *Alexandria: City of the Western Mind*. New York: Free Press, 2001.

Walbank, F. W. *The Hellenistic World*. London: Fontana, 1981.

————. *Polybius, Rome, and the Hellenistic World: Essays and Reflections*. Cambridge, UK: Cambridge University Press, 2002.

White, M. *Isaac Newton: The Last Sorcerer*. London: Fourth Estate, 1997.

Whitehead, A. N. *Process and Reality*. New York: Macmillan, 1979.

INDEX